BDQ

Essays and Interviews on Quebec Comics

BDANG

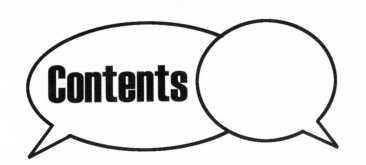

Contents

The Early Years:

The Middle Years:

The Nineties:

Modern Times:

Art by Simon Bossé

Many readers of this book will be unfamiliar with the rich history of comics making in the Canadian province of Quebec. Our goal is to expose you, dear reader, to this wealth of talent and resources. Quebec is a French-speaking province, with the cosmopolitain city of Montreal at its core. As such, much of the work being done in the area is in the French language (though not all), and the discourse around it is also in French. Conundrum Press has translated many graphic novels from Quebec artists through our BDANG Imprint, which has been successful in exposing English-speaking readers to French-language comics. This book of essays and interviews acts as a critical companion to the imprint.

BDQ is the term used to describe comics from Quebec, in the same way comics from Japan are called *manga*, or comics from China are called *manhua*. But specifically BDQ stands for *Bande Dessinée Québécoise*. The word for comics in French is *bande dessinée*, literally "drawn strip". So essentially, BD come from France (or Belgium), BDQ come from Quebec. It is important to make this distinction. Although influenced by the Franco-Belgian comics tradition, due to a shared language, Quebec comic artists are also heavily influenced by North American trends, especially the American underground of the 1960s (*comix*) and the zine revolution of the 1990s. BDQ reflect an amalgamation of these cultures, producing its own unique comics.

Of course the essays and interviews here are just a smattering of what could have been. It is my hope, dear reader, that this book will be a springboard into the wealth of the talent pool in Quebec.

I would be remiss if I did not credit the invaluable assistance provided by Helge Dascher, who not only translated most of the articles in this book, but provided invaluable editorial support, and even conducted an interview herself. So many thanks to her.

— Andy Brown, September 2017

THE EARLY YEARS

The Birth of BDQ

The Big Press and the Funnies
By Michel Viau

Originally published in:

Bears + Beer
mécanique générale, 2007

Translation by
Helge Dascher

Quebec comics appeared almost simultaneously in the Montreal newspapers La Patrie and La Presse in 1904. Can they teach us anything about Quebec society of the early 1900s, or were they just childish and insignificant distractions?

At the turn of the twentieth century, the Quebec press was influenced by American mass-circulation newspapers. In the US, press magnates Randolph Hearst and Joseph Pulitzer were engaged in a fierce circulation war. The Hearst-Pulitzer rivalry gave rise to many innovations that revolutionized the look and content of the dailies, including sensationalist reporting, sports, workers', and women's pages, banner headlines, the liberal use of illustrations and photographs, Sunday supplements, colour pages, and comics.

Eye-catching graphics were especially important. The US was experiencing an unprecedented immigration boom (23 million immigrants of all origins arrived between 1850 and 1905), and the visual aspect of newspapers helped to promote language learning and assimilation in the "melting pot."[1]

It was a no-holds-barred battle, and when a novelty like the comic strip appeared in one paper, it was quickly copied in the pages of the other. The owners also poached each other's star journalists and artists. In 1898, Richard F. Outcault, the creator of *Yellow Kid*, left Pulitzer's *World* to join Hearst's *Journal*. But when Rudolph Dirks, the author of *Katzenjammer Kids*, tried to take his characters in the opposite direction in 1913, he found himself caught up in a legal battle with William Hearst over their ownership.

In Quebec, an additional factor prompted newspapers to rapidly adopt these innovations. Quebec had by far the highest illiteracy rate among Canadian provinces (31.96% of the population over the age of 10, compared with 8.18% in Ontario).[2] The many illustrations in Quebec newspapers were thus intended as a pathway to reading.

As the two American newspaper magnates fought it out, giving rise to the development of comics at the dawn of the 1900s, a similar battle was pitting two Quebec newspapers against each other: *La Patrie* and *La Presse*.

Honoré Beaugrand

A bitter rivalry:
La Presse and La Patrie

In the late 1800s, newspapers in Montreal and Quebec City made no claims to the neutrality they aim to project today. Most dailies and weeklies supported specific and often antagonistic political positions. They were the reflections of a changing society in which ideas circulated, collided, and spread via the written word.

Among them, *La Lanterne*, founded by Arthur Buies in 1868, promoted the liberal and anti-clerical ideas of the Canadian Institute. This placed it in direct conflict with *Le Nouveau Monde*, a newspaper launched the following year by Mgr. Ignace Bourget, bishop of Montreal, and over which the clergy exercised absolute control. For their part, *La Minerve* and *La Vérité*, published by Jules-Paul Tardivel, promoted the ultraconservative and radical ideas of the right. These were met with vigorous opposition in *La Patrie*, founded by Honoré Beaugrand in 1879. A liberal mouthpiece, it advocated freedom of religion and access to education, going so far as to recommend a complete overhaul of the elementary school system as a solution to the social issues of the day.[3]

Israël Tarte, by Henri Julien

At a time when Wilfrid Laurier, leader of the Liberal Party of Canada, was trying to convince the general public and above all the clergy "that you can be liberal without being liberal" — an argument for various forms of liberalism — Beaugrand rapidly came to be seen as a radical element and a liability. In 1895, he was publicly repudiated by Laurier,[4] who would be elected Prime Minister of Canada two years later. Beaugrand went on to sell his newspaper for $30,000 to Israël Tarte, a prominent journalist and, above all, a member of Parliament and right-hand man to the leader of the Liberal Party.[5] Tarte immediately toned down the diatribe in its pages, initiating the shift from a partisan to an informative newspaper.[6]

While *La Patrie* was associated from the start with the federal Liberal Party, its rival, *La Presse*, founded by William-Edmond Blumhart on October 20, 1884, was connected with John A. MacDonald's Conservative Party. However, Blumhart soon distanced himself from the party, at least publicly. After several changes of ownership, the printer Trefflé Berthiaume purchased the Montreal daily in 1889.

A moderate-conservative newspaper, *La Presse* made space in its pages for the concerns of work-ers. In the late 1800s, Quebec experienced a period of intense industrialization and, with it, a major wave of urbanization. The working conditions of wage earners were virtually unregulated, and it was not unusual for factories to employ children under the age of ten. In his columns in *La Presse*, journalist Jules Helbronner, writing under the pseudonym Jean-Baptiste Gagnepetit, advocated for better working conditions and the organization of trade unions.

By the early 1900s, these newspapers no longer relied on political parties for their financing, but on advertising. Because advertisers were by nature less interested in polemics and averse to offending potential customers, the newspapers limited themselves to providing information without really taking sides. Opinion journalism gradually disappeared.

Jules Helbronner

Pioneers of the word balloon

From the second half of the 1800s onward, satirical and militant periodicals flourished in Quebec, publishing countless humorous illustrations and cartoons, as well as a few silent and captioned comic strips.[7] On April 21, 1900, *Le Monde illustré* published a captioned comic strip signed A. Lemoy, entitled "Pas le temps." On December 20, 1902, a wordless comic strip by Raoul Barré, "Pour un diner de Noël," appeared in *La Presse*. Long considered, erroneously, to be the first Quebecois comic strip, this short eight-panel story was nonetheless the first comic to appear in a mass circulation daily. But its publication was an isolated event, and it was not until 1904 that the first Quebecois comic strip with word balloons made its appearance. Published in *La Patrie*, it was "Les Adventures de Timothée," by Albéric Bourgeois.

> **"In Quebec, an additional factor prompted newspapers to rapidly adopt these innovations. Quebec had by far the highest illiteracy rate among Canadian provinces (31.96% of the population over the age of 10, compared with 8.18% in Ontario). The many illustrations in Quebec newspapers were thus intended as a pathway to reading."**

When "Timothée" debuted, the readers of *La Patrie* were already accustomed to stories told through images. Since 1903, the daily had published picture stories from France in its Saturday children's supplement. Its Saturday edition also featured occasional short wordless strips, told in three or four panels, by French artist Benjamin Rabier.[8]

It was in the US that Albéric Bourgeois learned the trade of illustrator and cartoonist. After settling in Boston in 1900, he published "The Education of Anne," a family strip about a young girl and her parents, in the *Boston Post*. It took all of Israël Tarte's powers of persuasion to convince Bourgeois to leave Massachusetts and a promising career to return to his home city of Montreal. Bourgeois joined *La Patrie* in October 1903 as a cartoonist and illustrator of various humour features (including "La population exotique de Montréal," "Le Tramway de 6:43," and "Les bouteilles").

Albéric Bourgeois

Albéric Bourgeois was born in Montreal on November 29, 1876. He studied at the Conseil des arts et manufactures de Montréal and, from about 1898 to 1900, at the Art Association of Montreal. From 1900 to 1902 (or 1903), he lived in Boston, where he trained as an illustrator with J.L. France. For the *Boston Post*, he created "The Education of Annie," a family strip about the tribulations of a middle-class couple and their daughter.

Back in Montreal in 1903, Bourgeois produced cartoons and illustrations for *La Patrie* before launching "Timothée" on January 30, 1904. He drew the adventures of this awkward dandy for a year before passing on the torch to Théophile Busnel.

Bourgeois left *La Patrie* in early 1905 to join its rival, *La Presse*, where he created numerous comic strips. However, his main contribution to *La Presse* started when he took over "Les Aventures de Ladébauche." He soon transformed the series into a humorous illustrated feature, and he continued to pen the page until his retirement in 1954. A collection of these pages, *Les Voyages de Ladébauche*, was published in 1907 and reissued in 1982.

A tireless worker, Bourgeois produced daily cartoons for *La Presse*, as well as a full page of comics for the Saturday edition, a column every two or three days, and short satirical pieces and prose poems that appeared under the title "Gazette rimée." From 1908 to 1909, he also contributed to the satirical weekly *Le Canard* under the pen name Passepoil.

Bourgeois' talents extended to music as well, and he composed some 100 burlesque and satirical songs, sometimes performing them himself as the character Père Ladébauche. A knowledgeable folklorist, he also organized and took part in numerous song, dance, and craft festivals both locally and abroad. In 1933, he wrote a radio show, "Le Voyage autour du monde de Joson et Josette," with characters inspired by the world of Ladébauche.

Bourgeois retired in 1954, after 49 years at *La Presse*. The following year, the University of Kansas awarded him a fellowship in honour of his exceptional work. The father of the French word balloon died in Montreal on November 17, 1962. A street in Pointe-aux-Trembles, in the east end of Montreal, is named after him.

"Timothée," "La Famille Citrouillard," and "Monsieur Phirin Lefinfin"

The Saturday, January 30, 1904, edition of *La Patrie* was 24 pages longs, measured 59.5 cm x 42 cm, and cost one "centin." The cover, by Jobson Paradis, depicted Montreal's tallest buildings. The comic strip "Les Aventures de Timothée" appeared on the top half of page 13, with the children's feature "Le Coin des enfants" below. This first episode of "Timothée" was printed in black and turquoise. Two weeks later, on February 13, the comic strip was printed in three colours, and as of March 5, in four.

On February 27, 1904, the children's feature, now entitled "Nos Chéries," left the "Timothée" page to make way for a puzzle based on the character, titled "Où est Timothée," and a wordless comic strip, "Histoire sans paroles," drawn in black silhouettes by René-Charles Béliveau. These short burlesque stories, told in three to four drawings, feature two little rascals playing tricks on a scrawny old man.

René-Charles Béliveau published five episodes of "Histoire sans paroles" before presenting, on April 2, 1904, a single episode of the series "Pourquoi la famille Peignefort mangea maigre le jour de Pâques." More bitter than funny, it tells the story of a working-class family obliged to make do with an Easter meal of bread and molasses after a dog steals the piglet they bought at the market. Two weeks later, on April 23, Béliveau returned with another new series, "La Famille Citrouillard," and this time he had a hit.

The Citrouillards, a country family, visit the city for the first time. Due to mishaps and misunderstandings, they quickly become regulars in the courtroom and police station, a sorry fate they share with Timothée. In fact, Timothée sometimes appears in their stories. On holidays such as Christmas, Easter, and Saint-Jean-Baptiste [Quebec's "National" Holiday, June 24], the characters of the two strips meet and the mayhem amplifies accordingly. These collaboratively created pages were signed by both Bourgeois and Béliveau, who each drew their own characters.[10]

On October 29, 1904, Timothée made way for "Monsieur Phirin Lefinfin." Drawn by H. Samelart, this short-lived series presents an urban intellectual who settles in the countryside in an effort to help reverse rural depopulation. As ill suited to the country as the Citrouillards are to the city, Monsieur Lefinfin takes along a pile of scholarly tomes for guidance. When the time comes to chop firewood, he consults various treatises on the art of woodcutting and heating; needless to say, he sets the house on fire. And pig-raising manuals are no help when he decides to become a pig farm-

Timothée

Timothée – a blundering dandy, unsuccessful but determined Don Juan, impenitent prankster, and card player – runs foul of the law, travels around the world, lives in Paris for a few months, inherits a Hollywood film studio, and rubs shoulders with celebrities. A sharp dresser with an impressive collection of hats, Timothée has no regular line of work. Instead, he mingles with high society in and around Montreal, punctuating his adventures with an emphatic "Au contraire!" He has a friend, Citronno, who helps him break out of prison, a fiancée, Sophonie, and a foul-tempered future mother-in-law. And sometimes, he is accompanied by a horrible dog, a boxer named Marquis. "Timothée" had several lives. Created by Albéric Bourgeois (1904 – 1905), the character went on to be drawn by Théophile Busnel (1905 – 1908), Arthur Lemay (1920 – 1925 and 1933), and Maurice Gagnon (1925 – 1926).

René-Charles Béliveau

The graphic artist, interior designer, portrait painter, and landscape artist René-Charles Béliveau was born in Montreal in 1872.[9] He studied painting in Paris at the Académie Julian, and returned to Quebec after a ten-year stay in Europe.

In 1904, Béliveau published five episodes of the series "Histoires sans paroles" in *La Patrie*, followed by a single episode of another series, "Pourquoi la famille Peignefort mangea maigre le jour de Pâques." On April 23, 1904, Béliveau returned with a new weekly series, "La Famille Citrouillard." Some 70 episodes would follow.

Béliveau left *La Patrie* in late summer 1905, but "La Famille Citrouillard" continued on, taken over first by Th. Bisson and then by Théophile Busnel. Béliveau died in 1914 or 1915.

er: no sooner does he buy a pig than it escapes. The series, whose graphic style prefigures Gahan Wilson, ran for only two episodes.

In early 1905, Albéric Bourgeois left *La Patrie* and went over to the "enemy": *La Presse*. There, he took over "Les Aventures du Père Ladébauche," drawn by Joseph Charlebois since March 5, 1904. "Timothée," however, remained the property of *La Patrie*. Israël Tarte chose a Breton artist, Théophile Busnel, to replace Bourgeois. But the sickly Busnel, who suffered tuberculosis, occasionally received discreet help from Bourgeois for the production of his weekly page. This unusual contribution, like the collaboratively produced strips, reflects the spirit of genuine camaraderie that existed among the cartoonists. René-Charles Béliveau, Théophile Busnel, and several other artists met regularly at Jobson Paradis' studio on Berri Street.[11] And when Busnel was given a dire prognosis by his doctors in 1908, Albéric Bourgeois, Jobson Paradis, and Napoléon Savard accompanied him to the ship on which he returned to his native Brittany.[12]

Père Ladébauche arrives in the pages of La Presse

At the turn of the century, Jules Helbronner was editor-in-chief at *La Presse*. It was under his direction that the first Quebec comics strips appeared, including Raoul Barré's "Pour un dîner de Noël" in 1902. But it was the publication of "Timothée" in *La Patrie* that incited *La Presse* to publish local comic strips. The paper did occasionally feature captioned strips from France; these were often anonymous, though some were signed by Benjamin Rabier, a strong presence in Quebec newspapers in the early 1900s.[13]

On Saturday, February 20, 1904, three weeks after the appearance of Bourgeois' character Timothée in *La Patrie*, *La Presse* inaugurated, on page 13, a special children's feature entitled "La ruche enfantine." Presenting stories, games, and illustrations, it occupied the lower half of the page, while the top half featured a comic strip. The first of these was entitled "Pourquoi il n'y eut pas de canard au diner." The 12-panel comic with word balloons tells the story of a couple's attempts to kill a duck for dinner. The strip was not signed, but Gilles Thibault has attributed it to Auguste Charbonnier (1859 – 1920).[14]

A week later, *La Presse* published another comic, "Un jour où M. L'oublieux a trop bonne mémoire." Although unsigned, it was probably an instalment of the American series "Mr. O.U. Absentmind" by John R. Bray. But it was the following Saturday that the great adventure of Quebec comics really got underway in *La Presse* with the arrival of "Père Ladébauche."

On March 5, 1904, *La Presse* published the first episode of "Père Ladébauche" by Joseph Charlebois. Although the character was not new (Hector Berthelot had created him in 1878 for his satirical weekly *Le Canard*), this was his first appearance in a comic. Unlike Bourgeois' "Timothée," which ran in *La Patrie*, Charlebois' comic did not use word balloons, except for the occasional exclamation. The dialogue was written in the style of theatrical lines and appeared under the panels. Notably, these lines did not include the narrative elements common to captioned strips. One could say that "Père Ladébauche" was midway between a captioned comic strip and one with balloons.

Printed in two colours,[15] the first episode presents Père Ladébauche stepping off a train, wearing an impressive fur hat. He has come to the big city to visit his nephew, Jean-Baptiste Lalumière. When he decides to celebrate his arrival

La Famille Citrouillard

The Citrouillard family, made up of father Baptiste, mother Pétronille, and son Gugusse, are from the countryside. Like many other rural families of their time, they decide to undertake their first-ever trip to the big city. The train ride to Montreal is an adventure in itself: language is a hurdle (the conductor speaks English) and misunderstandings ensue.

The Citrouillards are totally maladapted to city life: when they try to use modern appliances (telephones, gas stoves, magic lanterns, electric light bulbs) and urban contraptions (cars, drinking fountains, coal holes, tramways), the simplest devices turn into murderous objects; and their encounters with members of Montreal's ethnic communities (Chinese, Italian, Jewish, and African-American) inevitably end in a brawl.

with a drink, Ladébauche quickly finds himself in a skirmish over his hat, and everything ends, as it must, in front of a judge. The tone was set: in the two episodes that followed, Ladébauche again found himself in trouble with the law, and his hat continued to drive the story.

Like "Les Aventures de Timothée" and "La Famille Citrouillard," the Père Ladébauche series offered readers snapshots of the seasonal pastimes enjoyed by Montrealers. On April 4, 1904, Timothée visits a sugar shack; a week later, Père Ladébauche visits one as well. On June 4, both find themselves at a travelling circus, almost bumping into each other; on June 25, it is the Citrouillards' turn to go and set off a string of disasters.

From July 23 to November 12, 1904, Joseph Charlebois temporarily changed the strip's formula and title. Entitled "À chacun son métier,"

the weekly page became a pretext to poke fun at professionals, with Père Ladébauche now a jack of all trades: dentist, plumber, policeman, surgeon, peacemaker, jockey, nanny, paperhanger, mender of broken hearts, toreador, cook, lumberjack, "automedon," painter, coach driver, and bill poster.

On October 8, 1904, and February 4, 1905, the Père Ladébauche strips were signed Lennox Duffus; on the following February 11 and 18, they were signed Albéric Bourgeois. The 48th and last Ladébauche strip drawn by Joseph Charlebois appeared on February 25. The character then left the pages of *La Presse*, only to return a few months later, this time drawn by Albéric Bourgeois.

It is unclear why Joseph Charlebois put an end to the adventures of Père Ladébauche. Was it the editorial board's decision or his own? In his history of *La Presse*, published for the newspaper's centennial in 1984, Cyrille Felteau writes exten-

> **"Charlebois' comic did not use word balloons, except for the occasional exclamation. The dialogue was written in the style of theatrical lines and appeared under the panels. Notably, these lines did not include the narrative elements common to captioned strips. One could say that 'Le Père Ladébauche' was midway between a captioned comic strip and one with balloons."**

sively about Raoul Barré and Albéric Bourgeois, but makes no mention of Joseph Charlebois' work for the Montreal daily. Albert Laberge, in his work on Quebec painters and writers of the 1800s and 1900s, passes over Charlebois' contribution as well, although he and the artist were friends.[16]

"Le Petit cousin Charlot" and "Le Père Nicodème"

Several weeks after Busnel began drawing "Timothée," two artists at *La Patrie* took temporary leaves of absence from their respective series: Busnel used the break to create a character of his own, the little cousin Charlot, while Béliveau further developed a recent creation, Père Nicodème.[17] "Les Farces du petit cousin Charlot" is narrated

in the form of letters written by Aurore to her friend Berthe. Charlot, a troublemaker, plays pranks on everyone. There are no word balloons in the stories: the text is written directly inside the space of the half-page strip, crossing it from side to side and wrapping around the variously shaped panels, some of which have no frames.

Père Nicodème, for his part, is a bourgeois philanthropist and member of the animal protection society, always quick to intervene on behalf of the mistreated, both human and animal. But his efforts invariably backfire, earning him regular beatings. Nicodème made a fourth and final appearance in the April 15, 1905, episode of "La Famille Citrouillard," in which his efforts to car-

Théophile Busnel

Born in Brittany, probably in Saint-Briac-sur-Mer, Théophile Busnel immigrated to Canada, where he found work as an artist and illustrator at *La Patrie*. Starting in 1904, he created cover illustrations for the newspaper's weekend supplement, and on February 4, 1905, he took over the series "Les Aventures de Timothée," following Albéric Bourgeois' departure from the paper.

As of March 3, 1906, Busnel also drew the weekly comic strip "La Famille Citrouillard." He produced the two series separately for a brief two weeks before merging them, on March 17, in the first instalment of "Timothée et Citrouillard." From then on, Timothée and the Citrouillard family would experience their adventures together on a full page.

Busnel, who suffered tuberculosis, was often confined to bed and unable to draw his weekly page. In *Peintres et écrivains d'hier et d'aujourd'hui*, Albert Laberge recounts that Albéric Bourgeois visited Busnel seven or eight times to draw the weekly "Timothée" page in his stead.

When Busnel's health continued to deteriorate, his physician concluded that nothing more could be done for him; to protect Busnel's

wife and children from contagion, he advised the artist to return to France to convalesce with family and friends. One summer evening in 1908, Busnel's wife and several fellow-illustrators – Albéric Bourgeois, Jobson Paradis, and Napoléon Savard – accompanied him to the ship and watched him board. All except Busnel, who talked about his projects and plans, knew that he was condemned and would not return. "It was the saddest thing I've ever seen," Bourgeois later declared.

When he arrived in Brittany, Busnel continued to work with determination, sending new pages of "Timothée" to *La Patrie*. He died on September 4, 1908, two months after his return to Saint-Briac-sur-Mer. Arsène Besset's novel *Le Débutant*, published in 1914, was illustrated with his drawings.

LES AVENTURES DE TIMOTHEE

INFLUENCE DE LA LECTURE SUR LE CERVEAU DE TIMOTHEE

Le Père Ladébauche

LE RETOUR DE Q'JEBEC.

Ladébauche monté sur le "Canard" se fait remarquer par trois vapeurs de la Compagnie de Richelieu et d'Ontario.

Père Ladébauche

After spending "30 years with the *savages*," Père Ladébauche arrives in Montreal to visit his nephew, Jean-Baptiste Lalumière. Decked out in an impressive fur hat, Père Ladébauche is a *"Canayen qui a du poil aux pattes,"* a "hairy-pawed French Canadian" – hardy and resourceful. Always eager for new experiences, he tries out various sports and pastimes, including sailing, wrestling, skating, skiing, snow-shoeing, bowling, and billiards. Given his chronic bad luck, his athletic and professional endeavours invariably end in an accident or a brawl. Created by Hector Berthelot in 1878 for the satirical weekly *Le Canard*, Père Ladébauche appeared in numerous cartoons by Henri Julien, Albert-Samuel, and Arthur G. Racey before becoming a comic strip hero. In 1907, he was played on stage by an actor in a campaign to drum up subscriptions for *La Presse*.

ry out a rescue get him into trouble. The two new series lasted only three weeks (March 11, 18, and 25, 1905), after which Busnel and Béliveau returned to their regular series.

In late summer, 1905, it was René-Charles Béliveau's turn to leave *La Patrie*. "La Famille Citrouillard" continued on, however. After a first try on August 26, Th. Bisson took over the series from September 23 onward. His stint lasted five months, through to February 24, 1906.[18] Théophile Busnel replaced Bisson the following week, and for two weeks, he drew both of the newspaper's most popular comic strips, "Timothée" and "La Famille Citrouillard." He then decided to combine the two series, presenting the shared

adventures of the entire cast on a full page. The new series, "Timothée et Citrouillard," appeared weekly until June 9. The following week, Raoul Barré presented the first instalment of "Les Contes du Père Rhault."

Live from New York: "Les Contes du Père Rhault"

Raoul Barré, author of the comic strip "Pour un diner de Noël" that appeared in *La Presse* in December 1902, left Montreal in 1903 to live in New York, where he worked as a commercial illustrator. It was from the US that he sent his bi-monthly instalments of "Les Contes du Père Rhault" to *La Patrie*. The series, which featured the turbulent tykes Fanfan and P'tit Pit, ran until April 17, 1909, for a total of more than sixty episodes.

With Barré's "Les Contes du Père Rhault" and Busnel's "Les Aventures de Timothée," *La Patrie* in 1907 was offering its readers comics whose energy and efficiency were equalled by only a few American strips of the time. Little by little, Busnel modernized the layout of "Les Aventures de Timothée," giving it a personal and innovative touch. While Albéric Bourgeois continued to use a static, six-panel grid with full-figure characters shown in profile view, Busnel opened up the page to new possibilities. He played with the shape of the panels and the placement of the text, setting it in word balloons, under the image, and sometimes inside it. He also experimented with a variety of shots, including medium and three-quarter shots and even, in the July 25, 1908, episode, a close-up.

In 1907, Busnel broke new ground again. On June 8, Timothée, having received a large inheritance, sets out on a trip around the world, with his adventures chronicled in the comic strip from

week to week. This long 15-part story, entitled "Les Nouvelles Aventures de Timothée autour du monde," continued until December 21, when it suddenly broke off with no reason given. The next instalment of "Timothée," on January 4, 1908, returned to the one-page gag format, featuring our hero and the Citrouillard family. The series "Les Nouvelles Aventures de Timothée autour du monde" was thus Quebec's first serial comic strip.

Albéric Bourgeois' Adventures at La Presse

While the reasons for Charlebois' departure from *La Presse* are a mystery, we know the details of Albéric Bourgeois' contract with the newspaper, thanks to its reproduction in Felteau's above-mentioned account.[19] This three-year contract, signed on February 21, 1905 (after the publication of two pages of "Ladébauche" by Bourgeois and before the publication of the last page signed by Charlebois), required Bourgeois to "dedicate all his time, skill, and effort to the exclusive benefit of the *Compagnie de publication de La*

Joseph Charlebois
The cartoonist, draughtsman, illuminator, and illustrator Joseph Charlebois was born in Montreal on March 5, 1872. His father, Charles-Théophile Charlebois, was a painter and decorator. In 1897, Joseph Charlebois joined Montreal's roadways department, first as assistant chief draughtsman in the streets division, and then, in 1906, as chief draughtsman. He continued to work for the city for 23 years. From about 1899

onward, he created the illuminated addresses (hand-lettered texts of honour) that the city presented to its most illustrious visitors.

Alongside his work at the public roadways, he had a second career as a cartoonist. He started out at the journal *Les Débats*, drawing cartoons under the pen name Basibi from 1899 to 1903. On January 1, 1903, he launched a single issue of a cartoon magazine entitled *Le Taon*.

From March 5, 1904, to February 25, 1905, he produced the first comic strips featuring Père Ladébauche, a character originally created by Hector Berthelot in *Le Canard* in 1878.

In July 1907, Joseph Charlebois resumed publication of the magazine *Le Taon*, which came out at irregular intervals until February 1910. Charlebois also contributed cartoons to the Montreal publications *La Patrie*, *L'Action* (1911 to 1916), Olivar Asselin's *Le Nationaliste*, and *Le Canard* (1914). Many of these drawings were collected in small books that he published at his own expense, including *Nos*

p'tites filles, *La Bêche*, *Saint Jean-Baptiste d'autrefois*, *Montréal-juif*, and *Monsieur Gouin voyage*.

In spring 1920, Charlebois left his job with the City of Montreal to move to New York, where for eight years he worked as an illuminator for the firm Hayes and Robinson. He moved to France in 1928, but returned to Montreal at the end of his life. In his studio on Phillips Square, and later on Drummond Street, he continued to produce illuminations and religious works.

Considered one of the best illuminators of his time, Joseph Charlebois taught lettering at the École du Conseil des arts et manufactures de Montréal. His name appears in the catalogues of numerous exhibitions and salons held in Montreal in the 1930s, where he exhibited illustrations and, above all, illuminated texts.

Joseph Charlebois died on October 21, 1935, at the age of 63. His son, Roland-Hérard Charlebois, served as director of the École des beaux-arts de Montréal from 1945 to 1957.

Les Contes du Père Rhault

Poor Monsieur Rhault has to deal with Fanfan and P'tit Pit, two little pests who play pranks on their family and their Tante Frizine. But the adults give as good as they get. This lively and energetically drawn series presents a traditional or original story (such as Sleeping Beauty, Little Red Riding Hood, or Bluebeard) at the top of the page, setting the theme for both the kids' pranks and the ones they fall victim to. For comedic effect, the first of these stories was written in slang, but the experiment was abandoned the following week in favour of standard French.

Presse, Limitée." The contract specifies Bourgeois' working hours: from 8 a.m. to noon and 1 p.m. to 5 p.m., every day except Saturdays, holidays, and in emergencies, as required by the paper. Bourgeois' salary, however, is not mentioned in the contract.

Officially, then, Bourgeois began his career at *La Presse* on March 4, 1905, with the debut of a new weekly series, "Zidore." It ran for a total of 23 episodes, until August 5, 1905. The following week, Père Ladébauche was back in the pages of *La Presse*.

On March 11, 1905, hardly a week after the creation of Zidore, Bourgeois introduced readers to a new character, Toinon, an incorrigible little prankster who terrorizes the members of his bourgeois household. The series took an important turn on June 17, 1905, when Toinon's mother sends him to the country to spend the summer with the maid, Aglaé. Upon his arrival, he meets another little rascal, his cousin Polype. Together, they shatter the calm of the bucolic countryside. Another key character, Uncle Joson, entered the series in June 1906.

"Toinon et Polype" was Bourgeois' longest-running series. More than 128 episodes were published between March 11, 1905, and August 29, 1908.[20] Often, Bourgeois would blend in characters from his other series, with Zidore and Père Ladébauche, for instance, making cameo appearances at holiday get-togethers and on other social occasions (Christmas, Saint-Jean-Baptiste, April Fool's).

On August 12, 1905, "Le Père Ladébauche" reappeared in the pages of *La Presse*, this time in the form of an illustrated bi-weekly feature. Ladébauche travels the world, visiting heads of state and advising them on how to run their countries. This version of Père Ladébauche resembled Hector Berthelot's original character much more than did Joseph Charlebois' citified interpretation of him.[21]

In the course of his prolific career at *La Presse*, which lasted from 1905 to 1954, Bourgeois created numerous series. His early years with the daily proved to be especially creative. Later, his interests shifted to radio and theatre, though he continued to produce his weekly Ladébauche feature and daily cartoons for the newspaper.

Bourgeois also made many other series that were less significant, both in quantity and in terms of the elaboration of their world. The first was "Les Fables du parc Lafontaine." Freely inspired by La Fontaine's fables, the series consisted of short comic stories featuring animals with human behaviours. As in the French comic strips from France, the texts were typeset and appeared below the images. The strip appeared on an irregular basis, alternating with a feature presenting Ladébauche's reminiscences, from July 14, 1906, onward. (A week earlier, Bourgeois had already written and illustrated an animal fable that appeared in the place of "Ladébauche.") The Lafontaine series ran until August 1, 1908, for a total of 30 episodes. Bourgeois returned to the concept a few months later for a new series.

Alongside his work on "Toinon et Polype" and "Les Fables du parc Lafontaine," Bourgeois

Raoul Barré

Vital Achille Raoul Barré was born in Montreal on January 29, 1874. After studies at the Institut du Mont-Saint-Louis, young Raoul went to France in 1891 to further his education at the École des Beaux-Arts de Paris and the Académie Julian. While in Paris, Barré contributed to several humour magazines, including *Le Sifflet*.

Barré returned to Quebec in 1898, where he divided his time between illustration, cartooning, and painting. He collaborated with the Montreal daily *La Presse*, for which he published a regular humour feature, "En Roulant ma boule." Some of these illustrations were collected in a book in 1901. On December 20, 1902, he published "Pour un dîner de Noël" in *La Presse*. Barré's exceptionally dynamic and flowing style foretold his future interest in animation.

In 1903, Barré moved to New York, where he worked as a commercial illustrator. From 1906 onward, he sent episodes of a new comic strip, "Les Contes du Père Rhault," to the Montreal paper *La Patrie* every two weeks. In 1912, Barré created the animal strip "Noah's Arc" for a New York newspaper, signing it VARB (a pen name made of his initials). The strip, distributed by the McLure Newspaper Syndicate, was picked up by *La Patrie* and published in French from January 1913 onward as "À l'hôtel du Père Noé."

In 1914, he and William C. Nolan launched the Barré-Nolan Studio, one of the first truly organized animation studios, in the Bronx. He introduced many young animators to this new profession that he helped create, even offering them drawing lessons after hours. A few years later, one of his young apprentices, Pat Sullivan, would create *Felix the Cat* (1917).

Starting in 1915, he created dozens of films that combined live-action with animation, including two series, *Animated Grouch Chaser* and *Phable Cartoon*, for Edison Studios. In 1916, he partnered with Charles Bowers to found the Barré-Bowers Studio, where for three years he created animated adaptations of the most popular comic strip of the time, Bud Fisher's *Mutt and Jeff*. In 1919, after a falling out with Bowers, Barré left the studio and animation. He returned, however, in 1926-27 at the request of Pat Sullivan to help animate *Felix the Cat*.

Illness prompted Barré to return to Montreal in the late 1920s. He began painting again and took part in several exhibitions. In 1931, he published a few issues of the satirical magazine *Le Taureau*. Among the last projects close to his heart was the foundation, in about 1930, of a cooperative school, the Educational Art and Film Co. of Montreal, where students were paid to work on a film project, *Microbius 1ᵉʳ*. Barré died of cancer on May 21, 1932, at the age of 58.

"Quebecois comic strips made a brilliant debut in 1904, complete with numerous series, a variety of themes, and a host of colourful characters. But this period of intense activity lasted only six years, from January 1904 to November 1909. Paradoxically, the founding moment of BDQ is often referred to as its Golden Age, as though the richest time in its history was that of its birth."

Zidore

Zidore Laripaille is a country "hobo" who arrives in Montreal. Although he occasionally looks for work, he is generally more interested in schemes and scams. In one episode, he tours the city's stores to taste food samples, treating himself to a feast along the way. Another time, he pretends to save a life in the hope of getting a free lunch. Or he orders all items on a menu because of a sign outside the restaurant that reads: "Food and Drink Offered Here." His freeloading mostly gets him a kick in the pants or a visit to the police station, for which he is predestined by his "civil status." In the course of his urban adventures, he meets an acquaintance from back home, Mam'zelle Paméla.

Zidore shows her around, takes her on a boat ride to Saint Helen's Island, and drives her through the city – back in the days when cars were not welcome in its streets. Although the two seemed destined to fall in love, their story came to an abrupt end when the Zidore strip stopped appearing on August 5, 1905.

LA PRESSE SAMEDI 11 MARS 1905

Zidore s'offre un Diner Gratis

started another, more pedagogical series: "L'histoire du Canada pour les enfants." Published bi-monthly from January 19, 1907 to February 22, 1908, the series comprised 23 episodes. The concept was straightforward: an episode in Canadian history was told in text form in the top tier of panels, and a boy named Charlot relived the incident in a dream on the rest of the page. Each instalment ended with the boy's brutal awakening in his bed (or next to it). The narrative approach recalls Barré's "Les Contes du père Rhault," which appeared in La Patrie at the same time, and above all Winsor McCay's "Little Nemo in Slumberland." It wasn't the first time that Bourgeois adapted the premise of an American series for his own use. He had done so for "Zidore" (based on Burr's "Happy Hooligan"), but also for "Toinon et Polype" (inspired by Outcault's "Buster Brown" in the first episodes, when Toinon is alone, and by Dirks' "Katzenjammer Kids," after his cousin joins the series).

The world of childhood was never far in Bourgeois' work, and it took center stage in "Le Petit Monde," which debuted on November 28, 1908. This short-lived series (five episodes) featured the turbulent kids of a well-to-do family. The characters change from one story to the next, but a girl steals the show in the third, and her name, Lili, became the title of the final two episodes. In the last, published on January 16, 1909, Lili meets two little terrors who were surely still familiar to La Presse readers: Toinon and Polype. Together, they turn the household upside-down.

Toinon and Polype

The terrible twosome Toinon and his cousin Polype play pranks on other family members, including Toinon's father, his sister, Césarine, his spinster aunt, Cunégonde, her fiancé, Zéphire, the portly, balding, and moustachioed Oncle Joson, and above all the maid, Aglaé. The boys don't hesitate to electrify a turkey, lock a cat into a trunk, and set fire to a shed, all for a laugh.

Their mischief extends beyond the family, with victims including neighbourhood policemen and various shopkeepers and Chinese laundrymen. Only Toinon's mother, very rarely present, is spared.

The episodes always end the same way, with the two rascals receiving a well-deserved spanking (often administered with a cane).

Bourgeois was again influenced by an American series when he created the character of Monsieur Distrait, who first appeared on January 23, 1909. This time, the inspiration came from the series "Mr. O.U. Absentmind," by Jon R. Bray, an instalment of which was published in *La Presse* in February 1904. The stories are simple: Monsieur Distrait has an errand to run (such as mailing a letter or buying medicine), but he invariably forgets what he set out to do and mishaps ensue. Ending after just three episodes, it was Bourgeois' shortest strip.

On February 13, 1909, Bourgeois recycled the idea of the series "Les Fables du parc Lafontaine," this time under the title "Les Animaux savants." The stories in this new version followed the same formula, and again the texts appeared beneath the images. Only eight episodes were published before the series ended on April 3, 1909.

Bourgeois' last creation in the first decade of the 1900s came out sporadically between May 8 and November 6, 1909. It was the series "Pitou et son grand-papa." Pitou is yet another unruly boy who wreaks havoc wherever he goes. But unlike Toinon, who gets punished for his pranks, Pitou is spared every time, thanks to his grandfather's interventions. The series ran for 11 episodes, and the name "Pitou" returned for a single episode in April 1911.[22]

Bourgeois also marked holidays and other events with special pages that were not connected to a series, such as "En roulant ma boule," on June 22, 1907 (not to be confused with the illustrated Ladébauche feature, nor with Raoul Barré's feature) and "Comment on fait un journal," on October 16, 1909 (reprinted on September 8, 1910). It would seem that Bourgeois was free to use his full page as he pleased.

"Les Aventures de Timothée" and "Les Contes du Père Rhault continued to alternate in *La Patrie* until October 1908, with Busnel sending his strips from Brittany and Barré sending his from New York. On October 17, "Timothée" was replaced by an American comic strip, Richard F. Outcault's "Buster Brown." Then, on November 14, "Père Rhault" made way for "Le Jeune Ménage — et Bébé," a translation of George McMannus's "The Newlyweds," also from the US.[23] Bourgeois himself left comics in 1909 to focus full-time on his illustrated feature, "Ladébauche."[24] Thus the curtain fell on Quebecois comic strips in *La Patrie* and *La Presse*. It would be a few years before local comics made a comeback in their pages.

By way of conclusion...

Quebecois comic strips made a brilliant debut in 1904, complete with numerous series, a variety of themes, and a host of colourful characters. But this period of intense activity lasted only six years, from January 1904 to November 1909. Paradoxically, the founding moment of BDQ is often referred to as its Golden Age, as though the richest time in its history was that of its birth.

For lack of vision or new talent, or, more likely, for financial reasons, the editors of both *La Patrie* and *La Presse* went on to publish only foreign comic strips.[25] The Quebecois series and their creators were largely forgotten. In fact, when BDQ experienced a revival in the 1970s, many readers believed they were witnessing the birth of the genre. Only recently have researchers begun to take a real interest in these very first comics.[26]

And yet the artists who took part in this shortlived Golden Age — including Bourgeois, Béliveau, Charlebois, Busnel, Samelart, Bisson, and Barré — brought an exuberant originality and freshness to the medium. While the comic strips from France that appeared in children's publications were still weighed down by the use of captions below the image, the first Quebecois comic strips looked to American stylistic approaches for inspiration. Unfortunately, these strips were only read and appreciated locally, since they had no visibility beyond the newspapers in which they were published. And with no opportunities for further distribution, Quebec comics had no discernible influence in the broader French-speaking world. It would take another 20 years for French-language comics in Europe to adopt the systematic use of word balloons.

The strips published between 1904 and 1909 held a mirror to the concerns and social reality of their readers – an audience not limited to children. Unlike the comics out of France published in the same pages, the first Quebecois comics were also, if not primarily, for parents. Many of the themes, especially in the work of Bourgeois and Béliveau, touched on adult concerns that reflected the changes reverberating through Quebec society: urbanization, progress, the administration of justice, the increasing multiculturalism of the large metropolises, city pastimes ("La Famille Citrouillard," "Timothée," "Zidore," and "Le Père Ladébauche"), rural settlement ("Monsieur Phirin Lefinfin"), and the hardships of the working poor ("La Famille Peignefort"). They touched on the everyday reality of the readers of *La Patrie* and *La Presse*, offering a mocking and ironic reflection of their worries.[27] But this reflection could be reassuring, too: it showed readers that they weren't alone in their struggles to cope with a rapidly evolving world and a society undergoing dramatic transformation.

In the early 1900s, Quebec literature, both fiction and poetry, remained faithful to its recurring themes of the past and the land. Comics, by contrast, were firmly anchored in the present. With the growth of industrialization, the rural population dwindled; by 1921, it made up just one third of Quebec's overall population. And yet most novels published in the first half of the twentieth century focused on the traditional themes of love for the land and history (examples include *Maria Chapdelaine* by Louis Hémon [1914]; *Les Habits rouges* by Robert de Roquebrune [1923]; *Un homme et son péché* by Claude-Henri Grignon [1933]; *Menaud maître-draveur* by Félix-Antoine Savard [1937]; and *Trente arpents* by Ringuet [1938]), presenting an image of Quebec society that was both distorted and disconnected. Few novels examined urban issues,[28] and it was not until 1945 that the first great French Canadian urban novel, *Bonheur d'occasion* by Gabrielle Roy, finally appeared.[29]

And yet forty years earlier, comic strips had already addressed, with a light and mocking tone, the joys and miseries of city life. They chronicled the pastimes and distractions of the early 1900s, the spoken language with its patois and slang, the fashions, foods, and newfangled technologies, and the dynamics of interracial relations, while offering sharply observed social satire. As such, these first comic strips provide a truer portrait of Quebec society and have more to teach us about it than do the other literary forms of the time. ●

ENDNOTES

1. Gérard Blanchard, *Histoire de la bande dessinée* (Verviers, Belgique: Éd. Marabout, 1974), 170; and Maurice Horn, "Les origines de la bande dessinée," *Bande dessinée et figuration narrative* (Paris: Musée des arts décoratifs/Musée du Louvre, 1967), 19.

2. Jean-Paul De Lagrave, *Histoire de l'information au Québec* (Montréal: La Presse, 1980), 131.

3. Ibid., 134.

4. Luc Bouvier, "Les moments importants de sa vie," in Honoré Beaugrand, *La Chasse-galerie* (Montreal: Éd. CEC, 1996), 127.

5. Ibid., 129.

6. Pierre Godin, *La lutte pour l'information: Histoire de la presse écrite au Québec* (Montreal: Le Jour éditeur, 1981), 35.

7. The oldest known captioned comic strip is "Tribulations d'un cadet," attributed to Jean-Baptiste Côté. This wood-engraved comic strip appeared in *La Scie* in 1865. Captioned comics would go on to appear alongside wordless ones.

8. These were originally captioned, but the versions published in *La Patrie* appeared with both the captions and the artist's signature carefully erased.

9. David Karel, *Dictionnaire des artistes de langue française en Amérique du Nord* (Québec: Musée du Québec, Les Presses de l'Université Laval, 1992), 62.

10. This "tradition" continued when Théophile Busnel replaced Bourgeois as the creator of the weekly comic strip "Timothée."

11. Karel, *Dictionnaire des artistes de langue française*, 613.

12. Albert Laberge, *Peintres et écrivains d'hier et aujourd'hui* (Montreal: n.p., 1938), 64.

13. Benjamin Rabier's work appeared in the newspapers *La Patrie* and *La Presse*, and also in the satirical weekly *Le Canard*.

14. Gilles Thibault, "Avant les groupes," *La Barre du jour*, no. 46/47/48/49, 1st quarter, 1975, 39-46.

15. Starting on August 12, 1905, *La Presse* published its comics in four colours.

16. Laberge, *Peintres et écrivains d'hier et aujourd'hui*, 97-102.

17. Père Nicodème had already made an appearance in the July 16, 1904, episode of "La Famille Citrouillard."

18. One other work is attributed to Théophile Bisson: a pen and ink copy of a painting by Rubens, *The Last Communion of Francis of Assisi*, published in *Revue canadienne* in 1906 (Karel, *Dictionnaire des artistes de langue française*, p. 88).

19. Cyrille Felteau, *Histoire de La Presse: Tome - 1 Le livre du peuple* (1884-1916) (Montreal: Éd. La Presse, 1983), 353.

20. The collection consulted for this article was incomplete; additional episodes may have been published.

21. Over the years, the feature appeared under many different titles: "Les Voyages de Ladébauche" (August 12, 1905, to May 5, 1906); "Les Mémoires de Ladébauche" (March 30, 1907, to February 8, 1908); "Les Mémoires de Ladébauche, 2e partie" (May 16 to August 1, 1908); "La Revue comique par Ladébauche" (August 8, 1908, to January 9, 1909); "En roulant ma boule" (not to be confused with Raoul Barré's feature and book by the same name; April 10 to July 14, 1909); "L'Enquête royale du père Ladébauche" (August 7 to December 11, 1909); "Voyage fantaisiste de Teddy et de Ladébauche" (July 9 to August 6, 1910); "La Chasse-galerie"(October 29, 1910, to March 4, 1911), including "Voyage fantaisiste de Teddy et Ladébauche (October 29 to December 3, 1911) and "Voyage fantaisiste de Ladébauche et de son neveu Baptiste" (December 10, 1911, to February 18, 1912); and "En roulant ma boule, causerie hebdomadaire du Père Ladébauche" (starting on November 18, 1911).

22. "L'Éducation de Pitou," published under the pen name Max on April 15, 1911.

23. One last episode of "Les Contes du Père Rhault" appeared on Saturday, April 17, 1909.

24. Thereafter, Bourgeois created occasional comic strips, including the short-lived daily strip "L'Éducation de Pierrot," signed Max, which ran for six episodes, on December 22, 23, 24, and 28, 1915, and February 18 and 19, 1916.

25. The first of these imported strips originated in the US, but after 1910, most were from France.

26. Jean Véronneau was a precursor in the field, publishing "Introduction à une lecture de la bande dessinée québécoise, 1904-1910" in the publication *Stratégie* (nr. 13, 14), in 1976.

27. Strangely, despite the control exercised by the Catholic Church over most aspects of Quebec society, no comic published in *La Patrie* and *La Presse* during this time featured clerical figures.

28. Exceptions include *Le Débutant* by Arsène Bessette (1914) and *Les Demi-Civilisés* by Jean-Charles Harvey (1934).

29. Paul Gay, *Notre roman: Panorama littéraire du Canada français* (Montreal: Hurtubise HMH, 1973), 32.

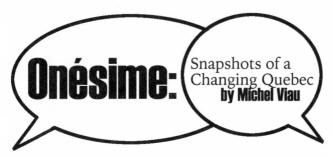

Originally published in:

Onésime: Les meilleures pages
(Les 400 coups), 2011

Translation by
Helge Dascher

In late 1943, as World War II raged on, a minor revolution was taking shape in a quiet Quebec farm magazine.

For more than 20 years, American comic strips had been invading most newspapers in the province of Quebec, crowding out the few Quebecois strips in their pages. But in November 1943, the opposite happened in *Le Bulletin des agriculteurs du Québec*.[1] The editors, who had been running American strips such as *The Captain and the Kids* (translated as *Les Jumeaux du Capitaine*) by Rudolf Dirks, decided to replace it with a local creation, *Onésime*, by Albert Chartier.

The illustrator got his start as a cartoonist in the Sunday pages of *La Patrie*. There, in 1936, the 24-year-old drew the strip *Bouboule*, written by journalist René O. Boivin. In May 1940, with $400 to his name and accompanied by his new wife, Chartier left Montreal to settle in New York City. For almost two years, he worked freelance, notably for *Big Shot Comics*, published by the Columbia Comics Corporation. But he also continued to contribute to various Quebec magazines. When the US entered the war in December 1941, Chartier decided to return home.

Back in Quebec, Chartier initially produced propaganda drawings for the federal Wartime Information Board in Ottawa. Before long, however, his New York experience opened doors for him in the editorial departments of various publications. He became a contributor to *La Revue populaire*, *Samedi*, the Montreal Star's Weekend Magazine, and Radio Monde, which he supplied with numerous colour covers, drawings, and comic strips.

In early 1943, on the advice of a cousin, he submitted samples of his work to the farm magazine *Le Bulletin des agriculteurs*. After hiring him to illustrate novels, short stories, and children's stories, some written by Gabrielle Roy, the editors invited him to create an original comic strip. He was given a free hand in all matters, including the choice of setting. Speaking as the guest of honour at Montreal's first comics convention in 1985, Chartier told Jacques Samson: "There were no restrictions. They just told me, 'Make something and we'll see how it goes!'"[2] Family and friends provided inspiration for his characters. One of his cousins was named Onésime. Another cousin, Aimé, was a tall, lanky man with a pronounced Adam's apple who smoked a curved pipe, and an uncle, Jules, had a big mustache. Chartier combined these elements and added his father's spectacles to create his hero.[3] Always inclined to play with physical contrasts (Bouboule was short and plump, and his wife, tall and skinny), he paired Onésime with a small, rotund wife: "A chubby wife and a tall, skinny husband; there's something instantly funny about that."[4] Again, Chartier looked to his family for a model and found one in "Aunt Éléonore, who weighed 300 pounds."[5] He gave his character a name often used by Albéric Bourgeois in his *Père Ladébauche* comics:[6] Zénoïde.[7] But the couple were not only opposites in appearance.

A note on the full page strips included here: In 2003 Chris Oliveros travelled to the home of Albert Chartier and scanned some of the original pages from *Onésime*. The strips were translated by Helge Dascher and relettered into English by Dirk Rehm. A sample of these pages were included in the *Drawn & Quarterly Anthology* #5 and are used here by permission of Drawn & Quarterly. © Estate of Albert Chartier.

"The power of the night-time effects, rendered with just a few cross-hatches, and the swirling, dynamic movement of the lines and specks, which turn a snow-storm into a whiteout in the wink of an eye, reveal a cartoonist passionate about the craft of storytelling and intensely aware of the graphic delights he is able to produce."

Where Onésime was impassive and thoughtful, Zénoïde was energetic and impulsive. She was the one who wore the pants in the mismatched relationship. In an interview, Chartier remarked, "In rural Quebec, it's the wife who controls the purse strings."[8]

Having created his protagonists, Chartier went on to define the setting. Since the strip would be published in a farmers' magazine, Chartier decided it would take place in the countryside – a choice that was all the more appealing since rural life was still a relatively unexploited theme. Drawing on childhood memories, he set about constructing the world of Onésime's adventures. As a child, Chartier had spent his summers at Lac Noir, in the Lanaudière region. "The first time I saw Lac Noir in Saint-Jean-de-Matha was in 1923. My father took me there in a pedal-operated Ford, a solid car that could handle the dirt and gravel roads of the day."[9] And so Onésime and Zénoïde became residents of Saint-Jean-de-Matha, home of strongman Louis Cyr. Chartier himself moved from Montreal to Lac Noir in 1951.[10]

In addition to giving Onésime an authoritarian wife, Chartier gradually peopled his world. It included a father (Grandpère Onésime) and mother, as well as a sister, Imelda, with whom they lived, and many nieces, a pretext for the cartoonist to draw beautiful young women. The brunette Frou-Frou, Imelda's daughter, let Chartier pit modernity against tradition, and the blond Gloria, who lived in the US, was proof that Quebecers had no need to envy the Americans. The couple themselves, however, had no children. As Chartier explained, "It would have changed the context completely. When there's a car accident, it's funny because there's only Onésime and Zénoïde. But if you had a bunch of kids in the back seat, it wouldn't be as funny. With kids, it would turn into a tragedy."[11] And there were

plenty of car accidents in the almost 60-year life of the strip, since Onésime was hardly a driving ace. The episodes in which he ran his car off the road were as memorable as they were frequent.

Chartier used India ink to draw his comics, along with white gouache for retouching. He'd prop a board on his knees – the same board he started out on in the 1930s – and lean it against the corner of his desk, using a fountain pen and ruler to draw on large-format illustration board. For almost a year, from September 1960 to August 1961, Chartier added a grey wash to his pages. But the cartoonist wasn't satisfied with the results ("it didn't turn out too well"[12]), and he quickly returned to the black-and-white that he mastered perfectly.

When he created the first pages of *Onésime* in 1943, Chartier was strongly influenced by the American comic strips of the time, with their chubby, boisterous characters. But toward the end of the decade, possibly as a result of the illustration work he was doing, Chartier began using a looser line and simplifying his characters, their curved forms undulating in the panels. Comics artist Jimmy Beaulieu associates this "chic" style with that of the *New Yorker* school of cartooning.[13] In the 1970s, the decors in *Onésime* became increasingly detailed, with Chartier sometimes opting for an almost realistic style. The nocturnal snowstorm scenes are remarkable: "The power of the night-time effects, rendered with just a few cross-hatches, and the swirling, dynamic movement of the lines and specks, which turn a snowstorm into a whiteout in the wink of an eye, reveal a cartoonist passionate about the craft of storytelling and intensely aware of the graphic delights he is able to produce."[14]

In his dialogues, Chartier used regional Quebecois expressions in order to re-create the spoken language of the countryside. However, he avoided the informal *joual*: "I could have had them saying "*toé pi moé*" and "*tabarnak*" and "*osti*"… but I didn't dare. Instead, I used a kind of proper rural French."[15] In his early appearances, Onésime had a stutter, but Chartier quickly grew tired of sustaining it in his scripts. In June 1961, Onésime stopped stuttering. When readers expressed their surprise, Chartier answered that Onésime had been treated by a chiropractor from Joliette: "It was just a nervous stutter and so the chiropractor cured him. It's as simple as that."[16]

Comedy in the *Onésime* stories often arises out of contrast and antithesis. Chartier constructed his gags around the physical differences between his characters, but also by playing with the conflicts between tradition and modernity, city stress and the quiet of rural life, men and women, young and old.

Numerous themes recur in the *Onésime* strips. According to Chartier scholar Jacinthe Boisvert, the artist "employed no more than some thirty themes, juxtaposed in various ways."[17] Topping the list are sports and outdoor activities such as camping, cross-country skiing, snowmobiling, canoeing, fishing, and hunting. In the latter, things generally turn out worse for the hunter than his prey. Onésime also makes regular trips to Montreal to attend hockey games and boxing matches, which invariably degenerate into general brawls. Religious holidays (Christmas with its midnight mass, New Year's, Easter) and other seasonal events like sugaring-off outings and Saint-Jean-Baptiste Day are also recurring subjects, along with natural catastrophes (floods, tornadoes), snowstorms, and fires.

Rural life, shaped by the rhythm of the seasons and annual festivities, was Chartier's subject in *Onésime*. But along the way, he also drew a portrait of Quebec in the second half of the twentieth century. "Onésime is… a chronicle of country life and, incidentally, a history of the evolution of mentalities in Quebec."[18] Onésime and Zénoïde visit Expo 67, attend the Olympics in 1976, and make their way to Quebec City in 1984 to celebrate the 450th anniversary of Jacques Cartier's first voyage to Canada. Like many Quebecers, the couple vacation in Cuba and visit Percé Rock in the Gaspésie. And once a year, Chartier sent his characters to tan on an American beach, initially in Cape Cod in the summer, and later in Florida

in the winter. Various public figures make brief appearances, including Quebec premier René Lévesque, singer Robert Charlebois, and hockey legend Maurice Richard. Even Batman has a cameo, stepping into the strip on the occasion of its fiftieth anniversary.

Chartier took part in activities in his region, and he enjoyed tipping his hat to local businesses in his comics: "I got a kick out of using real names."[19] And so the background of a panel might include billboards advertising the Potvin garage or the Gadoury grocery store. Over the years, *Onésime* also promoted many events in the Lanaudière region, among them the Saint-Jean-de-Matha sugaring-off festival, the Saint-Michel-des-Saints hunting festival, and the Saint-Gabriel-de-Brandon snowmobile festival. One festival in particular, however, inadvertently attracted considerable attention….

In 1980, Chartier created a strip for the Saint-Félix-de-Valois Poultry Festival. Onésime is on the beach with Zénoïde when an attractive young woman walks by. "See that cute chick [*poulette*]?" someone calls out. "*Poulette?*" thinks Onésime. He follows up with one of his signature minced oaths: "*Torbrûle!* What am I doing here? I almost forgot about the Saint-Félix-de-Valois Poultry Festival!" And that was all it took to unleash a storm upon Onésime and his creator.

The promotional comic, with a print run of 8000 copies, caught the attention of Marc R. Côté, interim activities coordinator at a local college. In an open letter to the *Joliette Journal*, published on June 6, 1980, he denounced Chartier's use of sexist stereotypes. "In this comic strip drawn by A. Chartier, the three men make SEXIST associations, which I find deplorable. The association of Women with chicks and Women with the Poultry Festival is crude and demonstrates a lack of respect for women" (capitals as in original).

He went on to take the festival organizer to task, demanding that the advertisement be withdrawn and an apology issued. Copies of the letter were sent to Agriculture Minister Jean Garon, the Council on the Status of Women, and the *Bulletin des agriculteurs*.

As the controversy grew, letters multiplied in the *Joliette Journal*. Some readers complained about Côté's lack of humour, while others, less numer-

"Onésime is... a chronicle of country life and, incidentally, a history of the evolution of mentalities in Quebec."

ous, supported his position. The editor of the *Joliette Journal* denounced what he perceived to be a witch-hunt. In the pages of the Montreal daily *La Presse*, Pierre Foglia weighed in with a column entitled "Down with the Sexist!", acknowledging that the strip lacked subtlety while ridiculing the author of the complaint. Popular radio and TV host Roger Baulu and comics scholar Richard Langlois of Université de Sherbrooke entered the fray as well, rallying to support Chartier.

A few months later, in January 1981, the contentious strip ran in *Bulletin des agriculteurs*, but with a new ending. When Zénoïde hears the expression *poulette*, she jumps up and berates the catcallers for their sexist behaviour.

In 1985, Chartier declared that he had benefited from the controversy. Whether provocatively or in mischievous reference to the incident, the term *poulette*, previously rare in *Onésime*, appeared ever more frequently in the months and years that followed. On one occasion, Chartier went so far as to include the dictionary definition in a footnote labelled "Attention feminists!"[20]

In the end, he recycled the controversy by integrating it into the strip. Women's issues now became a recurring theme, and Zénoïde emerged as a stalwart defender of women's rights, never hesitating to criticize her husband's sexist and "macho" behaviour.

With his pipe dangling from the corner of his mouth and his spectacles perched on the tip of his nose, Onésime bumbled through the pages of *Le Bulletin des agriculteurs* from November 1943 to May 2002. Throughout its run, the strip was hugely popular with the magazine's readers, as reflected in its exceptional longevity. In rural Quebec, four or five generations learned to read with *Onésime*.

When *Le Bulletin des agriculteurs* was bought by the newspaper group Maclean-Hunter in 1991, the editorial board decided to suspend the comic strip. But readers protested so vehemently that the new owner went back on his decision.[21] In

1994, the editor wrote the following in an article marking the strip's fiftieth anniversary: "*Onésime* is read by 85 to 90 percent of our readers, and when people address farmers at gatherings, many — including company executives — use *Onésime* stories to break the ice."[22]

Over the years, Chartier often redrew old scripts. A comparison of various versions of the same story (some storylines were recycled up to six times!) reveals the evolution of the cartoonist's style, but also that of Quebec society. In the late 1980s, Chartier began recycling the old pages themselves, applying white gouache in order to modify decors and integrate new elements alongside the old. This approach became increasingly frequent, and by 1995,[23] *Le Bulletin* was only publishing reruns and lightly retouched pages.

In 2002, Onésime finally retired, after 698 pages and a run that lasted 58 years and 7 months.[24] In June 2002, *Onésime* was replaced by Patrick Breton's *Les gens Delaville*. But Onésime himself did not entirely disappear from the pages of the bulletin, as the Delaville family lived next door to the esteemed retiree. Onésime and Zénoïde made a few appearances in the new series, which lasted through to October 2003.

Although *Onésime* totalled some 700 strips, only a fraction have been gathered up in book form. A first collection was published by Éditions de l'Aurore in 1974, on the occasion of the character's thirtieth anniversary. The 123-page album covered the period 1944 to 1963. A second, 64-page album appeared the following year, featuring strips published between 1946 and 1967. To celebrate the fortieth anniversary of *Onésime* in 1983, La Compagnie de Publication Rurale Inc., then publisher of the *Bulletin des agriculteurs*, issued a 146-page collection of strips published between 1943 to 1973, organized by themes such as winter, everyday life, the nieces, and sporting activities. To date, no strip drawn after 1973 had been reprinted in a book. And now it's done! ●

ENDNOTES

1. The *Bulletin des agriculteurs du Québec* began publication in February 1918.

2. Jacques Samson, "Rencontre avec Albert Chartier," *Actes: Premier colloque de bande dessinée de Montréal* (Montreal: Analogon, 1986), 64.

3. Albert Chartier, "Présentation," *Les Aventures d'un Québécois typique: Onésime* (Montreal: Éditions de L'Aurore, 1974).

4. Samson, 64.

5. Monique Brunelle-Ferland, "Onésime a 40 ans bien son-nés," *Le Bulletin des agriculteurs*, June 1984, 51.

6. The chronicle, sometimes entitled "En roulant ma boule," ran in the Montreal daily *La Presse* from 1905 to 1954.

7. Chartier.

8. Aubert Tremblay, "Torbrûle!" *Le Bulletin des agriculteurs*, November 1993, 8-11.

9. Louis Pelletier, "Un des premiers villégiateurs du lac Noir," *Joliette Journal*, January 23, 1985, 41.

10. Albert Chartier continued to live in the region until his death. A bridge over the Noire River is named after him.

11. Samson, 65.

12. Samson, 67.

13. Jimmy Beaulieu, "Ingénues," *Une piquante petite brunette* (Montreal: Les 400 coups, 2008), 5.

14. Richard Langlois, Albert Chartier, "*La bande dessinée made in Sherbrooke* (Sherbrooke: Musée des Beaux-arts de Sherbrooke, 1998), 45.

15. Samson, 65.

16. Samson, 65.

17. Excerpt from a talk given by Jacinthe Boisvert on June 4, 1994, at a family reunion of the descendants of Michel Chartier, in the basement of the Sherbrooke cathedral.

18. Michel Lessard, "Albert Chartier: Un grand-père vert," *Titanic*, no. 6, April 1984, 32.

19. Samson, 65-6.

20. Page published in April 1987.

21. Langlois, 43.

22. Aubert Tremblay, "Le grand-papa de la BD," *L'Actualité*, February 1994, 65.

23. The last page was entirely redrawn by Albert Chartier and published in March 1995.

24. *Onésime* was published continuously, except for interruptions in the months of August 1949, February 1950, October 1966, and May and November 1968.

THE MIDDLE YEARS

Réal Godbout

in conversation with Stanley Wany

Originally published in:

Trip #6
September, 2009

Translation by
Helge Dascher

I n April 2009, I sat down with Réal Godbout at ÉMI (École Multidisciplinaire de l'Image, the arts and culture school of Université du Québec en Outaouais) for an interview. It was one of the few times I've been back in the classrooms in which I spent most of my time as an undergrad.

I had two reasons for wanting to speak with Réal. First off, I think he is one of the most refined cartoonists around. At the Gatineau comics festival in 2007, I was amazed by his wealth of knowl-edge, not only about the medium and its various forms, but about history in general.

Second, given that I was familiar with the scope of his published work, I wanted to know why he had chosen to do an adaptation of Franz Kafka's *Amerika*.

This interview was recorded by Stanley Wany in April 2009 at ÉMI. The photos were taken by Marc Tessier. The interview was transcribed by Marie-Claude Mongeon and edited by Marie-Claude Mongeon, Stanley Wany and Réal Godbout in July 2009.

Photo by Marc Tessier

Stanley Wany: What made you decide to adapt Kafka's novel *Amerika*?

Réal Godbout: Well, publishing considerations aside, the fact is that it had been a long time since I'd written a script from A to Z all on my own. I feel like I can take any story and make it into a comic that's going to be interesting and make sense, but maybe I was a little paralyzed by the idea of going it alone. It's not the how that bothers me, but the what. What do I want to say? When I was writing *Michel Risque* and *Red Ketchup* for *Croc*, I was working with Pierre Fournier and we both had equal input in generating ideas. It's not like I was just there to draw his ideas. It was a true collaboration. But obviously, we'd keep each other fired up, so writer's block was never an issue. It was a special context, too, since we were doing a series for a magazine, which isn't the case now.

from *Amerika*

When it comes to subject matter, lots of cartoonists talk about their own life. That can make for some very interesting graphic novels, but I don't feel compelled to tell my life story in a comic. I'm not especially interested in digging up memories. So I returned to an idea I'd had for a long time, which was to adapt *Amerika* as a graphic novel. With graphic novels, there's no set page requirement, so you don't have to worry about format or length. You just start your story, and it takes as many pages as it takes. I wanted to do something more substantial, too — something that takes more than ten minutes to read.

SW: How did you go about writing it?

RG: I started with the idea of making a fairly traditional comic in line with what I had done before. In other words, something narrative, but where the narration is carried by action and dialogue. I didn't want it to be too literary, with large chunks of text. It was really more about staging a story based on the novel. I read and reread the novel and then I summarized it — I wrote a synopsis in my words based

from *Red Ketchup*

on my reading of the novel. After that, I put the text aside. You'll find virtually no lines from the novel reappearing in the comic book. Except I still tried to be true to the story... Obviously, there's going to be some transposition in moving from one medium to the other, but I tried to stay true to the story and the characters. I tried to preserve some of Kafka's spirit without pretending to be Kafka myself.

SW: That's just it. Do you find that the mechanisms of comics lend themselves well to rendering this kind of novel?

RG: I think they do. That's why I had the idea to begin with. I could really see it. It's not totally straightforward and you need to step back from the text, but yes, the medium lends itself to it. Especially since there's a very visual dimension to *Amerika*. And there's action, too. It's not a thriller, and still there's stuff happening. There's also a kind of humour that works well and that can be rendered visually. But yes, there are certainly times when it's a puzzle. Kafka's writing is

very distinctive, so you're always asking yourself, how am I going to tell this or set that up? There's a certain amount of reconstruction involved. You absorb the text the best you can and then you put it aside and you try to reconstruct and rewrite it. I rewrote it entirely in my own way, while trying to stay as true to the spirit of the novel and the storytelling as possible.

SW: I noticed on your blog that the artwork is in tones of grey. Why use grey tones instead of colour or just black and white?

RG: Because I was fed up with working in colour. [*Laughs.*] And I found that the subject matter lent itself well to it, though colour would have been fine, too. Plus it's a period piece, so visually, it's a bit like a black-and-white film. The Charlie Chaplin movies were the main reference for me. I definitely see some similarities with *Modern Times* and films like that. And the use of grey tones was similar to what I did in *Michel Risque*, so it was like connecting with my roots. Of course, it's a long book. It runs about 150 pages, so doing it in colour would have been a tremendous amount of work, plus very expensive to print.

SW: I'd like you to explain from A to Z how you approach a page. How do you start, how do you plan a page and lay things out....

RG: Let me go back a step to the writing. When I draft the script, which is based on the synopsis, I don't lay it out page by page. I have a story, I follow the thread of the story, and I work things out one panel at a time. For a story to take shape, you need to break it down panel by panel before you start drawing, and you plan the dialogue as you go. Let's say I've decided that each chapter is going to have about 150 to 200 panels. Alright, then I lay out my panels over a certain number of pages. I decide on an average number of panels per page, usually about six to seven panels, and then I try plan things out, with page breaks in the right places. Next I make a simple grid to work out the placement and size of each panel. So in this process I can already say, "This will be a large panel here. That will be a small panel there. I'll put a panoramic panel over there. I'll use a three-panel strip here, and a single-panel strip there," and so on…. As I'm going through this process, I'm already visualizing things. Why this frame here? Because I'm already starting to think about the next panel.

SW: When it comes to the text, how do you place the dialogue?

RG: The script is already broken down panel by panel. In other words, there will be "x" number of panels that I distribute into "y" number of pages and each panel has a certain size, and that just lets me arrange a layout. It's very rough, but it's a layout that establishes a certain framework for each panel. The fact of choosing one frame over another means I've already visualized each panel. From there, I do my sketches straight on the board… and I place my text at the same time, right from the start. I even letter it very cleanly from the outset so that the page is organized around the text layout and everything works together. You don't want to be doing all this nice artwork and then find out there's not enough room for the text! There's a relationship between the spaces occupied by text, by the characters, the backdrop, the framing and so on…. I do the first sketches fairly quickly right on my sheet. Then I trace them. To see the pencilling clearly, I erase my sketches as I go and I add details. When I get tired of sketching, I'll move over to pencilling. I always work in sequence, but I'll switch hats depending on my mood: sketching, pencilling, inking, grey tones…. I always work chronologically in reading order, though. I'm not going to go and do a panel three pages further ahead because I feel like working on that particular page…. I used to do that a long time ago, but I make a point

now of staying in line with the story as it reads. I find it works better that way.

Anyway, so I do the pencilling, and basically, that's the work that takes the longest to do. I rework the sketches where they're fairly tight and detailed. That's also when I integrate documentation, which can be significant since this is a period-piece comic. When I work with documentation, I never copy or transpose photos as such; it's just a starting point. When the pencilling is finished, I do the lettering and inking with a brush. One thing that's maybe a bit unusual is that I never use a ruler. It's more work, but a ruler-drawn line never seems to fit in with the rest. From time to time, I'll do some very detailed panels, which can be very time-consuming. I get annoyed when people tell me, "Oh, I saw a few pages. Wow, there's so much detail in them!" [*Laughs.*] Sometimes I feel like I need to add detail for people to appreciate the work.

from *Red Ketchup*

"I get annoyed when people tell me, "Oh, I saw a few pages. Wow, there's so much detail in them!" [Laughs.] Sometimes I feel like I need to add detail for people to appreciate the work."

And sometimes that gets frustrating. [*Laughs.*] It would be easier if I could draw very lightly. Maybe it comes down to insecurity, but I feel like I occasionally have to put the energy into drawing elaborately detailed panels.

SW: I just saw a panel in *Amerika* that shows a street in New York City. There's a policeman in the foreground who is directing traffic, and the perspective is just overflowing with details. On a page like that, how do you decide the level of detail you're going to include?

RG: For that panel, I took my cues from the novel, which has a fairly long description of the street. Without being too literal, I was trying to convey the equivalent in the drawing. I told myself that for this drawing, I needed to go all out. Earlier, when I was deciding how to lay out the panels, I knew that this one would be at least half a page. And a half-page means you're going to pull out all the stops. At that point in the process, I start working with documentation, but like I said, I don't copy photos as such. I use a variety of sources, I look for period photos on the Web, I pick the ones that inspire me the most, and I go from there. It all turns into something else, of course, based on the descriptions in the novel. But I don't always follow the text either: sometimes I'll make things up or add elements. For example, there's a scene in the first chapter where the character gets lost in a maze of passageways on a ship and can't find his way out. In the novel, he walks through the passageways and enters another part of the vessel with offices, rooms, and so on. To make it more visual, I had him enter the engine room, and you see the huge engines. There's a steam punk feeling to these massive steam engines in the ship's hold and it makes for a fairly impressive drawing. It fits, too, because the character in the engine room is interested in machinery, so there's a correlation, plus later on he meets a man working in the engine room, and that ties in too. But either way, at that point I felt like I needed to enrich the story visually. The book itself is a portrait of the times with a fantasy dimension, since Kaf-

ka never actually travelled to America. There are inconsistencies and he takes a lot of liberties, for instance with the geography. And so I went ahead and took some, too.

SW: Is there a message or a statement in all this? Does your choice of Kafka say something about you, or are you using this adaptation to address a specific issue?

RG: Maybe it's something to do with the main character. Kafka is a writer I'm attracted to for all kinds of reasons. There's that pessimism of his, and at the same time a kind of generosity. The writing is sober, too. The emotions are always contained, and there's an absurd dimension. People tend to think of Kafka as an avant-garde writer who was defying boundaries in literature. That's not necessarily something I'm trying to do — I don't see myself as a prophet. I like things that are avant-garde, but I'm not trying to deconstruct the medium. Formally, I'm pretty classic. I'm probably more classic as a cartoonist then Kafka was as a writer. Other than that, there's also the fact that I was very young when I first read the book. The novel is about an adolescent learning the ways of the world. And sometimes he reminds me of myself, even physically. When I look at some of the drawings of my protagonist, Karl Rossman, I say to myself, that's me! It's strange... something in the drawings makes me feel like I'm looking at a photo of myself at age 15 or 16.

SW: You say you're not interested in being avant-garde or a prophet. But at the 2007 Rendez-vous de la BD in Gatineau, an American from Texas said that you are one of North America's most important alternative cartoonists.

RG: I don't see it that way. I see what I do as something very, very classic. Clean line, Hergé-style.

SW: I have a different take on that. Still, you're a significant figure in the history of Quebec comics. Why do you think that is?

...at the spectacle of the street.

from *Amerika*

RG: Listen, I don't think I'm the right person to talk about how significant I am. [*Laughs.*] When I was younger, I did experimental work because I was interested in it and it was almost uncharted territory in Quebec. I was maybe a bit more marginal then than I am now. And marginal work was what I wanted to do. At some point I met people, I developed as a cartoonist, I tried different things, and then the magazine *Croc* appeared and everything changed. Even though I wanted to do marginal work, I also got the sense that I could use comics to reach a lot of people. That was probably truer back then than it is today. I felt like comics had a democratic dimension, and that I could connect with more people through comics than through painting. As it happens, *Croc* turned out to be a hit. Today, you've got all kinds of options, but having your work published in a magazine with a print run of 100,000 copies per month isn't one of them. So I did a serial for years. And of course that opened doors. If things hadn't turned out that way, I don't know what I'd be doing today.

SW: Still, *Red Ketchup* wasn't just about humour. Even though it was published in *Croc*, there was something about it that got people hooked.

RG: It was about humour…. Or maybe the choice we made, consciously or not, was that it would be humorous and satirical, but still have dramatic content. Some of the stories are pure parody and those can be pretty funny, but we wanted it to be more than that. *Michel Risque* started out as parody – it was a superhero caricature – but it turned into something else. As we went along, we began to believe in our characters. That didn't prevent us from exaggerating and doing broad comedy, but we were interested in credibility, too. Even the most overdone, outlandish aspects have a certain dramatic credibility. That's even truer in *Red Ketchup*. Obviously, satire is social commentary. It's a vision of the world you live in that goes beyond simple parody.

SW: How did you come up with the idea of the story "The Lawyer"?

Photo by Marc Tessier

from *Red Ketchup*

"Wanting to connect with the general public doesn't make you a sell-out. You just have to do what you want to do and make the books you want to make."

RG: That was in the context of a course. I was looking for a text to adapt, and since I was already toying with the idea of adapting Kafka, I flipped through a collection of his short stories. I wanted something very short that would lend itself well to the assignment, and this one really appealed to me. It's not as well-known as *The Metamorphosis* and it's much shorter, but I liked the idea of doing something about Alexander the Great's horse and reproducing images from the mosaic of the Battle of Issus. The mosaic shows Alexander the Great, his horse, and Darius, King of the Persians. It's a well-known work and I wanted to use it in a comic.

SW: Based on conversations we've had in the past, you don't seem convinced that we're seeing a "new springtime" in Quebec comics.

RG: Well, the term refers to Quebec comics in the 1970s. Are you talking about the 1970s or today?

SW: I'm talking about today. People keep saying that this is the springtime of Quebec comics.

RG: People said the same thing back in my day.... [*Laughs.*] I guess the expression has stuck. I do see a certain vitality. Of course, opportunities are opening up that we didn't have back then. It's different, but there are new opportunities.

SW: But it seems like the problems haven't changed. Printing costs, distribution...

RG: Well, with digital printing, it's easier to produce small quantities. Maybe that's the difference. Digital printing isn't free, but if you want to print fifty copies, you can. It won't pay the rent, but you can do it. And if you want to print 100, 200, or 1000 copies, that's doable too. Up to a certain quantity, digital printing is cheaper. In the past, if you wanted to publish a book, you had to print I don't know how many thousands of copies to make any money.

SW: Do people, whether they're here in Quebec or elsewhere, need to be able to live off comics for there to be a comics community?

RG: Maybe not exclusively, but it would allow for a certain continuity. It would let authors stay in the game longer and eventually focus on comics full-time. There are lots of people doing interesting work even though they don't make a living off it, and I admire that. It's tough going. It requires a lot of effort, because these are comics, after all. Sure, you can say poetry is tough, it's hard to write a poem or a song, but if things are going well, you can write a song in ten minutes. It doesn't always happen that way, but it's possible. Whereas in comics, even though a few people may be able to draw a decent page in ten minutes, generally speaking it takes more time than that. You've got no choice but to work full-time to pay the rent and put food on the table. I received a Canada Council grant for my book, but that was four years ago and the money is spent. The project is slow going, so I work on it alongside other jobs, illustration contracts, teaching, and everything else. I'd love to be able to tell you that I'm making comics full-time, turning out three pages a week, and I'll be done in a few months, but....

SW: But that's just not the reality for cartoonists in Quebec.

RG: That's right. There are ways to get published and be paid for it, but that's not happening for everybody. We need to try to get out of our closed circle and stop making work only for our small group. I don't think we have to make compromises just because we want to connect with the public at large. Wanting to connect with the general public doesn't make you a sell-out. You just have to do what you want to do and make the books you want to make.

SW: But what is the general public? That needs to be defined, right?

RG: Either way, there's not just ONE general public. When you talk about a general readership, you're talking about all kinds of people. I just mean a readership that's large enough for the work to be viable. I don't see why that shouldn't be possible....

SW: But like you said, Quebec comics seem to be aimed at a small market.

RG: Quebec isn't a big market to begin with, and if we limit ourselves even further to our small group, our little clique, we're not going to get very far.

SW: What do you think this phenomenon is due to?

RG: Well, Quebec's population is relatively small, so that just makes for a small market. But I wonder why we can't connect with everybody.

SW: Is it a matter of perception?

RG: Maybe.

SW: For example, I think *Red Ketchup* and *Michel Risque* are pretty accessible, but it seems like the readership is limited to a certain number of people.

RG: Yeah, but that's always the case. "General public" doesn't mean everybody, and it never will.

SW: Of course it doesn't include kids, but it seems to me that most of today's comics are for older readers anyway. For instance, if you take what's coming out of Europe today, it's not for readers aged 7 to 77.

RG: No, but that's not what you want to aim for, either. Of course, you're still likely to get bigger print runs with kids' comics. Despite all the effort that's been made, there's still a perception out there that comics are for kids. Or if they're not for kids, they're for teenagers. Not everybody thinks so, but many do. And when a comic book is specifically for adults, people figure it must be a porn comic, but that's not it. Take Michel Rabagliati and his *Paul* books. Michel really connects with people, you could say he appeals to the public at large, and at the same time his books are for adults, he's creating auteur work, and he's very well known. His books sell well and he's relatively successful, but he still has a hard time living off comics. He's making something that is super accessible, widely reviewed, popular, and good, and it takes all that for him to earn his bread and butter. Others just set their sights on Europe instead, and so you get a few people making things like *Les Nombrils* [Series by Maryse Dubuc and Marc Delafontaine, pub-

lished in English as *The Bellybuttons*.] I think what they're doing is totally fine. They make books for young adults that are very accessible and published in Europe, and at the same time, they've got an authentic flavour. They're making a decent living from it, and I think that's great. When somebody's a commercial success and they're making something that's good, all the better.

SW: But meanwhile they're working with a European publisher.

RG: Sure, but they got their start here, and then things took off for them in Europe. Which is great. Sure, their work is for teenagers, but there's nothing wrong with that.

SW: What do you think about the trend of European publishers setting up divisions in Quebec, like Glénat Québec?

RG: I don't know much about it. I figure what Glénat does here will probably be similar to what they do in Europe, and personally, it's not for me. I'm waiting to see the results. Maybe down the road they'll help Quebec artists reach a bigger market, which is a good thing. I haven't seen anything conclusive yet, but I'm not really up to date, so I'm not the right person to ask.

RG: Have you heard about the Quebec version of the Tintin book *Coke en Stock* [published in English as *The Red Sea Sharks*]?

RG: Yeah, that's a strange one.... I know Tintin has been translated into various dialects, but Quebecois isn't a dialect. It's a way of speaking French. So can you really translate something into Quebecois? I guess you can if you play with it. Some people were shocked by the idea. It doesn't really bother me. I take it for what it is, a game.

SW: Perfect. I think the idea of playing games is a good place to end the interview. Thanks! ●

from *Michel Risque*

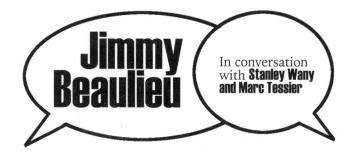

Jimmy Beaulieu

In conversation with **Stanley Wany and Marc Tessier**

Originally published in:

Trip #6, 2009

Translation by Helge Dascher

Stanley Wany: Jimmy, do you think it's spring-time or winter for Quebec comics? [A reference to the famous Quebec springtime of comics (1968-1975) which started with the Chiendent group and is considered a renaissance period for Quebec *bande dessinée* (see Sylvain Lemay's *Du chiendent dans le Printemps*, published in 2016 by MEM9IRE)].

Jimmy Beaulieu: It depends. In economic terms, it's always more or less winter, but in terms of creativity. I teach at Cégep du Vieux-Montreal [One of Quebec's network of cegeps, or post-secondary schools, that offer technical and pre-university programs.], so I'm always seeing inspiring new artists — people like Vincent Giard and Julie Delporte, who make huge strides in a year. So I can't really say it's winter. I'm still fired up.

Marc Tessier: Are we coming out of winter and headed for a new spring?

JB: You could say so, but I can't really complain about any of the periods during which I've been active. Things have gotten so much better over the past ten years. I never thought I'd be making books the way I am now. We never thought we'd be on television talk shows or getting this much attention in the press. And we've got a certain presence in bookstores, too. Of course there's always room for improvement. I see the glass as half full. We've come a long way, and there's still a ways to go. But I see people who have the energy and motivation to take their turn at being the Jean Drapeaus of comics, like I was.

MT: The Jean Drapeaus?

JB: Denis Lord once called me the Jean Drapeau of Quebec comics. [Mayor of Montreal from 1954 to 1957 and 1960 to 1986, who brought Expo 67 and the Olympics to the city.]

MT: Why?

JB: Well, because I'm ambitious and I always have some big project in the works. Denis came up with that line when I published *Plan Cartésien*. I was happy to play the role for ten years, but if somebody else wants to wear that hat, I'd gladly give it up.

SW: Economically speaking, why is it so hard to produce quality projects in Quebec? The quality is improving, but we're still

Photo by Marc Tessier

jimmy 5 mars 2005

45

"I've been getting offers from European publishers since 2004, but if I accept them, I'll be giving up on the possibility of building something in Quebec. I have a hard time accepting that."

not making hardcover albums. It's like we can't bridge the gap in terms of financing.

JB: I'm not especially interested in making hardcover books or colour comics, so that hasn't been an issue for me. Except I would have liked to print on thicker paper or have sewn bindings, but the cover price would have gone from $15 to $30.

MT: That's what La Pastèque is doing.

JB: Yes, but they get their books printed in Asia, and I'm not willing to do that. And so MG [Mécanique générale, a comics imprint headed by Jimmy Beaulieu from its launch in 1999 to 2009.] became obsolescent in a way. Everybody else was making beautiful books that were printed outside Quebec. I'm not comfortable with that. I'd rather stick to the underground and make comics that are digitally printed and perfect-bound, on recycled paper.

MT: Would you say that MG comics were "overground-underground"?

JB: Yes. It's strange because things have changed. The big seller in Quebec is Michel Rabagliati, not *13* or *Largo Winch* [Titles by best-selling Belgian genre author Jean Van Hamme.].

MT: Like the MG books, Michel's *Paul* books aren't hardcover. They're perfect-bound and black-and-white.

JB: We tend to associate commercial success with books like the *Largo Winch* series. But it's a whole other story in Quebec. Michel Rabagliati's *Paul* books are what sells here. My books sell respectably. The marketing model is different than it is in France, the US, or Japan. In countries other than those three, it's all very small scale, but you'll have books that seem marginal because they're black-and-white and softcover, with edgy content, and yet those are the ones that sell.

MT: It's worth mentioning that the term underground goes back to Spiegelman, Crumb, and Shelton. It refers to a whole movement that revolutionized comics in terms of content and by taking a more personal approach. The MG catalogue has a lot of titles along those lines, like Philippe Girard's books and Benoit Joly and Luc Giard's formal experiments. David Turgeon does experimental work that isn't always conclusive, but it's great that there's a forum for him to try things out.

JB: In a way, MG was about imagining that we could make something mainstream. Not "underground comics," but "comics," period. By that definition, everything else, like the traditional sword-and-sorcery stuff, would be "genre comics" (and if something is just bad, it's *"bédé"*). Things are categorized the same way they are in literary publishing. There's commercial fiction, literary fiction, sci fi, young adult fiction, and so on. MG was crazy enough to want to help put graphic novels, aka underground comics (which I just call "comics"), in the centre. And in a way it worked. It was up to the authors to decide, and creativity always came first. Right up until a book was actually printed, I never thought about how I would market it. In a perfect world, you'd only start thinking about sales after a book rolls off the presses. I never said to an author, "We'd sell more copies if you put in this kind of scene or if the book was longer or shorter." I did say: "Add two or three pages so we feel more connected to your character." That's the kind of advice I'd give.

MT: Did the authors listen to you?

JB: Yes and no. Since sales were modest and there wasn't much marketing support, I didn't really insist. I'd make suggestions. The key thing was for the end product to be the book the author had in mind. So I'd back off quickly if there was conflict, even if my instincts and experience were screaming for me to hold my ground. I regret it a bit today because my instincts were sound and my experience was a good asset. I just said sales were modest, but things were actually going pretty well, and they were getting better and better. In the last year we were selling out print runs. Zviane and Catherine Lepage's books did very well. But the books that were driving sales weren't enough to make up for the more daring and difficult books. When the publisher I worked for, 400 coups, was bought out, everything changed. I decided to step down as head of the comics section and MG. I needed to pull back and take a break.

SW: How do you balance producing graphic novels and genre comics and making sure they sell? In Quebec, 3000 copies is a success.

MT: Actually, 500 copies is a success.

JB: Personally, I'm thrilled when I sell 500. I call my authors and we pat each other on the back.

SW: Why do you think it's like that?

JB: People read comics, but they don't necessarily buy them. And not many people read in Quebec. We don't have a lot of bookstores. We've got one chain that bought out all the others, and the independents are suffering. I've worked in bookstores, so I know how hard it is to move the books you love off the shelves.

MT: Is there a recipe for success when it comes to comics in Quebec?

JB: Keep making good books. Stay in the game. But there's always the temptation to publish abroad. And I'm starting to get tempted, because they're offering €10,000 to €12,000 for things where in Quebec, I'd get $500. At a certain point, you'd have to be crazy to try to create something here. I've been getting offers from European publishers since 2004, but if I accept them, I'll be giving up on the possibility of building something in Quebec. I have a hard time accepting that.

SW: Is it because of the market that no Quebec publisher can offer a $12,000 advance?

JB: We have a mistaken conception of publishers here. Publishers make money by selling books. If they produce books that don't sell, they eventu-

ally run out of money. Some authors want to be paid $1500 a week to work on their books, as if this was Hollywood. Dream on!

MT: Those are American rates.

JB: And they're asking for them before they've even drawn a single page!

MT: What do you do in those situations? Smile and say nothing?

JB: I answer the best I can and try to be as respectful as possible. I don't want to discourage them too much or burst their bubble.

MT: Is making comics here today an art form? Is it something people do out of passion, because they feel a need to express themselves, and not for the money?

JB: Take a book like *Le moral des troupes* (mécanique générale, 2004). I worked on it for two years, and I got paid as much for it as I've earned on illustration and advertising jobs I've done in half a day (and sometimes even in an hour). You can make as much money in a couple of hours as you do on something you slaved over for two years, giving it your heart and soul. Making comics in Quebec is basically a vocation, and it was seriously crazy of me to have tried to make it viable. But people like

47

La Pastèque are managing pretty well.

SW: In Finland, the system is competition-based. You submit your project to the government and it pays for printing.

MT: That's almost a communist system.

JB: We can't compare ourselves to the Scandinavian model. It's paradise. We live in a country that voted for Stephen Harper and Jean Charest. So we can either sit around and complain or try to keep doing things, try to get people thinking. Like: do you really want to vote for Harper? I talk about that in stories like "Démodé" [Published in *Le tour du monde en bande dessinée* (Delcourt, 2009).]. Art needs government support in Quebec because we don't consume culture the way other people do. There's no patronage. In English-speaking culture, people value neighbourhood libraries as community resources that bring people together. They have book clubs. We don't value culture the same way here in Quebec.

MT: Have things changed? Was culture more highly valued in the 1980s than it is today? What value does culture have in today's society? Nobody has managed to clearly show how culture contributes to the well-being of a nation. What would it take to convince politicians and the public in Quebec that culture matters and we need to invest in it? During the last round of budget cuts, artists spoke out, and even though they said a few nice things, I wasn't convinced.

SW: There was no concerted action. Everybody did their own thing. People didn't go to Ottawa to present their grievances. And then you've got the government setting aside $25 million for awards to foreign artists on the one hand, and cutting funding on the other. You've got foreign artists coming here to exhibit, and at the same time, the government is cutting grants and preventing local artists from exhibiting elsewhere.

JB: Our relationship to culture is bizarre. Here in Quebec, we tell ourselves that culture is vital because we're francophones or whatever, but it's all bullshit!

SW: Last year, Halifax ranked second as Canada's cultural city.

JB: In the 1970s, there was a need to define our identity, to create something that could be called Quebecois.

MT: I read comics as a kid and when I'd find something from Quebec, it made me proud. It inspired me to make comics. MG will make its way, and a whole generation is going to discover your books and be inspired by them.

SW: Still, it's strange that it's taking so much time for Quebec comics to become accessible and available. MG books are in the bookstores, but booksellers still point you to the latest reissue of Tintin. There's even going to be a Quebecois version of *Coke en stock* [Quebec sociologist Yves Laberge "translated" *Coke en stock* (*The Red Sea Sharks*) into Quebec French; his controversial adaptation, *Colocs en stock*, was published by Casterman in 2009.]. What the hell?

MT: Right. For example, Glénat Quebec is part of Hachette Canada, and most foreign guests at festivals are managed by Hachette. It's almost a monopoly. So if Hachette is distributing Tintin, everybody is going to be talking about the Quebec edition of *Coke en stock*.

"You see it right away in my drawings, which can be loose, tight, deep, or all over the place. It's destabilizing. My work isn't an easy chair you can settle into. It's more like a hamster wheel, except it's square, triangular, or diamond-shaped... Whatever..."

JB: I think the appeal of the Tintin books is their familiarity. They take people back to when they had the time to be interested in culture. We keep rehashing the past because we don't have time to be curious anymore.

MT: Jimmy, the students at ÉMI [École multidisciplinaire de l'image, an arts and culture school in the Université du Québec network.] talk about your work. You take a stand that's more critical and political – you use comics to communicate. Generally speaking, the students are less into that. Not because it's not as good, but because they've been shaped by fiction. When you're that age, it's harder to take a stand, to be transparent, to put yourself into your stories. You worry that you'll be judged if you talk about yourself and your everyday life.

JB: Making comics forces me to take responsibility for what I say. When I started out, I didn't understand why people thought it was brave of me to talk about my life the way I do. It was pretty rare in comics. I use the word "journal" for my work instead of "autobiography:" it's a personal account, it's things I see. I'm not the subject. I use an avatar of myself to talk about what's going on around me so I can talk about the world I live in. Autobiography means telling the story of your life, but what I'm doing is using my own existence to talk about existence generally. I use fiction the same way. I think self-representation really obliges you to own what you say. I like that transparency. It can create monsters, though. Lots of bloggers talk about their lives without being especially brilliant. When autobiographical comics were a trend more than five years ago, we were criticized for being complacent and self-centered. That bugged me, but it's turning out to be true.

MT: During the first wave of autobiographical comics, with Chester Brown, Joe Matt, and Julie Doucet, critics were already slamming the trend and waiting for it to end. Literary writers have always broken taboos and helped society evolve by talking about their own lives. In literature, it's a legitimate approach that has endured through time. But in comics, it gets treated like a trend that has to be nipped in the bud. Except there are thousands of authors, and everything depends on the depth, value, and humanity of a person's perspective. For instance, cartoonists can take a documentary approach like you do in *Les balcons de Montréal*. You talk about an aspect of Montreal without putting yourself into the frame. It's as though you were filming a documentary with a camera on your shoulder. When it's you talking...

JB: It makes people uneasy. I don't know why. When Felix Leclerc sings songs about his son, nobody ever says, "That's so egocentric!"

MT: That's because songs are all about pure emotion. Drawing is more provocative, more in your face.

SW: In what sense?

MT: In the sense of revealing yourself. In class, I get students to talk about themselves more, to dig deeper. I have them go from genre comics to stylistic exercises so they can start thinking more deeply about everyday life and how they see it.

SW: Whether it's comics, literature, or any other medium, being an author is about revealing yourself. It's not always immediately apparent, but authors have to reveal themselves. And Jimmy, that's a role you've always taken on.

JB: That's really true. I don't see any difference in scale between taking the problems you've got with your mother and transposing them onto a naval battle. Or transposing political issues onto an intergalactic war. You can reconstruct and transform things or leave them as is — one way isn't better than the other. When you deal with issues straight on, you're saying, "There's no time to waste or play it safe." When I try to make something political or social, it's like I'm forcing myself to take a position. "Okay, I'm going to take a stand here and say it as it is." That doesn't mean that what I do is only literal. It has many layers. If you want to look closely at my work, you can spend a lot of time digging through aspects that are more intuitive and poetic. But it's really important to me for the message to be clear on first reading, like in *Le moral des troupes* (translated as part of *Suddenly Something Happened*, Conundrum, 2010). It has to be something I can't run away from. "Yes, that's what I said. Even if I was wrong." That matters to me. When I make a mistake, I admit it in writing. In *Le moral*, I show how the protagonist evolves. He starts out hating Montreal; he has all kinds of prejudices. And then at some point, his prejudices are shattered.

SW: Is that autobiographical, confessional approach a conscious choice?

JB: It's really a matter of personal preference. It's about what you want to do, tell, and show.

MT: If you look at Michel Rabagliati's work, it's "fake fiction." He's a good observer and he's sensitive. He makes stories based on what's happening around him. He condenses and edits. But he never says, "This is my life." As opposed to you, where it obviously is.

JB: You're right. It gets under people's skin.

MT: In the case of the *Paul* books, the author is older than the character. He's wiser and more experienced. He's not necessarily trying to provoke. Michel has created a character with eyebrows like his own, but if you don't know Michel, you can't know that his books are autobiography disguised as fiction.

JB: Well, I'm fighting for my right to exist. "You all want me to be a robot like yourselves, you want me to buy your hyped-up crap, you want me to be humble. Fuck you! I exist." [*Laughs.*] That's part of it, but at the same time, I'm not that much of a blowhard. It's not all about me. It's weird: people think a guy driving his SUV to the mall is the essence of individualism. But buying an SUV isn't a celebration of the self, it's a celebration of robotization. It's like you're celebrating the fact of becoming a robot and blending in with the crowd. I think there's an important distinction to be made between individualism and self-centeredness. I think I was influenced by *The Prisoner*…

MT: In your books, you describe yourself as an egotistical monster who craves attention. But to people who know you, that's not the image you project. I think you're a mirror for us all.

JB: I try to be honest.

MT: *Au lit les amis* is my favourite book in the Colosse collection [Collosse is a publishing collective dedicated to experimental comics and ephemeral book projects.]. It's full of narrative experiments, and some are really great. Long stories like *Ma voisine en maillot* (translated as *My Neighbour's Bikini*, Conundrum, 2014) don't seem to lend themselves as well to formal experiments. In your Colosse books, some pages are just sketches, things go in all directions, there are false narratives and dialogues collaged onto the images, but it still holds together. It's an amazing laboratory.

JB: It's interesting for you, and for about twelve other people.

MT: Twelve other people?

JB: Maybe 120 people. I print a hundred copies at a time, and I sell them all.

SW: Let's go back a bit. Even though you and Michel Rabagliati start out with similar intentions, your work touches me more. Your approach is more personal, so it's easier to identify with the story. Why is that?

JB: Michel thinks about readers, whereas I'm really thinking about artists. I don't work for someone who's strictly a spectator. I appeal to the reader's creativity and imagination. Michel takes artists into account, but he also makes it easy for people who just want a story. If you're reading *Ma voisine en maillot* and you're expecting suspense or fireworks, you'll be disappointed. There is a first level, but if that's all you're reading, you'll think, "So what?" If you're more creative, you'll consider the drawing and the writing, and you'll wonder why I bothered to tell the story and what I'm trying to say, so it will probably speak to you more.

SW: Does it really take a specialized background to get it? People say Michel is great because they've experienced the things he talks about. That kind of identification happens with your work, too, so why does your work touch only 120

from *My Neighbour's Bikini*, translation by KerryAnn Cochrane

people when Rabagliati's touches so many?

JB: Again, it comes down to how you approach the work.

MT: I'm not sure I agree with Stanley. I like Michel as much as I like Jimmy. Michel experiments with form, too. The bit about the history of Mac computers in *Paul Goes Fishing* is a good example. He touches people, he's able to reach out to them. It's like Kurt Vonnegut, who started writing when he was in his fifties. Michel was over forty when he started making comics. He brings a different perspective to them. He freelanced as a graphic artist

for a long time so he knows how to connect with people. But that doesn't mean he lacks content.

SW: True, but my question is this: given that he starts out with the same intentions as Jimmy, how come his work touches so many people?

MT: Maybe because he uses fiction?

JB: His work is carefully constructed. It's a well-oiled machine, like a Hitchcock movie.

MT: His graphic design experience taught him how to be accessible. And when he makes comics, he taps into that experience. Recently, on a beautiful fall day, at the corner of Fabre and Laurier, I saw a young girl sitting on a stoop reading a *Paul* book. That's fantastic. I'd rather see her reading one of Michel's books than *Asterix* or *Tintin*. It's time we put our own authors ahead of those from Europe (who manage to make a very good living off of comics). I hope that one day, after they've read the *Paul* books, Quebec readers will ask themselves what other comics are being made in Quebec.

Jimmy, you wear your heart on your sleeve. When you're depressed, when things aren't working out, when you're on the verge of crying, you

show it. You're totally transparent, but not everybody is into that. Michel tends to be discreet, and Jimmy is more shameless. Age is part of it, too. When you're younger, you want to be hardcore and shake things up. At the launch for Michel's book *Paul Goes Fishing*, people were older, in their 30s and 40s. He connects with people his age, and they're influential people who talk about his books afterward. Like I said, when students read Jimmy, they feel uncomfortable because they're confronted with the question: "Would I be capable of this level of transparency? I'm afraid of being this transparent." That's what I'm feeling. Years ago, everybody was talking about Julie Doucet. When I show her books to students today, nobody knows who she is. They look at her books like they're from another planet.

JB: That's terrible.

SW: Do you think it's the graphics or the drawing that turns readers off?

JB: Neither. It's really the structure, the architecture of the thing. Whether it's welcoming or a bit more raw. You see it right away in my drawings, which can be loose, tight, deep, or all over the place. It's destabilizing. My work isn't an easy chair you can settle into. It's more like a hamster wheel, except it's square, triangular, or diamond-shaped... Whatever... I like weird films, too. I like when things are a bit uncanny.

SW: Poetry and desire, anima and animus? Those elements all show up in your work.

JB: Yes, more and more. The older I get, the more of an old pervert I am. It's terrible. [*Laughs.*]

SW: Is that why you talk about sex — because you're an old pervert?

JB: Again, it's a question of urgency, of not wasting time. When you're working from an intensely personal place and you're not censoring yourself, things constantly slip into the realm of desire. It's part of my life. I'm married to a woman I find absolutely amazing. And that's just how it is: when I sit down at the drawing table, what motivates me is desire, life force, and all that. It's what gets me to the drawing table. If I'm not feeling great, if I'm feeling dead, I'll sit at my computer and poke around on the Internet. When you're feeling up, you're alive, you're walking around outside, you're drawing women, you want to have sex. And when you're feeling down, you poke around on the Internet, you watch TV, you stay home and order out.

MT: When things are going badly, do you draw on sexual desire to cheer yourself up?

JB: I try to sometimes, but I just end up making these really lame monsters. Often I'll convince myself that I'm doing okay, and then I'll draw some hot babes and it turns out ugly. I give it a go, it's like therapy, "Life is beautiful, let's draw some naked ladies and everything will be great!... (Heeeelp!)" Other times it works, it calms me down, but it's not a given. It really has to be celebratory. When things are going well and I'm in a good mood, the only thing that matters is drawing women or a setting or this street I love so much. That's how I end up being in the picture, because I'm celebrating and documenting things I love. The street, a park, whatever. I want to leave a mark. Twenty years from now it will all make sense. I'd love to read what Pierre Fournier would have done if he'd made an autobiographical comic about his "acid blue" years, or Chartier if he had done stories about his trips to New York, when he went there with his wife to show his work to the *New Yorker*. Imagine if he'd made comics about that, set in Montreal's Parc Lafontaine and in New York City as it was back then.

MT: In your comics, when you mention women, it seems like you're expressing your feminine side. In other words, you cast yourself as a woman in your erotic stories.

JB: That's absolutely true!

MT: There's something tantric when you talk about channelling life force energy into your erotic drawings. Does your wife mind you drawing those erotic scenes?

JB: It's not her favourite thing, but she knows it does me good and calms me down. Obviously there's a bit of her in what I'm drawing.

MT: I had a look at the comics Zviane made in response to your erotic stories. Instead of two women, there's two men. They're great. It would be interesting if she kept it up. There's something down-to-earth about the way she deals with eroticism that takes the drama out of sex and nudity. I think it's an approach that makes people less uptight. Sex is usually so overblown, or it's used to sell things, or it's super melodramatic, even though it's actually mostly cool and fun. It seems to me that the minicomics you make, with print runs of a hundred copies — like *Appalaches, Au*

from *My Neighbour's Bikini*, translation by KerryAnn Cochrane

53

"Twenty years from now it will all make sense. I'd love to read what Pierre Fournier would have done if he'd made an autobiographical comic about his 'acid blue' years, or Chartier if he had done stories about his trips to New York, when he went there with his wife to show his work to the New Yorker. Imagine if he'd made comics about that, set in Montreal's Parc Lafontaine and in New York City as it was back then."

lit les amis! And *Demi-sommeil* — would sell well in France. I'm surprised that Delcourt hasn't approached you. Have they seen them?

JB: I sent them to my editor there as a gift, that's all. What really works in France is autobiographical stories with a political slant. They're not looking for spy stories these days (not mine, anyway). They'd like me to do political autobiography. It's the new golden cow because it has credibility and it's good for sales. It's the kind of thing that gets you onto television talk shows and it sells a lot of books. But right now, a political autobiography would be more artificial for me than a book like *Appalaches*.

MT: Can't you play with their requirements?

JB: Sure. And at some point I'm going to have to start making money again. But if you want to make a comic, you need to be doing good. You really have to be in the right frame of mind.

SW: I totally agree.

JB: You need to have felt down to get inspired. But at a certain point, you need to be feeling calm so you can concentrate and draw. That's how it is for me, anyway.

MT: When you were head of comics at 400 coups, were you really getting 200 emails a day?

JB: I tend to exaggerate. It was more like 80 or 100.

MT: Still! When I have to answer 10 to 15, that's already a lot.

JB: These days I get about 20. There was a point where I just didn't answer my emails at all.

MT: So how do you manage to feel calm when you have so many projects to manage?

JB: I don't. When you're young, you can make a book like *Le Moral des Troupes* on the corner of a table while the emails pile up. You do it all – you answer your emails, pull all-nighters, have a girlfriend, watch movies. I'm going to be 35 soon. Things started going downhill at about 32. I couldn't drink till 4 a.m. anymore and wake up the next day at 10 a.m., ready to get to work. Now I feel like ideas need to incubate if I want to do something longer that has the same quality of writing and drawing as *Appalaches* and *Demi-sommeil*. It's like I'd need to be in a cottage with a rifle and shoot anybody who comes near. For now I'm doing a lot of very short stories – one-pagers with a single drawing, or two-, three-, or ten-pagers. That way I can take three or four days and really focus. But the emails and bills keep coming in.

MT: It took you two weeks to do *Ma voisine en maillot*. You preface almost all of your recent books by saying that you carved out two or three weeks of time here and there to draw them. That's a drag. Where's the pleasure? Imagine if you could work on a book full-time for three months, just for the fun of it.

SW: Can you even have that kind of fun when you're both an author and an editor?

JB: I'm pretty sure that somebody in better shape than me could manage. I was spreading myself too thin: I was writing reviews, teaching, publishing and making comics. And despite all that, I was one of the two most prolific comics artists in

Quebec for five or six years. I released a new book every year, I put my work online, I collaborated on all kinds of projects. I was really extremely active. You have to be incredibly healthy to work that way, and you burn out quickly. I got pretty sick. It was all stress-related: asthma, heartburn, eczema. The stress and responsibility just wore me down. When you're an editor, you're responsible for somebody else's work. If you're not paying attention, you're being negligent with something that matters. I found myself in a place where I had to be negligent sometimes, because when you're responsible for twenty authors, you can't always give 100% to a book that was published two years ago. But that book is still a big part of the author's life and output. If you don't have somebody to back you up, it'll be a flop.

MT: Doesn't the author have responsibilities as well? I thought publishing was becoming increasingly collaborative.

JB: You need to figure out who's going to be worth your energy and who'll be a waste of time. It might sound harsh, but it's the truth. You'll always get people who aren't very resourceful, but whose work is so important that they're worth the time you put into them. But you need to choose carefully.

MT: The work you do as an editor needs to be demystified. People tend to think it's only about success and money.

SW: The Bachelor in comics program at EMI should also be training publishers.

JB: Or it should at least let people know what to expect in the world of Quebec publishing. We need to get rid of the myth of the cigar-smoking publisher with pockets full of cash who'll step in and take care of everything. That's not how it is, especially not in the guerrilla environment we've got in Quebec.

MT: Are the people you work with – your closest collaborators — aware of all the work you do?

JB: We were part of an existing editorial structure called Les 400 coups, and since their books are in bookstores, there's an assumption that everything works by magic. Les 400 coups publishes a lot of books, but not every book is a bestseller. A book that was made with a lot of love often sells only 200 or 300 copies, with $6000 invested. And so they systematically lose money on most of their books. Sometimes you need to get the publisher excited about an artist. I know that Serge Théroux, the former head of Les 400 coups, agreed to do books like Benoit Joly's *Hiatus* out of love for the work. I presented the project, and he said, "We have to do it. We won't sell more than 150 copies, but we have to do it." The strange thing is, even if you don't need more than 300 copies, printing fewer than 1000 makes no financial sense, because you won't qualify for the same level of government funding. It's truly perverse.

MT: That's to get rid of some people (the authors who don't sell) in favour of others (those who do).

SW: But those kinds of measures seem out of touch with reality.

MT: The publisher Alain Stanké suggested eliminating all subsidies for publishers, so that the only books in bookstores would be the ones that sell. That's a totally commercial approach. It denies the value of art and literature, and the fact that they don't always connect with the public. You mentioned Benoit Joly — he's an incredible author. He was years ahead of everybody else, a kind of Réjean Ducharme of comics. At some point he had a breakdown. He disappeared from the scene until Jimmy brought his work back to public attention by publishing him. He has more books out now, but not many people know about him, which is a paradox. Our collective memory isn't very long when it comes to the arts and comics. There's not much in-depth analysis to guide readers, even though we're lucky to get the newspaper coverage we do. But without decent criticism, how can anybody go into a bookstore and find the best comics?

JB: You end up buying whatever's being promoted. Journalism here is all about hype. But I'm glad it exists. I didn't expect to see it in my lifetime.

SW: What will be MG's legacy?

JB: Remaindered books that even discount booksellers don't want! [*Laughs.*] I know we inspired people to make comics, and that makes me happy. We opened doors for young authors and we gave them the illusion that things are possible. We upheld the illusion of: "Go, do your own thing, and everything will work out."

SW: What would you say to somebody who's getting started in publishing?

JB: This is basic, but make a daily schedule for yourself and stick to it. I really destroyed myself by feeling responsible for other people's work. That's why I've decided to focus on my own books and let someone else do the dirty work of editing. When you're an author-editor, your friendships become poisoned by expectations and maybe even insincerity. Production at MG was constant, so the number of authors with demands on me kept increasing and I felt responsible for everything all the time. Meanwhile, on the business end of things, I was being asked to produce all kinds of documents, to prioritize books that sell, and to plan my publishing schedule years in advance. And the authors wanted to see their books quickly, which is understandable. The creative and the management/business aspects were always in conflict. I was getting more and more worn out, and the criticism didn't let up. It became a downward spiral, and I had to get out of it. I might go back to publishing, but…

MT: If you went back, what would you do differently?

JB: The *Colosse* collection is the answer to all that. What really matters in this whole mess? What matters is getting together and making books. Being together and being solid as a group, that's what matters to me. Get people involved: you pay for your own books and you do your own advertising. If we make enough money, at some point we'll hire a marketing person. But let's get back to what matters: let's get the job done, let's make books. And let's be part of a network where we get to discover each other's work. When Pascal Girard makes a mini-comic, I like that — I feel inspired to make one, too. Having a group dynamic is important because our work is so solitary. That was the idea behind MG, before it got stuck in a business model with a "real publisher." The basic philosophy couldn't thrive in that environment.

SW: Can artists survive in it?

JB: Yes, but put a dozen starving people in a room and throw in a piece of meat. A gracious person will die of hunger while the others eat. There's not much money in publishing, but there's a lot of people who want to live off it. Some books pay for themselves. Other books deserve to exist and almost break even. And then there are books that

deserve to exist even at a loss, like *Hiatus*, because it's a masterpiece. You have to be able to pay for all those books.

MT: What's the strategy at *Colosse*? How are you able to print books, sell them, and cover your costs, without going through the usual distribution channels?

JB: I look at what did well in the past. If I print 100 copies of my book before an event like Expozine, it costs $1000. I go to Expozine and sell 50, which is half my print run. I sell them for twice cost, so that covers the printer, and everything else is profit. You need to see if your printer can give you a week or 30 days to pay, or else you need some cash to get started, and you do what you can to avoid losing money.

MT: Are you saying that your printer gives you 30 days to pay?

JB: Not on the first two or three jobs, but after that, most printers can give you a 30-day account.

MT: Do the other *Colossus* authors get the same terms?

JB: Yes. Since we print books on a regular basis, we get better terms. We each pay for our own books, and they don't always cost a $1000.

MT: In terms of sales, does everybody manage to make a profit?

JB: Pascal Girard can sell out in a few seconds. I think everybody pretty much breaks even. The thing is, you wouldn't be able to sell books this way in bookstores. Our books retail at two times the cost of production. As a rule, publishers price books at five times cost. The bookstore gets 40% of the cover price, the distributor gets between 15 and 20%, and the artist gets 10%. That's how it usually breaks down. If you want to get out of that system, you can't sell in bookstores in the usual way. If I were to give bookstores 40%, I'd have to retail *Appalaches* at $48. That's not feasible.

MT: So your market basically consists of comics festivals and events like Expozine, where you can sell your books without a middleman and make a profit.

JB: Exactly. I only sell directly — or through bookstores that take a reasonable cut. At Expozine, you can break even in the first few hours.

(And that's a good thing, because I work from zero!) Just before an event, I'll make some new material, or I'll pull together a few things I've done for my blog and add some original work. I assemble it all, I go to the printer, and I hope I'll sell enough copies to cover my costs.

SW: It seems to me that a lot of work needs to be done at the level of distribution and promotion. It would take a comics rep to speak with the government and with bookstores. It's like something is missing for Quebec comics to get established. People talk about the springtime of comics, but I wonder if we've really seen it yet. It seems to me that there's no direct link between financing and the government.

JB: No, there isn't. And I'm not sure it would be a good idea, either. With one person handling things, you'd end up with infighting and cliques. The system we have now, where artists and publishers each apply for their own funding, is a pretty decent system. Except there's not enough money to go around. Despite everything, bookstores have been pretty supportive. It's relative, though. When I go into a bookstore, I come out heavyhearted. I could just cry. Take Chartier's book, *Une piquant petite brunette*. I worked on it for a whole year, I gave it everything I've got. I thought it would be an important book, a real

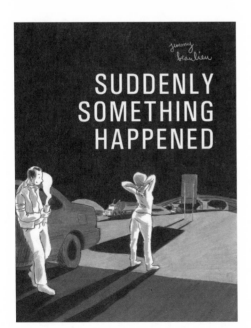

event. So far, I've looked in a few bookstores, and the only place I've seen it is Fichtre! I was in France the month it came out. That's how long a new book lasts: one month. When I got back, I went to the bookstores. They might have sold the copy they'd bought, but none had reordered. *Burquette* was a hit because it tied in with current events [Les 400 coups published two volumes of Francis Desharnais's comic *Burquette*, in 2008 and 2010.]. But my publisher refused to do any advertising for Chartier. We should have run an ad in *Le bulletin des agriculteurs*, which published Chartier for decades. Albert Chartier's readers are loyal fans, and 80% of them knew of him via the *Bulletin*. But the publisher refused to take out an ad. It would have cost $100 or $200. That wasn't a brilliant move. I'm still angry about it.

MT: They're probably so cash-strapped that they can't afford to advertise. They keep publishing books, but they don't have enough money to promote them.

JB: You're right. At some point, you need to publish fewer books and try to do them well. I would have needed help with marketing. I'm not much of a promoter. I'm resourceful, but I've got my limits. I would have needed to pass the puck to somebody as far as promotion goes. Especially since production was already taking up all of my time.

MT: When I look at your work with MG and the exhibitions you've organized, like the ones at the Maison de la culture Mont-Royal and the Cégep du Vieux-Montreal, including the last one, *Bagarre*, you've done more than is humanly possible. There's no reason for you to feel guilty.

JB: But some people have stopped talking to me because I didn't do enough.

MT: There's the author's ego, too. When you make a book, it's your baby, you have to take care of it. But you also have to put it out there and let go. It's not easy.

JB: It's like they're handing off their baby to a nanny. At the time, I was being paid $12,000 a year and working at least 75 hours a week. That's a lot of hours for a salary so far beneath the poverty line.

MT: Every author should self-publish to see the other side.

"Some books pay for themselves. Other books deserve to exist and almost break even. And then there are books that deserve to exist even at a loss, like Hiatus, because it's a masterpiece."

JB: Publishers tend to think: "Be thankful that I'm investing my precious dollars in your little project." And meanwhile authors are thinking: "You lousy, rich bastard: I'll let you get your dirty hands on my work if you make me a star." But neither is true. And I was stuck in the middle. Both positions are equally justified and exaggerated. And both sides saw me as a traitor. But I managed anyway. Things were coming along.

MT: Did the sale of 400 coups put an end to it all?

JB: No, it wasn't because of the new owners. They actually wanted to double our comics production.

MT: So what happened?

JB: The new owners didn't really understand what we were trying to do. They were only looking at the numbers. Trying to explain to them that their Excel sheets should have a column for artistic value was like talking to them in Klingon. For example, they wanted me to do a comic based on *Les Boys* [Quebec-made hockey film that spawned three sequels and a television series.]. They didn't see *Burquette* as a big driver, even though the sales were more than respectable. Their business approach was: "Make a safe product that looks like it will sell, and then release it without promoting it." The approach I would have liked is: "Make daring books, create a market for them, and go all-out with promotion." It just wasn't for me anymore and I didn't have the energy to put up a fight.

MT: In other words: minimal investment and maximum return. That's treating culture as a commodity.

JB: Comic book adaptations of *Capitaine Bonhomme* and *Patof* [Two popular children's television series.], and comics as spin-offs: it's not a recipe for masterpieces.

MT: Now that you're a simple cartoonist again, can you tell us what your plans are? I'd also like you to talk about young artists to watch.

JB: There's Vincent Giard and Julie Delporte, who work together. Their work is sweet and fun. There are a lot of people in my workshops at the Cégep du Vieux Montréal, like Luc Bossé and Delf Berg. I like reading François Dunlop. The best thing about teaching is that the moment you think everything has gone to hell, you discover something fresh and new. It keeps me motivated. My big goal is for those guys to accept me as one of their own. Even though I've had it hard and taken a fall with group dynamics. I want to get back on my feet and be part of this crew of young artists. I don't see it as, "Work hard, kids, and one day you'll be part of my gang." It's more like: "Even though I'm a has-been, can I be part of your gang?"

MT: C'mon, no false modesty.

JB: It's not false modesty. I really do feel like a has-been.

SW: In what sense?

JB: The last months were really difficult emotionally, with the buyout of Les 400 coups and all the changes that followed. I had to admit that maybe I wasn't such a great editor after all.

MT: You can take a break from publishing and come back to it one day. Maybe you'll get some of your own books published in Europe and they'll invite you to be head of a collection, with a lot more means at your disposal. That would let you bounce back.

JB: I hadn't made a book in a very long time and I didn't have the energy for it either. Now I feel up to it again. When I was working on the short stories in Saint-Malo, I felt better than I had in a long while.

MT: I read the stories yesterday on your website, jimmybeaulieu.com. There's the one that stirred up some controversy, "Intra-Muros." It made me laugh — it's just a few soft sex scenes.

JB: The downtown part of Saint-Malo is called Intramuros. The name makes you wonder what happens behind the walls. That's what inspired the story. And then the mayor of Saint-Malo came to see this exhibition of young Quebecers who'd been invited by the city, and he called it "a bunch of filth!" [*Laughs.*] What's really strange is there were rape scenes in an exhibition by Blacksad. If you mix sex with violence, it doesn't bother anyone. But my story had fun, celebratory, consensual sex. And that was controversial.

MT: Actually, that kind of sex doesn't get shown a lot. Sex is always associated with violence or something negative. You're the total opposite. I think the way you deal with sex in your comics is the way of the future.

JB: That's what interests me. Something that really bugs me is the way people tolerate sex when it's closely associated with extreme violence.

SW: That's a pretty deep topic. It's like people shouldn't be too in touch with themselves. Better for them to be in touch with something outside themselves, or else…

JB: And you're supposed to keep teasing them, keep them in a state of constant frustration so they keep consuming things. I like to show the aftermath, the moments after sex. In porn, you never see the small talk that happens after sex. But that's what's interesting – that's intimacy and life. I'm trying to make something that's soothing.

MT: Was "Simon," the story about the kid at the pool who has no swimsuit, in the same exhibition? It's such a cute story. "Intra-Muros" is more provocative and experimental, whereas "Simon" is very gentle, with intimate moments that are almost invisible.

JB: The script was by Pascal Girard. We were working on the same table at Saint-Malo and we kept talking about things like that — desire, discomfort, perceptions of male desire. That's what sparked that story.

MT: Will there be a sequel to *Ma voisine en maillot*?

JB: There should be. But I'm so interested in doing weird stuff right now that going back to *Ma voisine en maillot* isn't exactly exciting. I've got 125 pages written, but I made the mistake of writing them well, so I've already created the book — it's written, it's done. When I get around to drawing it, I'll be the employee of my story.

MT: What do you feel like doing? Do you want to improvise stories like the ones in your *Colosses* books?

JB: Yes, but I want to try to flesh them out a bit more to create a kind of unique book, something that's very specific and also very targeted at artists. I'll have to find the balance between the two.

MT: That kind of exploration can generate a lot of energy for artists.

JB: I'd like to do a story like *Mousseline* [*Mousseline et le metteur en scène*, a comic by Jimmy Beaulieu, first published in 2010 by Colosse.]. A fake genre story. A kind of *Bonnie and Clyde*-style road movie, with a gang of bank robbers.

MT: There's a dreamlike dimension to that story — an absurd narrative, something that breaks up the chronology of traditional storytelling.

JB: That fascinates me, too. I'd like to do a fake Elvifrance comic [Italian publisher of gore and porn comics.] or something like that — something really tasteless. The books had just two or three panels per page, with these crappy adventures, and loads of them came out every week in the late 1960s, but nobody remembers them anymore. The provocative, shit-disturbing part of me wants to do something like that, some cheap pulp story along those lines. That's the way of the future. [*Bursts out laughing.*]●

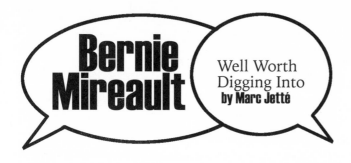

Bernie Mireault

Well Worth Digging Into
by Marc Jetté

Originally published in:

Trip #8, 2014

Translation by
Helge Dascher

The adventure starts

Bernie Mireault was born in 1961 to an English-speaking mother and a French-speaking father, both of whom were serving in the Canadian Forces. The family travelled frequently and relocated every three years in Quebec and Ontario, depending on their assignments.

When Mireault was 12 years old, the family settled down in Rawdon. He read a great deal, though not many comics, since they were hard to come by in the region. Telling himself he could do better than what he was seeing in that vein, he took up drawing with serious intent in his free time. He went on to study art and photography at

Dawson College in Montreal and work full-time in a seniors' residence.

He diligently attended comics conventions while sending his portfolio around. His future came into sharper focus in 1984 when he met Mark Shainblum and Gabriel Morrissette, who decided to publish him in their *New Triumph featuring North Guard* series.

After this debut, Mireault was frequently published in the US, and he began earning a living with drawing-related jobs. He worked in animation, notably on the first *Heavy Metal* movie. In the late eighties, he became a colourist, colouring DC titles such as *Batman* and *Green Lantern* alongside *The Flintstones* and *The Jetsons*.

His career as a cartoonist developed along two paths: work-for-hire and personal creations. Publishers including Comico, Caliber, Dark Horse, and DC have hired him to work on their series, and he has collaborated closely with well-known cartoonists, contributing to titles such as *Grendel* by Matt Wagner and *Madman* by Mike Allred. Neil Gaiman, acclaimed author of the Sandman series, recently mentioned that his all-time favourite comics page was from a *Riddler* story "When Is a Door," drawn by Mireault and published in the *DC Secret Origins Special* in 1989.

Even though Mireault has had no major breakthroughs, his career trajectory has been an interesting one, and a look at his production suggests that he has not made stylistic concessions to the editors who have hired him. Mireault's work depicts a personal universe that is distinctly quirky and charming. In 1999, he stuck to his highly stylized approach in his illustrations for stories spoofing the blockbuster horror movie *The Blair Witch Project*, published by Dark Horse.

But Mireault's standouts have been his own series, including *Mackenzie Queen*, inspired by *Doctor Strange* and published by Shainblum and Morrissette in Montreal, *Bug-Eyed Monster*, created for the *Nickelodeon* magazine, and the delightfully entertaining *Dr. Robot*, published by Dark Horse. The latter chronicles the adventures of a kind-hearted scientist who builds robots to assist him in his domestic chores and to help residents of a neighbouring town in various ways. Mireault uses a radiant colour palette to light up the pages of this wordless series. His masterpiece, however, is *The Jam*, the story of a Montrealer by the name of Gordon Kirby who is passionate about comics and often winds up helping others while wearing a patched-together superhero costume.

The Jam

Throughout his career, Mireault has returned periodically to his series *The Jam*, whose 16 issues have been published successively by no fewer than six publishers. *The Jam*, which tells the not-so-ordinary stories of ordinary people in their everyday lives, introduces the main character Gordon Kirby and his girlfriend Janet. Kirby manages a small band in the local music scene, guiding it to a brighter future. Somewhat eccentric, he dons a jogging outfit that his sister one day transformed into a ragtag superhero outfit for Halloween. He occasionally wears it as a joke, or to walk his dog Harvey (a regular presence in the series), or to listen to music on the roof of his house. And sometimes he happens to do good deeds while wearing the costume, such as talking a man out of committing a murder or scaring off two thieves in order to rescue an elderly woman, Jane Marble, who later sets him up with various very odd jobs. Despite sad events such as a break-up and domestic violence, Kirby often seems a bit too happy, and so Mireault has the Devil come into his hero's life as well.

The pleasure Mireault gets out of making comics is abundantly on display in *The Jam*. The series is funny and imaginative, with inspired visual effects that give the images a surrealist feel and a psychedelic touch.

The independently produced work is, however, occasionally uneven. Some pages appear hurried, and the story seems to go off track over time. Nonetheless, *The Jam* is a title well worth discovering in the Quebec comics scene. Mireault has created a personal series that displays his skills

to their full advantage and includes a number of outstanding issues. He particularly recommends numbers 6 and 10.

To Get Her, or the art of showcasing all your talent in a single book

Gordon and Janet return for new adventures in a graphic novel entitled *To Get Her*. A large-scale and impressive project, it is the product of many years dedicated to the challenging craft of making independent comics. It also reflects the tenacity of an artist who has earned his credentials through an impressive body of work and his single-minded pursuit of the goal he set for himself at the start of his career.

To Get Her is the work of a skilled cartoonist at the top of his game, making it an excellent point of entry for discovering Mireault's prodigious talent and mastery of the comic book medium.

Wherein the author expertly pursues multiple objectives at once

1) In this graphic novel, Mireault analyzes the human condition and recounts personal experiences through his protagonist, Gordon Kirby. And yet *To Get Her* does not come across as autobiography, except perhaps in the prose introduction and the other interspersed text passages, the gist of which is distilled in small symbols or drawings at the start of each paragraph.

The story, which starts off dark, lightens up despite the various tragic events that occur. The ending offers an opportunity for a new beginning that is a play on the words of the original title. Thus, *To Get Her* could be the first volume of a series to come, just as it is a continuation of Mireault's preceding series, *The Jam*.

2) Mireault reconnects with Gordon Kirby, a character he clearly identifies with, given that both are cartoonists living in Montreal. As such, we're back in the world of "the jammer." Kirby, however, has now put away the superhero costume he used to wear while walking his dog, since his girlfriend has grown exasperated with his behaviour. (Like being an artist or a cartoonist, being a superhero isn't a real job because it doesn't bring in money.)

3) Mireault introduces readers (and perhaps also publishers) to a range of characters, stories, and series that are worthy of publication. Through his cartoonist-protagonist, Mireault casually displays his expertise and humorous touch in a variety of formats, including full stories, half-page sequences, comic strips, and a comics jam broadsheet.

Nested comics

As such, the comic spawns other comics created by Gordon Kirby, aka Bernie Mireault. Or are they by Bernie Mireault, aka Gordon Kirby? They include the following:

1) A 16-page story entitled "Internal Dialogue": A man, unable to get up out of bed one day, realizes that the meeting he thought he had scheduled is not with the people he needs to see that morning. The story fully exhibits the author's skill, especially in regard to dialogue. An entertaining and downright funny read.

2) A half-page strip entitled "Ass Hole," featuring a panhandling clown. Of course, all the passers-by enjoy the show, including one in particular.

3) A series entitled *Hi-Hat*, comprising five half-page stories. A giant but friendly insect encounters humans whose friendliness is questionable.

4) Several seven-panel strips, positioned at various places throughout the book, that tell the sto-ry of a reader reading *To Get Her* while Mireault intervenes, not always happily.

5) A sequence running several pages, in which Mireault documents the making of a comic book page created by several artists at a comic jam at La Sala Rossa in Montreal. This sequence lets Mireault introduce fellow Montreal cartoonists, both through their drawings on the collaboratively improvised page and in an appendix featuring their strips. It is an expression of Mireault's loyal support of local artists, some of whom were published in the pages of his comic book *The Jam*.

Wherein the comic book takes on a philosophical and urbanist slant

In what may be a reflection of Mireault's own life, the book's prose-style introduction reveals the difficulty, or perhaps even the impossibility, of being a cartoonist while also keeping up a romantic relationship. It is followed by riffs on the meaning of life, God and heaven, generous souls and profiteers, and the importance assigned to money. Readers in general — and comic book artists in particular — are sure to relate. Along the way, Mireault suggests that the difficulties of living in society are partly due to an environment unsuited for human health. He makes the case with reference to Montreal, which he suggests is not the prettiest or healthiest of places — or, at the very least, one far removed from the ideals of the Renaissance, with its prescriptions for the construction of a perfect city based on the

proportions of the human body (see the Vitruvian Man, drawn by Leonardo de Vinci in 1492).

We interrupt this program…

To Get Her is occasionally interrupted by sections of prose text. One of these, extending over several pages, explores the author's doubts about his presumed goodness and lets him reflect on the fate of his relationship and his path in life.

The same passage goes on to give a brief history of comic books, supplemented by an analysis of the medium and a how-to guide for creating a comic book. This interruption should probably have been placed in an appendix. As is, the tangent slows the pace of the story and risks losing the reader's interest.

The starting point

The story begins when Gordon Kirby gives his relationship a second chance while also committing full-

from *The Jam*

time to making art, a decision his girlfriend deeply disproves of. The narrative arc is constructed out of scenes of their life as a couple, encounters with friends, and dog walking. As time passes, various events punctuate the story and maintain the reader's interest.

It becomes clear that good times and romantic notions are a thing of the past. Kirby and Janet, who have lived together for a decade, go to the Blue Angel to listen to the band they saw on their very first date. The evening is intended to mark their renewed commitment to one another, but

ends up reflecting what their everyday life has become, with all its accusations and animosity.

The story seems to lose its way when a police detective appears out of nowhere to talk about events that occurred in past stories. In a prose passage that follows the drawn sequence, the detective's identity is revealed. The device is awkward, as is another one used to mark time in a scene showing the couple in happier moments. Aerial views of the city repeat from one image to the next, presenting different times of the day. The effect gets monotonous after a while, stripping some of the impact of the sequences.

"To Get Her is the work of a skilled cartoonist at the top of his game, making it an excellent point of entry for discovering Mireault's prodigious talent and mastery of the comic book medium."

The absurdity of life

The denouement revolves around Collin, a troubled individual who is obsessed with Kirby's girlfriend, Janet Ditko. A true nutcase from a wealthy family, he likes to dress in historic attire, depending on his mood. His frequent calls to Janet, an old flame from college, create problems, especially since Kirby always picks up the phone first.

A tragicomic character, Collin resurfaces several times in the first section, always in different outfits, offering a counterpoint to the overall seriousness of the story. Perhaps he is meant to portray the absurdity of life, serving as a rogue element that derails things just when everything seems to be moving along nicely. He causes Kirby to have a near-death experience and is partly responsible for the gripping ending, which is one of the story's high points. The outcome brings sadness for Kirby, but also a certain freedom and renewed inspiration. The jam Kirby was in is resolved, if only temporarily.

It is worth pointing out that Kirby and Janet's names are those of two renowned American comic book artists, Jack Kirby and Steve Ditko, who designed several Marvel Comics characters. Readers familiar with comics history will wonder if it might not have been more fitting for Janet to be named after Stan Lee, the Marvel editor-in-chief and illustrator against whom Kirby held a grudge. Kirby's dog Harvey is likely named after Harvey Kurtzman, the founder of *Mad* magazine. All three have been a major influence for Mireault.

Mireault, master of hand-drawn and computer-generated art

Visually, *To Get Her* is a major achievement. Mireault uses inner stories within an outer story to present several visual styles and express himself in a variety of genres. His drawings reflect his mastery of the medium, including composition, anatomy, and perspective. It comes as no surprise that he cites Escher as an influence.

The art in *To Get Her* is created digitally, featuring a clear line technique, a highly detailed approach, and a wide range of grey tones that nicely render the objects and their textures. Clearly, Mireault is an ace at computer-assisted drawing. The 16-page story contained within the book proves that he is able to use this tool to achieve a less polished style and rougher lines as well, for an entirely different appeal.

Mireault also has fun showing his alter ego Gordon Kirby working with old-school tools of the trade. When Kirby uses an ink-laden nib to draw on Hi-Art paper, Mireault reminds readers how perilous the method was, smears and all.

His narrative approach is classic: one panel leads logically to the next. Still, he indulges the occasional flourish by changing the shape of frames to emphasize the tone of a scene and enhance its effect. Flights of fancy also characterize the personality of the character who idolizes Janet. They suggest the artist's desire to escape the gravity of his subject and expose the absurdity of life (it is known that many introverts, from a young age, seek refuge in reading and drawing to escape a reality perceived to be threatening.)

To Get Her demands a sequel. Mireault has created an intriguing world with a cartoonist at its centre. This clever idea lets him showcase various comic book styles within the same story and put the full range of his talent on display. In the case of an artist as versatile as Mireault, that in itself is compelling. A series based on the book would be a perfect vehicle for him and surely the work of his lifetime — or at least of his life so far. ●

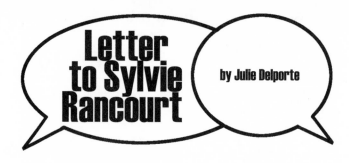

Letter to Sylvie Rancourt

by Julie Delporte

Never before published

Translation by
Helge Dascher

The comic *Melody* follows the autofictional adventures of its author Sylvie Rancourt, a nude dancer in Montreal in the 1980s. Often unfairly described as naive in content and form, *Melody* is in fact revolutionary — especially in the power of its female gaze.

Dear Sylvie, I've decided to write this text as though I were writing you a letter of admiration. In our small world of contemporary independent comics, I think we've too often looked at your work from the superior perspective of comics experts. We only welcomed you recently, after the rerelease of your *Melody* magazines (6 issues), originally self-published between 1985 and 1986 and reissued by the French publisher Ego Comme X in 2003. Your comics surprise us. I think they challenge the ways we've come to understand the history of our language. In comics theory, we literally forgot about you — you wouldn't be the first woman that has happened to — and until recently, you had not been counted among the pioneers of autobiography, although you were a practitioner of it more than 30 years ago. Here you are now, scrutinized after the fact, like some alien object, out of synch, an outsider (as things stand, it wouldn't take much for you to be classified as an outsider artist as well). We describe your style as charming, childish, and naive; and we acknowledge the brilliance and efficiency of your storytelling, despite your supposed naivety. That's the gist of the introductions to the reissues of *Melody*. To establish your credibility in the eyes of the public, these introductions were written by prominent men: the superstar Chris Ware on the English side, and Bernard Joubert, a writer and specialist on censorship, on the French. Chris Ware writes that you let us see "a venal adult life through the eyes of a child." Joubert states that you are familiar with, but don't master, the form of expression that is comics. "That is one of the charms of the

following pages, the naivety of their author." These words that try to pin down *Melody*'s distinctiveness sound to me as though they were spoken behind your back, and with a touch of paternalism. I would like, by addressing you in the form of a letter, to try to keep myself from that kind of analysis.

When the English edition of the *Melody* compilation was put out by Drawn & Quarterly in 2015, I interviewed you in front of an audience at the Montreal Comics Art Festival, in Parc Lafontaine. Having hosted a radio show about comics for ten years, I usually find that kind of exercise as relaxing as drawing a big-eared dog. But I have to say that with you, Sylvie Rancourt, it was a bit more intimidating. I had never interviewed anyone like you. I had a hard time following all the stories you were telling into the mic. Was it because you have a nice Abitibi accent, and I was there with ears trained in France? To be honest, I don't really remember what was said during that encounter. Except — and I remember this very clearly — for a question I hadn't planned to ask and that I think surprised us both: I asked if you were aware of the feminist significance of *Melody*.

I hadn't thought about it before, but it struck me as we were speaking: *Melody*, a feminist work! That must be why you've fascinated me since I discovered you, back when I was working at Fichtre! The owner of that now-defunct Montreal bookstore (1996 – 2010) had put out a hand-bound anthology of *Melody* comics that I was able to borrow. So you had been available all

mélody

Drawing by Sylvie Rancourt in Julie Delporte's copy of *Mélody*

"Here you are now, scrutinized after the fact, like some alien object, out of synch, an outsider... We describe your style as charming, childish, and naive; and we acknowledge the brilliance and efficiency of your storytelling, despite your supposed naivety. That's the gist of the introductions to the reissues of Melody. To establish your credibility in the eyes of the public, these introductions were written by prominent men."

that time for comics lovers in Quebec, but the edition created by Yves Millet was too luxurious for general consumption (it's the volume that Chris Ware mentions in the introduction to the D&Q edition of *Melody* — the one he found at Quimby's in Chicago). Afterward, I kept asking Quebec publishers why they weren't taking the book under their wings, until one day it appeared in an edition out of France, an inspired move by publisher Ego Comme X. As luck would have it, the company folded last year, which means that here, in your French-language homeland, you're back at square one.

When I talk about your work with people around me, I get mostly two comments. There's the naivety of your style, as mentioned above, and the fact that people judge you for staying in a relationship with a moron like Nick (your alter ego's lover in *Melody*). Comments about the personal lives of female authors are not uncommon. When I read *Reunion*, not only do I not allow myself to say that the author, Pascal Girard, is a jerk, but I unconsciously assume that there is a distance between the author and his character. Why doesn't it occur to your readers that *Melody* is part caricature? Or that Nick's pathetic behaviour is exaggerated? After all, it's obvious that you, too, are capable of being funny, and that you know how to stage a good scene. It reminds me of when I was invited to talk about my book *Journal* on a Montreal radio show, and the two hosts were more interested in asking about my love life than

sylvie rancourt
mélody
ego comme x

about my colour choices. I'm also thinking of the many questions about your work as a stripper that open an interview from the 1980s, available online. The journalist, amused by his own joke, notes that, of course, you're there that day fully clothed! The way he talks to you and his use of the informal "*tu*" reminds me of the treatment that novelist Nelly Arcan was subjected to by the media. Thinking about the two of you makes me dream of the day when women's literature gets more attention than their sexuality.

Hopefully people today would be less inclined to judge the work you did as an *effeuilleuse* (a stripper, conjuring the image of one leaf — *feuille* — removed after the other). I heard the word in another YouTube clip, this time a television report from 1987. You were great in that report. Not naive, not childish, not out to lunch. No. You were beautiful, sure of yourself, inspiring, uncomplicated, professional, hyperactive, and original. And you seemed to be quite ambitious. "I want to be a big brand," you said. "With playing cards, and with shoes and outfits for dancers." It gives me a better idea of the role your friend Jacques Boivin might have played in your career. You were moving fast: drawing and publishing six 48-page magazines in the space of a year (you would have liked to make one a month) is more than productive. No wonder you wanted Boivin to draw and colour your covers to keep up the pace. And when American publisher Kitchen Sink would only publish your stories if

Boivin drew them in his more realistic style, you probably didn't hesitate. Many readers in Quebec and elsewhere came to know you in that form, in an aesthetic not quite in line with the intellectual tastes that have since rehabilitated you.

Initially, I was a little bothered by Jacques Boivin's presence in your world, especially when I found out that the rights to your work are negotiated through him. I thought: "Another guy exploiting a talented woman!" But I get the feeling he's more of an agent and a friend than a profiteer. There's nothing unusual about having a mentor, and men often play the role. At the start of my career, cartoonists like David Turgeon, Jimmy Beaulieu, and Vincent Giard (in the roles of teacher, publisher, or life partner) sometimes gave me a hand. But in my head there's this parallel universe where Julie Doucet, Diane Obomsawin, and you, Sylvie Rancourt, would have been my guides. It still takes so much energy for women to succeed as artists — and simply to live under patriarchy — that they have little left to give to the next generation of artists. And there are other barriers to change: the poor self-esteem and modesty imposed on women by their education (under the circumstances, how can you want to teach your vision of art?), combined with a lack of confidence from the outside (who can you systematically turn to for advice about comics? Who gets approached and hired when teaching opportunities arise?)

During our interview, you rejected the adjective "feminist," one I've come to think of as the most powerful of all. I may be wrong, but could it be that a certain feminist resurgence has since let you feel more at peace with this qualifier? Bernard Joubert notes in his introduction that you tried to convince your colleagues to set up an association for nude dancers in Quebec. But that's not where your feminism ends. I almost laughed when I heard you were being published by Drawn & Quarterly: for me, *Melody* has become the anti-*Paying For It (A Comic Strip Memoir about Being a John)*. In his graphic novel, Chester Brown addresses a subject I'm tired of hearing cis men talk about. But I'd love to put a pencil in the hand of every woman involved in any way at all with sex work. In the field of cinematography,

Julie interviews Sylvie, MCAF, 2015

director Jill Soloway has written in recent years about the omnipresence of the male gaze: "Movies are the male gaze. Movies show how it feels to be a man for the most part. Directing is about nothing if not desire. When you're a director, you have to go, 'I want to see this. Now, I want to see that person. I want to cast that person. I want this colour. I want this camera.' You have to say, I want, I want, I want, over and over again. And women are so disconnected from their desire because desire is shamed for women, that just women starting to talk about how it feels to be alive and to tell their own stories, to me, that would revolutionize the world." I'm going ahead and applying feminist concepts from film, since comics has no real equivalent yet. In 1985, the female gaze wasn't exactly dominating the field of comics. Julie Doucet says it all when she repeats in an interview that she more or less left that world out of exasperation with its boys' club atmosphere. I can't find the words to explain just how much *Melody* means to me, both historically and in today's context. As such, maybe the right word to describe *Melody* would be revolutionary (not naive!).

Your lack of bias in *Melody* also exemplifies how diametrically opposed your approach is to Chester Brown's. While the author of *Paying For It* spends dozens of pages arguing for the benefits of prostitution, you have no other agenda except to entertain us with your stories. *Melody* isn't based in propaganda for the self or claims of victimization — despite the occasionally challenging situations that arise. Bernard Joubert is right when he says about you: "At no point does her account of her difficult experiences seem intended to evoke pity. She takes responsibility for her life." And if you're not making a sex-positive argument, it's because you're not looking for approval, either.

That aspect of your approach is what inspires me most. It takes a lot of courage to put oneself out there, to honestly tell one's own story, especially as a woman. The online and paper versions of my book *Journal*, probably because it deals with depression and relationships, elicited unsettling comments. Some people interpreted my sharing of my inner world as a cry for help, which was the last thing on my mind. To be able to keep doing this kind of work, I often think of the advice of Jean-Christophe Menu, former editor-in-chief of L'Association: just write and don't think about the readers. I could look to you, too, as a model to follow. Whenever I publish autobiographical material, I feel like I'm jumping off a cliff, into the void. If you think about it too much, you'll never do it.

I have to tell you that the more I reread *Melody*, the less naive it seems to me. What I see instead is a sensitive intelligence that lets you draw, with nuance and humour, the hard work you did (you said it yourself: it takes a good morale and good health to do the job). Jacques Boivin's drawings, on the other hand, feel crass to me, so I've never been able to read you as inked by him. Maybe people use the word naive to mean a kind of drawing that is unschooled, uninfluenced, self-taught. Mine is self-taught as well — or it used to be, in any case. I think the same is true of many cartoonists in Quebec. François Dunlop, for instance. But do people keep insisting that *Pinkerton* is naively drawn? I don't think so. That aesthetic of imperfection, of unforced amateurism, has more artistic value than we tend to admit — it is present, for instance, in

the Japanese notion of *wabi sabi*. I recently came across these words by French director and actress Valéria Bruni-Tedeschi: "I think perfection scares me." Perfection and seduction, she says, "can be an obstacle to emotion — they block humour." And isn't humour the thing that has driven comics from the start?

Before writing this text, I wanted to have coffee with Virginie Fournier, a literature student who is active in feminist circles and a regular in the Montreal comics scene. "Whenever I read *Melody*, I laugh a lot — it's total tragicomedy to me. The pimp, the manipulative boyfriend, is the butt of the jokes. Melody is the badass, and he's the one who keeps screwing things up," she said. She also talked about the realism she sees in the *Melody* stories. "Relationships often play out that way in real life: there's nothing more normal than trusting somebody who doesn't deserve it. Melody tells us: 'This is my life, here's what I did. It didn't work out, but I'm still here — life continues and I can tell you what happened to me.'"

Virginie and I tried to describe your humour, which is refreshingly, even provocatively, uninhibited. "She makes these bad jokes, and it's like she's saying, 'Me and my puppets know a couple of dirty jokes, too! It makes you uncomfortable? Fine!'" I'm guessing you heard jokes like those every day from your customers at the strip club. To me, your own use of that kind of humour was an assertion of power, since your customers were your first readers. You were dishing it right back to them, in a way.

I often try to imagine the moment when you decided to turn your everyday experiences into a comic. I always figured it was an act of resistance for you, a desire (even if it was unconscious) to call out your bosses' and customers' assumption that their power was legitimate. In your draw-

"I have to tell you that the more I reread Melody, the less naive it seems to me. What I see instead is a sensitive intelligence that lets you draw, with nuance and humour, the hard work you did (you said it yourself: it takes a good morale and good health to do the job)."

ings, they're both caught in the act of their abusive behaviour, and shown as ridiculous. It's one of the points that Jill Soloway puts forward when she tries to define the female gaze, which is not simply the opposite of the male gaze as defined by Laura Mulvey in 1975. Soloway breaks down the female gaze into three parts: "feeling seeing" (in which the feminine becomes a subject by seeing the world through her own body — I'll get back to this); "being seen" (which communicates the experience of generally being an object of the male gaze — what is the effect of being looked at like that?); and lastly the "I-see-you gaze" (in which the feminine returns the male-gaze-that-is-looking, transforming it in turn into an object). It is totally enjoyable for me to think about *Melody* using Jill Soloway's filmic language, because, even without a camera in play, the universe of strippers is essentially about the gaze.

During our conversation, Virginie Fournier had a different take on the idea of resistance that I associate with your speaking up: "Maybe dance wasn't just an alienating practice for Sylvie Rancourt, but also, in a way, a means for her to express herself artistically. Maybe that's why she decided to make a comic about it," she said. You probably thought the strip-club life was a bit crazy, and that its stories should be told. You've always drawn, and comics was an intuitive language for getting started on *Melody*. Either way, I've come to believe, following critic Christian Rosset's thoughts on this subject, that comics are the most corporeal of all literary forms. They help us tell stories in which the body is present and, what's more, those, like *Melody*, in which the body is at issue in power relationships.

As I mentioned earlier, for Jill Soloway, establishing a female gaze begins with "reclaiming the body." "As a director I help make this happen by staying in my body as the actors work, by prioritizing all of the bodies on the set over the equipment or the money or the time." It seems to me that in *Melody*, you do more than create your character; you also play the part — and you play it well. I published a drawn article about the film *Wanda* by Barbara Loden (1970) in the Quebec comics journal *Planches* in spring 2017. To me, the fact that the film's director also plays the lead role intensifies the presence and impact of the female gaze. Barbara Loden's gaze and body fuse to make Wanda a true subject. Through the particular presence of sexuality and thus the body in *Melody*, you, Sylvie Rancourt, also switch on this strong female gaze. Jill Soloway correctly notes about women, "We don't write culture, we're written by it." *Melody* is an exception. ●

The Rituals of Luc Giard

Profile by
Jean-Marie Apostolidès

Originally published in:

Bears + Beer
mécanique générale, 2007

Translation by
Aleshia Jensen

Luc Giard's work still has not received the attention it deserves. A talented artist, Giard is mainly associated with comics, placing him even further on the fringes. Though the comic arts have gained recognition over the past quarter century, the general public is slow to acknowledge the medium as an art in itself, for all age groups and not just children. Luc Giard's frequent use of *joual* also isolates his work even further, though this article will attempt to clarify the reasons for its strategic use. A better understanding of Giard's unique, powerful work is essential for it to be recognized as it should. In the following pages, I offer an interpretation of it, taking a non-systematic approach so as not to weigh down a process that is more implicit than methodical for Giard. My starting point is the concept of *ritual*, in relation to the personal ceremonials to which Luc Giard and his characters devote themselves.

Biographical Notes

Luc Giard was born on July 7, 1956 in Saint-Hyacinthe, Quebec.[1] He spent his early childhood in Sainte-Rosalie. His father was a neurologist and professor of medicine. Luc has three siblings: his sister, Micheline, his brother Guy, and his brother Marc, who often shows up as a character in his work. Early on, the Giard family settled in Montreal East, the neighbourhood of the city's future Olympic Stadium. They then moved to Outremont, a middle-class neighbourhood with

a large English-speaking community. Luc Giard did not attend a specialized art school; he went to Collège Jean-de-Brébeuf in Montreal, where he met Father Marcel Lapointe, who taught Giard to develop his talent for drawing: "When I met Marcel, everything changed, and I never stopped drawing."[2] For over thirty years, Luc Giard's art career has included drawing, collage, painting, sculpture, and comics. He uses comics the way Jean-Michel Basquiat used tags and murals in New York: as material to create personal art that doesn't fit into official categories. After publishing somewhat more obscure work in the 1980s, in which he appropriated characters from his childhood—Batman, the Thunderbirds, and especially Tintin—he came out with several books in the early 2000s that gave readers insight into his cohesive imaginary world.[3] His work has an autobiographical aspect that makes these notes worthy of mention. His work is, however, most often fictional biography, making it difficult to distinguish fact from desire or fantasy.

Drawing Tintin

To understand Luc Giard's more recent work and the role that certain intimate rituals play, it is necessary to understand what an important place Hergé held in his life. In the beginning was Tintin. His discovery dates back to Giard's early childhood. The artist has dedicated numerous works to the young Belgian reporter, but we will start with a page illustrated in colour, published

in *Drawn and Quarterly* magazine. It is a representation of an Arumbaya fetish from *The Broken Ear:*

from *Drawn and Quarterly*, vol. 1 no. 7 (1992)

Looking at it closely, Giard does not represent the fetish as Hergé created it; he reworked it based on childhood memories. In his imagination, the statuette is an animate being rather than an inanimate object. While in the Tintin comic the statuette is thin, almost spindly, Giard sees it as round. It looks more like a teddy bear than a statuette—almost like the teddy bear the author has said he sleeps with even today.[4] The Arumbaya fetish incarnates the *transitional object*, as defined by Winnicott.[5] The fetish continues to be important to him. Even today, it comes up numerous times, such as in *A Village Under My Pillow*. In the third part of his story *Les aventures de monsieur Luc Giard*, the author writes about his marriage to Diane. As Luc's old girlfriends are dancing wildly, a disturbing shadow enters the adjacent room. It is Ticoune, a double of the artist who we'll come back to. He grabs the most precious object on display in a glass cabinet — the Arumbaya fetish—for which he has apparently been searching for ages. When he finally has it in his arms, he speaks to it as if it were a woman he loves:

Finally, there you are, darling. Do you know how many moments have perished in your absence? But we will never be apart again. Never, never ha ha ha ha. How could those fools think they could keep us apart? Ha ha ha.

To keep anyone from taking it from him, Ticoune sends the fetish to the Orient, and then Giard uses a few vignettes from *The Blue Lotus*. While for Hergé the Arumbaya fetish characterized a single adventure, for Luc Giard it moves from one work to another, one character to the next, as though it were a precious object, treasure, or even a loved one.

To better understand the importance of the Arumbaya fetish for Giard, we need to go back to the Tintin book where it first appeared. *The Broken Ear* is an unusual adventure in the early Hergé period in the sense that Tintin loses a bit of his imaginary power in the story. He also finds himself confronted with a world of "twinness." Hergé weaves a story like an incessant variation on the "doubles" theme; we find this symmetry not only with the Thom(p)son brothers, but the whole of reality, which is structured around this notion of duality. Twins are constantly fighting to obtain a unique object or individual, whose sacrifice will allow one group to triumph over its rival. Tintin and the Arumbaya fetish are part of this *Unique* category that sets them apart from most other people, and they are put in danger by doubles and symmetry.[6] For the Arumbaya people, the statuette is a special object endowed with a soul, or *mana*, making it sacred and blessed with beneficial and harmful powers. Equally so for Westerners, mainly due to its broken ear and the diamond found inside the statuette. In other words, it is an empty object that can be used to hide something precious.

Tintin et son ti-gars,[7] an older Luc Giard book, develops this theme. The author tells the story of a family united under Tintin. The grandfather shows characteristics of Hergé's hero, as does the father, who is named Tintin, and Tintin's son, Ticoune. Professor Calculus (Professeur Tournesol), an intellectual who finds the solution

"Picasso is still a strange case… One foot in the 19th century, two feet in the 20th, and another foot in the 21st. He copied everyone, and influenced everyone. An interesting paradox. Probably the key to the mystery. When we let it all filter through us, it all comes out on the other side. Simple and efficient. Maybe that's what genius is: knowing how to be nothing."

to the Tintin family's problems, also appears in the story. The mother figure is only present in the image of a great goddess who is discovered on a far-away planet and possesses all the knowledge of the world: "All of a sudden, the muse Ava Gardner, Goddess of the Earth, Fire, and Water, brought him to her breast and revealed to him the many secrets of a time past."[8]

The entire book deserves an analysis, as it allows for a better understanding of Giard's fictional genealogy. To sum up the work, Tintin's son, Ticoune, comes face-to-face with a giant hollow statue that resembles the Arumbaya fetish. He goes inside, finds a control panel, and presses the buttons. The statue takes off like a rocket, sending the boy up to mysterious worlds, where his father has to come find him. Tintin succeeds in doing so with the help of a moon rocket that Professor Calculus lets him use. After braving all danger, Tintin finds Ticoune. They then lay low in the family home at 775 Wilder Street, immersed in the pleasures of childhood — mainly reading comics — more like two brothers than father and son.

In his work, Giard associates Tintin with the fetish for its protective abilities. The artist is fascinated by scenes where Hergé's Tintin is hiding or imprisoned, but at the same time protected from the view of others, like the diamond inside the statuette. The back cover of *A Village Under My Pillow* reproduces an archetypal Tintin adventure scene in four vignettes: the hero is in prison, no doubt condemned to death. He wonders how he'll manage to get out of this. It is not a specific scene, as Tintin is often imprisoned and shackled up. Giard distills all the elements of various stories into a single image, highlighting his close relationship with Hergé's character through the concept of imprisonment. One scene recurs often: Tintin is a prisoner of the Bird Brothers in

the dungeons below Marlinspike Hall. Using a beam, he manages to break through the wall keeping him prisoner. This adventure sometimes takes on a straight-out sexual nature in Giard's work, like in his comic *Un pull crado pour une crapule*, where after breaking through the wall, which in the original comic leads to the castle's old chapel, Tintin finds himself in what is probably a brothel and is greeted by a woman. The battering ram he used to break through the wall transforms into an enormous phallus able to give him access to the forbidden woman trapped on the other side of the wall.

from *Un pull crado pour une crapule* (Éditions Ticoune, 1999)

In his paintings of Tintin, Luc Giard often portrays the character enclosed in a circle. This tendency can be read as an homage to Hergé, who made the circle a primary form, charged with different meanings.[9] We can also interpret it as a celebration of envelopment: Tintin is *enveloped* in a circular shape that keeps him prisoner and serves as a protective armour. Thanks to this, Tintin-Luc feels stronger. In one of his numerous fictional self-portraits, Luc Giard is represented in the form of Tintin, at school, inside a circle, staring wide-eyed at his surroundings, but also protected, as much by the picture frame borders as by the enormous books beside him.

A Village Under My Pillow (Drawn & Quarterly, 2003)

To recap: the theme of being encircled is a link between the identities of Luc Giard and Tintin. Tintin is a hero, a *superchild*, and imprisonment is just a single episode in his quest for accomplishment. By blending Hergé's character with the Arumbaya fetish, it becomes clear that Giard himself is haunted by a desire to be shut away, inside Tintin or the statuette — a single entity in his universe. He wants to curl up inside an *image of strength* to become one with it. Tintin thus becomes a protective armour that the child uses to feel stronger and protected from the brutality of the outside world. Hergé's hero serves as a psychic cocoon, or a skin-ego, to use a concept developed by Didier Anzieu.[10] Without Tintin at his side, the child feels exposed, fragile, and open to attack. But these attacks don't only come

from the outside world, but also sometimes from within. The magical act of uniting Luc and Tintin is carried out through the process of drawing. By redrawing Tintin, the artist creates a boundary between himself and the outside world; the lines allow him to differentiate that which belongs to him and to the other. While Hergé is an expert at clear lines and his borders are clear-cut, Giard does not really emphasize the contours, so that the life of his characters shows through in all its violence. Drawing Tintin and *becoming Tintin* is a ritual that allows Giard to slip into a protective armour. It serves as a frame for his imagination. By becoming an all-powerful hero, Giard not only relives the adventures that are beyond him (pleasant or not), but he makes himself visible, projecting himself into a sort of Mythological Self, a source of pleasure and anguish. With Tintin, he puts a face to his fears and feels able to confront them.

In the 1980s, Giard used Hergé's heroes in abundance, but legal difficulties forced him to change the ritual slightly. This is how he came to create another character, Ticoune Ze Whiz Tornado, a Robin-Tintin hybrid. This creation should be seen as a step toward separating the imaginary world of childhood and the adult world. By abandoning Tintin, Giard shows that he has internalized the character's main traits. At the same time, he acknowledges the part of childhood associated with the ritual. Luc and Tintin are no longer distinct characters, one stepping into the shoes of another. They now form a new being, Ticoune Ze Whiz Tornado, who is the idealized version of an almighty power, known and accepted as a childhood dream. The hero continues on his path for several years, never completely disappearing, though his importance eventually begins to dwindle.

The Invention of Luc Giard

Ticoune Ze Whiz Tornado was a step toward the discovery of a new character, Luc Giard, who first appeared in *Les aventures de monsieur Luc Giard*. As the title indicates, the book is a fictional autobiography, i.e. a mix of real events and fictional adventures that the reader is unable to distinguish between. However, the book reveals a new perspective, with a hero who goes on adventures that are still mostly fictitious but within the realm of the possible. Luc Giard's character is no longer Ticoune Ze Whiz Tornado, the all-powerful individual gifted with magical abilities. We get the impression that the author has based the work on daily activities — drawing, choosing paper and ink — in order to nourish the existence of this double. The comic also gives the reader a chance to discover several characters who are emblematic of Luc Giard's personal mythology: Hart Crane (literature); John Coltrane (music); and Calder, Motherwell, Giacometti, Duchamp, Picasso, and Jasper Johns (painting and sculpting). Many of these characters were later the subject of large gouache portraits sometimes exhibited at Montreal bookstores. Giard often has the characters go on imaginary adventures, as a way for him to include them into his imaginary world. This is how in *Les aventures de monsieur Luc Giard*, Picasso becomes a cartoonist. Wishing to reboot the adventures of Spider-Man, Picasso tries to land a job at Marvel, though management is still not convinced of his talent:

Discouraged, Pablo came back from Marvel and said: They can all eat shit, I'm gonna make more money than them, an' gonna be in the dictionary.

Then he went to read a DC comic. Ha!! What a story

from *Les aventures de monsieur Luc Giard* (mécanique générale, 2003)

Giard once again takes the figure of a known artist and uses it as a mask. But it works both ways; he appropriates Picasso's world, but also forces the painter to magically enter Giard's imaginary world. His Picasso character reappears in *Le pont du Havre*. The text deserves to be cited here: "Picasso is still a strange case," Giard writes (*PDH*, 78 a). "One foot in the 19th century, two feet in the 20th, and another foot in the 21st. He copied everyone, and influenced everyone. An interesting paradox. Probably the key to the mystery. When we let it all filter through us, it all comes out on the other side. Simple and efficient. Maybe that's what genius is: knowing how to be nothing" (*PDH*, 78–79). This important passage tells us as much about Luc Giard as it does about Picasso. Giard (playing the detective) seems to have solved a mystery he'd been trying to decode for a long time: the mystery of Picasso. And, just like when Tintin discovers the solution to a problem, Snowy suddenly appears to get affection from his master (*PDH*, 79 b-c-d). We can thus associate these different homages to artists, both alive and dead, to different rituals that allow for confrontation of the outside world. Luc Giard invents imaginary relations who gradually take the place of his biological ones; this time he is not simply given them, but chooses. By inventing his relations (meant here in the sense of the Latin word *invenire*, to bring about, to bring out), Giard also reinvents himself as a fictional character of prominent lineage. Once again, we see the creation of a Mythological Self that allows him to face the violence of reality. This more realistic double is the hero/narrator of his more recent and highly accomplished work, *Le pont du Havre*.

Le Pont du Havre

With *Le pont du Havre*, Luc Giard gives us a better understanding of the cohesive inner workings of his imaginary world. The celebration of the bridge theme is reminiscent of another artist Giard admired, Hart Crane,[11] and the mood is reminiscent of Réjean Ducharme's novels, especially *Dévadé*. *Le pont du Havre* is above all a fictitious autobiography. The following overview of the book serves to better identify and elaborate on rituals in the life and work of Luc Giard.

Many subthemes can be identified, but two seem particularly significant: the Jacques Cartier Bridge, which the book is named after, as well as *the run*, which comes up throughout the book. We also encounter the subthemes of music represented by Miles Davis, and art through Pablo Picasso's brush strokes. And a new theme appears: the theme of the book itself—the book to be acquired during the run, and the book to be created. Quebec writers Jacques Ferron and Victor-Lévy Beaulieu are also in the book, as is an object never mentioned in the written text but which comes up numerous times: the armchair. None of these themes make sense on their own, but their recurrence creates associations. Created with the help of Jimmy Beaulieu, who helped establish the sequence of the story, Luc Giard's book is presented as a series of seemingly improvised themes that constantly intersect. Each holds a place in the overall score. Confronted with these themes, the reader grasps the book as a whole. Giard's work offers an open and profoundly new style of writing, even more enticing in that it is difficult to analyze.[12]

"When they built the Pont du Havre, the boats passing under it were small. Now they're big. So we jacked up the bridge like we jack up a car. Fantastic. Then we called it the pont Jacques-Cartier."

The book's first *topos*, beginning with the title, is the bridge. Giard turns it into a mythical being, both mechanical and biological. In mechanical terms, it is a solid, closed structure that came into the world on a certain date: "a) On May 27, 1925 construction began on the South Shore. b) In December 1929, the marvellous work was complete. c) On May 24, 1932, Mackenzie King baptized it 'Pont du Havre'. d) On the first of September, 1934, it was renamed 'pont Jacques-Cartier'" (*PDH*, 8 a-b-c-d). Because of its solidity, the bridge also escapes time: "Time goes by, snow falls, and it maintains its gracious curve of well-bolted steel... Our ancestors must have been mad to have anchored it so well" (*PDH*, 37). The bridge is presented as a seemingly modifiable machine (the author reminds us of the changes it has undergone):

When they built the Pont du Havre, the boats passing under it were small. Now they're big. So we jacked up the bridge like we jack up a car. Fantastic. Then we called it the pont Jacques-Cartier.

from *Le pont du Havre* (mécanique générale, 2005)

The bridge also takes on the appearance of an enormous and magnificent living being. This humanization seems at first to be a kind of seduction: "The bridge laughs to itself" (*PDH*, 11 b). There's something attractive and feminine about its smile, reminiscent of Ava Gardner in *Tintin et son ti-gars* (the bridge, as Luc Giard sees it in certain images, looks like two enormous lips). One has to be wary of it, because the bridge has the last word. In the final image, the bridge's smile shifts to a triumphant laugh. Because of its dual nature (biological and mechanical), the bridge overshadows humankind. It is stronger than them, and will outlive them. It challenges them with its overwhelming presence over the entire city: "The pont du Havre snickers before small humans of skin and bone. Its erect, riveted metal pulled in every direction has seen many generations, with their small cars that stink, that sully its splendour. But it laughs, because time goes by, gone forever" (*PDH*, 118). Because of the name given to it, Jacques, the same first name as the writer Ferron, and because of its steel structure, the bridge seems an immense male power. The terms the author uses (such as "screw" and "jack") can have a sexual (phallic) connotation. But the bridge is also presented as giant lips, like a bodacious being on the water, able to emerge from the river to catch those who pass within its reach. In one of the first images of the book, the bridge looks like a stretched out body, a sort of white whale likely to swallow people down into its belly.

In *Le pont du Havre*, the bridge thus also has a female persona. It evokes both Melville's Moby Dick, the mythical whale that Captain Ahab pursues until death, and the sea monster who devours Pinocchio and Geppetto in Collodi's tale.[13] As a male figure, the bridge is a steel structure; it allows people to get off the island of Montreal, to leave in a straight line, and to travel. In this story it serves the same purpose as the car in Giard's previous book, *Les aventures de monsieur Luc Giard*. But the recurring desire to travel is perhaps only a dream: "The pont du Havre conjures up an old nostalgic desire for a departure that will never

be" (*PDH*, 41 a). Its biological nature means the bridge is a being that grips, encloses, and holds tight. The workers who built the bridge were its first prisoners, and later the narrator is held inside its structure, as though a steel jaw were closed around him.

For this reason, the bridge makes us think of the armchair, another mythical object in Luc Giard's imaginary world. The bridge holds the same importance for the city as the chair does for the house, one in a public space and the other at the centre of a private space. The two are promises for escape never satisfied. Like the bridge, the armchair is a mix of mechanical and biological; it is massive, stable, and solid. Like Beckett's character Clov, Giard's narrator admits: "I sit, looking at my wall" (*PDH*, 35 a).[14] The armchair is, however, a living entity; it has arms that close around and keep prisoners and it laughs just as the bridge does: "It laughs too, a dark laugh that never ends" (*PDH*, 35 c). The chair thus has the same capacity to envelop as the bridge, except that the chair envelops the individual while the bridge can enclose an entire city, enveloping a whole community.

The Run

The run is the most fleshed out ritual in the book. At its core, the run is a North American cultural reference to a milk or ice cream seller's route.[15] But the expression has taken on different, more modern connotations with expressions like "run

for your life" and film titles such as *Run Lola Run*. "The run…. Strange thing to call it, but makes sense when you think of *run for your life*" notes Giard's narrator (*PDH*, 13 a–b).

Like most of Giard's rituals, the run dates back to childhood. If we assume the narrator to be the author, it began when he was ten years old, after the Giard family moved to the Montreal neighbourhood of Outremont: "The origins of the run date back to the 775 Wilder era, in May 1966. We'd just moved to Outremont. I was ten. We still went to Lucerne, the motel pool on the corner of Viau and Sherbrooke. We lived close to Van Horne, where there were three little stores. Three *dépanneurs*. That's when the run first started. Three ordinary little stores I used to go to with my brother Marc, my first companion. […] You might call it the adventures of Ticoune and Marco." (*PDH*, 15 a to 16 b). The run is an activity with geographical boundaries and the end goal of discovery. It is a source of both despair and pleasure. Giard celebrates it with a sort of prose poem: "You meet people / You forget people / You buy books / You forget the hurt / You go to Dunkin' / You read the book / You go home to your wife / Tomorrow / And you start all over…" (*PDH*, 13 c to 14 d).

The run is a *psychogeographical* exercise, the combination of physical wandering and mental activity.[16] It resembles the situationist practice of *dérive* ("drift" or "drifting") but it also greatly differs. The *dérive*, a concept created by Ivan Chtcheglov, Guy Debord, and Gil Wolman, is an activity of urban movement on foot. Debord defines it as "a mode of experimental behaviour linked to the conditions of urban society: a technique of rapid passage through varied ambiances. The term also designates a specific uninterrupted period of dériving."[17] The ritual sparked the creation of the Letterist International collective, as the *dérive* was one of the group's most important activities, along with the practice of *détournement*.[18]

Starting in childhood, the run surfaces as an activity where the artist finds satisfaction through the acquisition of an object — the book — which he will immerse himself in to give him the strength he needs to brave reality: "Neil Adams' Batman was so grim. I wanted it so bad it hurt." (*PDH*, 16 a). It involved, above all, acquiring comics and as many magazines as possible. Soon the neighbourhood of Outremont grew too small: "After, the run extended down Bernard Street to 'National Shop,' where there was a stack of comics six feet high" (*PDH*, 16 c). The results of the quest were promising, and the run became a customary activity that continued on into the present: "The run has kept going, ever since that summer" (*PDH*, 16 d). But by associating the run with past confidences, it is made clear that the quest is never-ending. The narrator will cease to be tormented only once the collection is complete. But he will never be able to acquire every single comic ever published. Unable to complete the collection, the run itself becomes a closed space; it is closed because it takes place inside a city, Montreal, and also because the route has been carefully delineated. At this point the practice of the run diverges most from that of the situationists. The *dérive* finds its end from within, as it is a search with the single goal of experiencing the moment. Moreover it involves an open space; we never know where it will take us, as Ivan Chtcheglov learned the hard way. The end goal of the run is to complete an imaginary collection that will give its owner magical absolute power; it is an endless activity that is also limited in time, built from stops and rituals that merit a closer look.

The Space of the Run

The route for the run is quickly established, in spite of the constant evolution of Montreal's downtown. It happens "partly on St. Cath's, between Guy and McGill" (*PDH*, 17 a). Every step has a dedicated station, like the Stations of the Cross. They don't, however, detail a stop on the way of the cross, but a quest at each used bookstore between Atwater and Place des Arts. Depending on time, the run is carried out on foot or by metro:

The metro. Luc's favourite stations are "Mont-Royal" for "L'échange," "Guy" for "Concordia," "Peel" for the girls, and "Côte-des-Neiges" because it's my house. I like the metro. I like the bus.

The runner, or wanderer,[19] has his customs, including stopping in at Dunkin' Donuts on Peel Street for a donut or apple fritter and a coffee, then leaving again:

a: We take a break at Dunkin' on Peel. My brother Marco calls it my office.

b: I spent so much time reading on the second floor. Had a good laugh with others, cried so much and so hard,

c: ate apple fritters like a pig.

d: And a large coffee, please, thanks, and then we pee and head home.

As the run is carried out in a limited space, it goes in circles. It is always the same bus routes that lead the wanderer from the neighbourhood of Côte-des-Neiges to Sainte-Catherine Street, always the same metro stops (Guy-Concordia, Peel, and McGill), and always the same streets that the narrator counts obsessively:

The run's circular space becomes an abstract model for the whole of existence. It is a vicious cycle from which the narrator cannot escape. From the run, all

> "The basic structures in Luc Giard's work are organized around the juxtaposition of the mechanical and the biological. The narrator, Luc or Ticoune, is a being of flesh and bone who wants to become as solid, strong, and permanent as something mechanical. He is the opposite of the Star Trek android, Data, who dreams of turning into a man: 'Data wants to become human, poor fool!'"

human practices, real or abstract, take the form of a circle for the artist. Giard's most powerful images are those where the artist describes the circular traps he seems imprisoned within:

The circular activity is also present during the whirlwind that takes hold of Luc's mind earlier in the book upon discovering the work of great artists such as Miró, Richard Prince, Bernard Krigstein, Ben Shahn, Matisse, and Roy Lichtenstein:

Books and Time

The main goal of the run is to uncover a book, a literary work or even more so an artistic work, that will broaden the wanderer's horizons. In one sense, he hopes the book will help him escape the confined space he occupies and leave the known world to go beyond, appropriating unknown artists to become part of his fictional family. It is thus a spiritual quest that will end in reinforcing the Mythological Self with the sacred object of the Book, if we understand this word to be the books as a whole which constitute a personal history of art, Luc Giard's artistic gospel. Similarly, the whole of Tintin's adventures form a single adventure, always beginning again just like the run: "You buy books / You forget the hurt / You read the book / and you start all over…" Once discovered, the new piece becomes part of the whole of the collection and is imprinted with the owner's stamp:

When I buy a book, I stamp it with my name. It's like a diary… otherwise I forget.

Stamping the book is a way for the narrator to make it his own and control time. The new book thus becomes part of a spatial (Luc's apartment) and temporal (the day of its purchase) order. Reading a book is similar to watching water flow under a bridge; the passage of time is immediately evident: "The ellipses of time are fascinating. When I open a book, I suddenly see time pass. Then I remember…" (*PDH*, 19 b). The act of reading opens a gap in the continuum of time. It allows the reader to leave behind the weight of the present, the pain, by permitting another time to emerge: childhood, the time of origin that is the true goal of this quest. The ability to seize this early period promises to answer the questions of the present and perhaps dissipate

"The run becomes this constant departure. Day after day, a journey that never ends. Collecting books and little cars just means death comes a little slower."

the pain and madness. "A book is like a watch," writes Giard (*PDH*, 19 d); in other words, it indicates an intimate time and assigns a place in space. The gap in time that the book opens cannot close until the collection is complete, an impossible task that would mean death. This is why all of the books on the shelves around the bed turn the room into a tomb:

In this tomb is a crypt, the artist enclosed in it like the living dead, escaping humankind's standard temporality. He is living in another time. Seen in this light, the run is a preparation for death, or rather the symbol of death itself: "This never-ending quest hums the melody of my death" (*PDH*, 26 b). Even if the wanderer is oblivious to this deeper meaning, he feels as though he is going in circles and that the run is a path to the land of the dead.[20] It is a celebration of the

power of darkness: "We come back, we run, but we still understand nothing. The darkness stares at me from the depths of its eye. The black mass brushes against the ceiling and the yellow glow of the light bulb. It's late tonight." (*PDH*, 30–31). The run takes the place of the bridge. While the bridge shows a desire for travel that has roots way back, and which the author knows won't take place, the run becomes compensation, always beginning again, which the wanderer himself admits: "The relationship between the pont du Havre and the run? The pont du Havre conjures up an old nostalgic desire for a departure that will never be. The run becomes this constant departure. Day after day, a journey that never ends. Collecting books and little cars just means death comes a little slower" (*PDH*, 41).

The Quest for Women

The goal of the run is to achieve the implausible dream of completing a book collection to create a Unique Book, but it also represents the hope of meeting the Woman who will bring a unique love. The Lady, in the medieval sense of the word, is a crucial side mission in the Quest: "The run is also an interminable quest for the princess, the faithful wife, and love" (*PDH*, 28). But once again, this is an illusion — an attempt to close the circle, block the senses, and avoid pain by completely shutting in. While the run can serve as a ritual, it cannot stop water from flowing under the bridge, nor the people we want to hold in our arms from fleeing: "The looks, one after the other, the lips, curves, breasts, hips, boots... A woman appears then quickly disappears again. Feverish moments that are too furtive, too seductive" (*PDH*, 28-29).

By associating unconditional love — perhaps a duplication of maternal love? — to the book, the reader discovers that the run has only one goal: to attain the Woman-Book, which Giard selects

the flowing water brings us face-to-face with the passage of time: "At Ste-Ursule, there are falls. We have a BBQ near the trains. We put our heads under the cascades. We have fun. We take Viau home to 42nd" (*PDH*, 38 d). Happiness resides in the day-to-day, and the narrator realizes this as he remembers his attempts at living as a couple with Louise or making travel plans with Sandrine: "When Louise does the dishes, Luc comes up behind her slowly, and lovingly takes hold of her breasts" (*PDH*, 39 a). But the narrator is tormented by the need to *go in circles*. When he decides to go home after an unsuccessful quest, he wonders whether someone will be there waiting for him: "Is she there waiting or am I alone?" (*PDH*, 25 d).

He learns the contradiction between the love in his day-to-day and the quest for the Woman-Book whose face he's searching for: "I love a girl, you see, a pretty little wisp of a woman. Loving is dangerous. You should know when to yield, but you want more, you're tired. But love is connection, a destiny that you feel, that you can't deny or quell" (*PDH*, 58–59). Immediately after this lucid statement, the narrator realizes that the run is at odds with everyday love, which requires compromise and acceptance of the world's incompleteness. The run is a way to escape time, the weight of daily life, history, travel, and the water that keeps flowing. It is linked to the desire for absolutes and immortality. A conquest of time, the Book, the Princess, it translates the desire to enclose oneself in armour that the author discovers looks like a mother, at once loved and hated: "The run stays. Waiting like a mother who knows we'll always come back. A mother we both love and hate" (*PDH*, 60 a-b). The run is the unconscious desire to return to the maternal womb to be enclosed, inside the belly of Moby Dick, the devouring whale, or the arms of Ava Gardner, the Goddess-Mother.

as the unique being/object that will completely fulfill his desire, for love and for knowledge. It is a woman whose sexual body is able to open up like a book, and who will reconnect him with the world:

But love is connection.

The Unique Woman, like the Unique Book, is an amalgamation of all the narrator's former female loves, whose presence he evokes in the majority of his works: Louise, Diane, Sandrine, and all the others who passed through Ticoune's life one after the other like metro stations abandoned one after the next. "Each time, the fire of love / Each time, the fire of hurt / Stuck with the pain / The pain in your chest," recounts the narrator (*PDH*, 89).

Girls don't want to take part in the run, they prefer to travel, escape, leave the circle. The author is well aware of this as he remembers a trip to Mont-Royal Chalet with Louise (*PDH*, 38 c) and a visit to the falls at Sainte-Ursule, where

By looking too hard for unconditional love, refusing travel (i.e. the passage of time), the narrator ends up alone with his madness. The run pulls him into a vicious cycle where he must face his demons, even though he can't make them out. Death seems the only escape:

So this is your life.
Your name is Ticoune
and you die every single day.

Basic Structures

Le pont du Havre is constructed much like a jazz piece, seemingly improvised. It invents itself as it goes. It is reminiscent of Kurt Vonnegut's *Breakfast of Champions*, a cult classic for Giard and a book he purchased eight copies of. He recalls, "When I bought my first copy of *Breakfast*, I was going through a very difficult time in my life. It was 1981. My job at the museum had ended. I was in a crisis about my art. I was watching *The Price is Right* in Diane's bed. I lived on Notre-Dame. Diane lived on Saint-André. I hated Notre-Dame. Strangely, I didn't fall into madness, just depression. But I had Vonnegut" (*PDH*, 80 d). From the seemingly disjointed text, a logic surfaces bit by bit and we begin to grasp its organizing principles. It aims to establish the ambivalent nature of the personal *topoi*, presented here as private rituals. Each ritual is an organizing element of Luc Giard's ceremonials.

The basic structures in Luc Giard's work are organized around the juxtaposition of the mechanical and the biological. The narrator, Luc or Ticoune, is a being of flesh and bone who wants to become as solid, strong, and permanent as something mechanical. He is the opposite of the *Star Trek* android, Data, who dreams of turning into a man: "Data wants to become human, poor fool!" (*PDH*, 92 d). The wanderer wants to become a machine, his limbs outfitted with tools that would allow him to become all-powerful and protect him from the brutality of the outside world. He wants to be like Inspector Gadget, the Jean Chalopin character on whom Giard bases his narrator's physical appearance. In *Le pont du Havre*, Gadget (though never mentioned by name) has the same purpose as Tintin in earlier work; he serves as a protective cocoon. The narrator sometimes becomes an appendage, a simple piece of the bridge.

Two paths are presented to Ticoune, two directions which are alike yet opposite. One takes the shape of a line, inviting travel, escape, and separation; it provides a way into the story and

into invention, creativity, and the unknown. We can characterize this path as paternal, without needing to make the term absolute or associate it with a particular Father figure. Everything mechanical can be associated with this first sphere: construction, tools, drawings, and anything that can cut, slice, or detach. The bridge is the clearest example. The second path takes the shape of a circle, which implies the run, i.e. a ritualistic and repeated activity. It is no longer the search for a story but a celebration of memory. It is the quest for origin and the absolute, presented as repetition and fusion. It stems from religion in that it relates to ritual and celebration. In this context, it is associated with writing, where Luc Giard uses the text to emphasize the narrator's voice.[21] The positive side of the second sphere takes the form of the Goddess-Mother, a sacred figure who fulfills every desire. The negative side is a deadly and all-devouring whale (Moby Dick) that brings death or swallows one into its belly (the sea monster in Pinocchio). Its power is both maternal and biological.

Between the two, there is neither complete opposition nor incompatibility. The mechanical becomes the biological and vice versa. The pont du Havre takes on the appearance of a sea monster and laughs at the tricks it plays on humans. It creates the illusion of a departure to elsewhere, to the United States, the world of Herman Melville, Kurt Vonnegut, Hart Crane, Edgar Allan Poe, John Coltrane, Miles Davis, Alexander Calder, Robert Motherwell, or Jasper Johns, who are all part of the father genealogy Luc Giard has invented. But the departure is an illusion. The Jacques-Cartier Bridge remains the pont du Havre, i.e. of France, origins, the Mother, mouth, vagina, soft protective belly, which encloses and suffocates.[22] This is why it shouldn't be trusted. It is impossible to differentiate between the paternal and maternal spheres, as they are unstable and prone to inversion. They also each have advantages and disadvantages that must be taken into account. However, the wanderer is fully aware of this; if he wishes to grow as an artist, he must leave the vicious cycle, escape the infinite repetition, change the run into a more creative activity so it does not stifle his talent. In other words, he must escape a fusing universe to enter one defined by separation, relativism, and castration.

Does the solution to the problem not lie in reversing family relationships, or perhaps just practices? Jacques Ferron leaves Longueuil to visit Victor-Lévy Beaulieu, his friend and spiritual son.[23] Does he cross the bridge to give himself over to the run and choose a young author to be his spiritual son? The narrator of *Le pont du Havre* imagines meeting Jacques Ferron in a bookstore. They start talking together:

Ah, Luc! How nice to see you again!

Through the magic of this encounter, Jacques Ferron, who was a doctor, becomes Luc's fictional father. Ferron rightfully belongs to the artist's spiritual family — both men attended College Jean-de-Brébeuf: "There must be something good about Brébeuf if Doctor Ferron and I turned out alright" (*PDH*, 46 d). Luc feels justified in his artistic and spiritual endeavours with the approval of Jacques Ferron, who christens him *sub specie aeternitatis*: "Quebec literature would be lost without you, my dear Luc! You know dear friend that a brush stroke like yours is rare nowadays" (*PDH*, 44 a-b). Doctor Ferron tells Victor-Lévy Beaulieu of the artist's talent, saying, "Come on Victor, it's clear that Luc is a genius!" (*PDH*, 44 c)

Proud of this endorsement, the artist can see a future beyond the impasse of the run. He is given numerous signs encouraging him to choose the straight path over the continual circle, such as when his biological father survives a heart attack and Sandrine asks him to leave town to visit the Hemmingford Safari park. It's the first time he embarks on the impossible journey. They drive over the Jacques-Cartier Bridge in Sandrine's car, an act which holds the promise of freedom and love: "Time goes by, I sleep peacefully" (*PDH*, 100 b). The artist can then devote his whole self to his art. The book ends in an explosion of colour: gouache paintings of trees, a telephone pole in the snow, a teddy bear, and the women he loves fill the last pages. The author can look more objectively at his past. Separation can finally take place. The once all-powerful child accepts castration and incompleteness. He splits into two: Luc, the narrator, and Ticoune, the melancholy and depressed little boy. The two characters start talking, in a sort of reconciliation. Luc adopts Ticoune's *childhood* language of *joual* and speaks to him, making peace: "Today, I met Ticoune. He was coming back from Nova with his latest Frank Miller and a Motherwell book from Green. He was all excited. So we grabbed a coffee at Dunkin'. It's his office he said. The one on Peel Street. He didn't want me to touch his comics! It was snowing so much outside that he was scared the books would get wet. Ticoune gabbed away for three hours. Damn Ticoune! I listened. He let me look at his Motherwell book in the end. He told me about all the paintings and drawings. Motherwell was happy even though he's dead. But you're never dead if someone is reading your book. It was still snowing outside. The lights of the city were laughing too. It was a nice afternoon. For once, Ticoune was happy. Everyone in Dunkin' was happy. Wow!" (*PDH*, 116–117)

I read Luc's acknowledgement of Ticoune as a sign that the artist is distancing himself from his own childhood to look at the outside world through the eyes of an adult.

Demain matin, Montréal m'attend![24] ●

ENDNOTES:

1. The source of biographical information is Jimmy Beaulieu's preface to Luc Giard's book *Le pont du Havre* (Montreal: mécanique générale, 2005), 4–5. References to this book will be cited as *PDH*. The number refers to the page, and the letter to one of the four panels on the page, when the page is divided in four.

2. *PDH* 46 b.

3. The works referred to are *Les aventures de monsieur Luc Giard* (Montreal: mécanique générale, 2002); *Donut Death* (Montreal: mécanique générale, 2005); *A Village Under My Pillow* (Montreal: Drawn & Quarterly, 2005); and *Le pont du Havre* (Montreal: mécanique générale, 2005).

4. "For twenty years, Luc has slept with his teddy, Steiff." (trans.) *Les aventures de monsieur Luc Giard*, 69.

5. "I have introduced the terms 'transitional objects' and 'transitional phenomena' for designation of the intermediate area of experience, between the thumb and the teddy bear, between the oral erotism and the true object-relationship, between primary creative activity and projection of what has already been introjected, between primary unawareness of indebtedness and the acknowledgement of indebtedness." D. W. Winnicott, *Playing and Reality*, 2nd edition (Routledge, 2005).

6. More on this subject can be found in my study *The Metamorphoses of Tintin or Tintin for Adults*, trans. Jocelyn Hoy, (Stanford University Press, 2003), 79–89.

7. Luc Giard, *Tintin et son ti-gars* (Montreal: Éditions du Phylactère, 1989).

8. Giard, *Tintin et son ti-gars*, 34.

9. J.-M. Apostolidès, *Tintin et le mythe du surenfant* (Bruxelles: Éditions Moulinsart, 2003), 65–69.

10. Didier Anzieu, trans. Naomi Segal, *The Skin-Ego* (Karnak, 2016).

11. Hart Crane, *The Bridge* (1930). An examination of the theme of the bridge in American literature would be an interesting endeavour. It would include a wide range of individuals, such as Henry Longfellow, Ambrose Bierce, Herman Melville, Thornton Wilder, and Arthur Miller (non-exhaustive list).

12. A more in-depth study of the work than mine would surely highlight the opposition between the text and images in Luc Giard's work.

13. For more on Pinocchio mythology: my study "Pinocchio ou l'éducation au masculin," *Littérature*, no. 73, Feb. 1989, 19–27.

14. When Clov announces to Hamm that he's looking at the wall, Hamm replies, "The wall! And what do you see on your wall? Mene, mene? Naked bodies?" to which Clov retorts, "I see my light dying." Samuel Beckett, *Endgame* (Faber and Faber, 2012).

15. See references to the milk run in Thorton Wilder's play *Our Town* and to the ice cream man in Eugene O'Neill's play *The Iceman Cometh*.

16. "The study of the specific effects of the geographical environment (whether consciously organized or not) on the emotions and behaviour of individuals" in *Internationale Situationniste*, no. 1. Re-edition. Paris, Fayard, 1997, 13. Trans. Ken Knabb, "Definitions." *Situationist International Online*, www.cddc.vt.edu.

17. *Ibid.*

18. Guy Debord, «Théorie de la Dérive», in *Les Lèvres nues*, no. 9, November 1956, 6–13. Re-edition. Allia, Paris, 1995.

19. My homage to "*La rôdeuse*" ("the wanderer"), the Guy Béart song performed by Monique Leyrac at the time Luc Giard was doing the run.

20. Luc Giard and Grégoire Bouchard, *Vers le pays des morts*, (Montreal: Éditions du Phylactère, 1991). The last page of this book shows a revolver on a blank page, where we're meant to think the narrator will write his final words. Under the drawing is written "I don't know where I'm going but I'm going."

21. Usually a child's voice. Hence the author's frequent use of *joual*.

22. "*Havre* is usually used in French to describe a sea port (v.1138) and regionally can also describe a small natural or man-made port; as of the 12th century the word took on the meaning of a safe haven (v.1190, *hafne*) in marine terms, hence its figurative meaning (v.1420) of "shelter", "refuge" (haven of peace), and its literary use." Trans. of passage from *Dictionnaire historique de la langue française*.

23. The only book of Beaulieu's mentioned in *PDH* is "La trilogie de la Grande Baleine Blanche" (PDH, 42 b), the essay on Melville and *Moby-Dick*.

24. (Tomorrow morning, Montreal awaits me). Well-known Quebec reference to Michel Tremblay's famous play and its musical adaptation.

THE NINETIES

The Old Codgers' Corner

A Round Table on 1990s Quebec Comics
Led by Marc Tessier

Originally published in:

TRIP #9, 2016

Recorded
November 14, 2015

Translation by
Helge Dascher

The 1990s were a decisive time for BDQ, spanning humour comics, the Quebec underground scene, and the emergence in full force of autobiographical comics. The period opened the way for a burgeoning independent publishing movement and a modernization that is still reflected in all aspects of Quebec comics today.

Henriette Valium put out *Iceberg* in 1984 and *Milles rectums, c't'un album* in 1987. In 1986, Marc Tessier and Stéphane Olivier founded Gogo Guy Publications, and in 1988, Julie Doucet launched her fanzine *Dirty Plotte*. In 1990, Simon Bossé founded *Mille Putois* with Alexandre Lafleur. Siris started publishing comics in 1988, and introduced his iconic character "la Poule" in 1995. Hélène Brosseau, one of Quebec's leading comics booksellers, came to Montreal from Quebec City with Denis Lord in 1988 to co-direct a number of collectives, including *Les vidangeurs d'images*, *DJABE*, and *L'enfance du Cyclope*. Jean-Claude Amyot, who studied visual arts at Université du Québec à Montréal (UQAM), founded the magazine *Noir Sire* with Frédéric Schmitt in 1991.

Also appearing on the scene in the 90s were Richard Suicide, Éric Thériault, Martin Lemm, Marc Richard, Jean-Pierre Chansigaud, Thibaud De Corta, Caro Caron, Luis Neves, Yves Millet, Rodz, David Bacha, Carl Bacha, Rick Trembles, Eric Braün, Luc Giard, Rupert Bottenberg, Billy Mavreas, Obom, and many others. A bit of digging reveals artists who are still active today and who, at the time, changed the landscape of BDQ for the better.

To talk about it, *TRIP* convened Stéphane Olivier (**SO**), Marc Tessier (**MT**), Alexandre Lafleur (**AL**), Hélène Brosseau (**HB**), Jean-Claude Amyot (**JC**) and **SIRIS**, along with guests **FREDC** and **LPRZ**.

MT: In the articles about Quebec comics that were written for La Pastèque's fifteenth anniversary and Drawn & Quarterly's twenty-fifth, journalists didn't go back further than the year 2000.

1992: **Back** (l-r): Lafleur, Bossé, Siris, GB Edwin, Olivier, **front**: Tessier, Brown

JC: It's like the 1990s didn't exist for comics. But what about *Croc*? And *Michel Risque*? There were other things before us!

HB: *Croc* was a HUMOUR magazine that included comics!

MT: What are your thoughts about the 1990s?

AL: I'm fascinated by how many fanzines there are today compared to the 1990s. There were about 20 of us back then, 30 at most.

SO: That's a generous estimate. There were never 30 of us.

SIRIS: Those cartoonists were just starting to emerge in 1995. They saw the whole evolution of BDQ, with La Pastèque and mécanique générale. Autobiographical cartooning was on the rise in France and Belgium, too. L'Association and Drawn & Quarterly set that machine in motion and it hasn't stopped since. It was making waves.

And technology changed as well. Everything used to be very complicated. The first comics we put out (*L'Organe*, *No. 1*, 1987) were super expensive to make, with all the money going to printing. The fanzines we made were photocopied, and the quality was pretty average. Digital printing has made a huge difference in terms of cost and quality. Screen printing and other mediums are making a comeback, too.

AL: Like Pritt glue!

SO: Even Pritt glue is better than it used to be! [*Laughs.*]

SIRIS: The cover Stéphane made for *Mac Tin Tac No. 3* in 1992 with a drawing of mine is a good example. You did it on the computer and it took you what, 18 or 20 hours?

SO: Yeah, it was crazy. Layers didn't exist yet.

MT: What did you use to make it?

SO: FreeHand. It came with the early Macs.

SIRIS: He did it with a mouse. Pens didn't exist yet, either.

SO: I still use a mouse! [*Laughs.*]

HB: You've gotten pretty good at it!

JC: The Internet has made marketing much easier, too.

LPRZ: You're talking about format and distribution. What about content — has that changed as well?

SIRIS: You bet! There are more women making comics, and their content is different. Guys like us were making urban comics that were a bit trashy around the edges. Women found them boring.

MT: What about Julie Doucet?

HB: And Caro Caron and Geneviève Castrée? And *Misery and Vomit* by Chantale Doyle...

SIRIS: Julie is an exception.

AL: Julie influenced us all!

SO: Personally, I don't think the content has changed very much. Today's concerns seem the same as the ones we had.

Alexandre Lafleur, 2016

SIRIS: There's a female audience today that we didn't have twenty years ago. It developed around Michel Rabagliati's comics.

SO: That's true.

HB: It's a worldwide phenomenon. Wherever comics are made, more women are making and reading them. It's not just here — it's everywhere. Cartoonists like Chantal Montellier were a rarity in the 1970s. They were feminists, and they had a whole other discourse. Today, women are making comics whether they're political or not, and they're not all talking about the same thing.

SIRIS: Take Julie, though. Guys wouldn't have talked about menstruation. And that appealed to women, too.

HB: Yes!

AL: Every cartoonist in the underground scene was different. Things didn't look alike. We weren't all making piss-and-shit-and-hair stuff.

HB: Actually, we did make a lot of it. Because it was part of the underground tradition.

SO: My daughter is into photography, not comics, but she makes zines, too. It's funny how there are always zinesters from one generation to the next. Their content reflects what matters to them, so in her case it's feminist content. You can see their concerns in their zines, and it was the same thing in our day.

HB: One thing about our group is that, with the exception of Marc,

Cover image: Richard Suicide

we were artists more than writers. These days, cartoonists are more well-rounded. We were more focused on the drawing than the storytelling, so of course the work didn't appeal to everybody.

FREDC: Was it more experimental?

SO: I think so.

SIRIS and **HB:** Yes, absolutely.

AL: Our biggest influences were the 1970s, the American underground, drugs, and psychedelia.

MT: *Cibole*, I haven't changed much! [*Laughs.*] Alexandre, you told me that when you look at books like *Le theatre de la cruauté*, they still seem "heavy" today, even though we made that one in 1993.

AL: Political correctness appeared on the scene in the 2000s, and people started worrying about what was presentable and what wasn't. We didn't give a shit. We concentrated on the pleasure of making things. That's what we got out of it — that was our salary.

HB: When you don't have an audience, you don't give a damn. You just do whatever you want.

AL: [*Laughs.*] Down with readers! All 200 hundred of them!

SIRIS: We didn't have readers, *câlisse!*

MT: There's a bigger readership today, but when I see what's out there, I get the feeling it's tailor-made for that audience.

FREDC: Exactly!

MT: It's cleaner — there's less texture, less detail, less content. It's very light. You can read a lot of those books in 15 or 20 minutes, and they leave you with an empty feeling. You end up thinking, why publish that, except to meet grant quotas?

AL: I was making comics for myself. It was all about figuring out where my limitations were and how to transcend them in my work. It's not like we had a choice. At Cegep, my art professors would tell me that comics weren't art.

HB: Same here!

Cover of *Mac Tin Tac* #3, art by Siris, 1992

JC: We made *Noir Sire* at UQAM [Université de Québec à Montréal]. When we started the magazine, we had a drawing instructor who had nothing but disdain for us. One day, somebody said to him, "Hey! You draw. Do you want to contribute to the magazine, maybe do a few pages?" And he laughed at us! I'm talking about a university professor!

MT: Now that comics are in, do you think he would say yes?

HB: I think he would be more open. He would definitely give it more thought.

JC: It's true that things have changed a lot. Cartoonists have taken comics to a more accessible level, so yes, the instructor would take it more seriously. But I still can't get it into my head that a university prof would ridicule you for making comics.

MT: That was the climate in the early 1990s. It was a widespread attitude. American underground cartoonists like Dan Clowes, Peter Bagge, and Charles Burns have all said the same thing about the perception art professors had of comics. In the visual arts, comics were not a viable option.

SIRIS: I was publishing my comics in the magazine *Krypton* at the Cégep du Vieux Montréal, and I would draw them in the professor's class. He'd say: "What the hell is that? It's shit!" He didn't get it at all!

MT: He really said that?

SIRIS: Yes. "It's crap, you won't go far with that." It was the same stuff I was hearing from the woman I was renting a room from!

HB: Back then, was there a comics category for funding?

SIRIS: I got my first grant in 1992, and it was for comics.

SO: We got a provincial grant for *Mac Tin Tac* in 1990, and it was in visual arts. There was no comics category.

SIRIS: By 1992, there was a comics jury.

"I was publishing my comics in the magazine Krypton at the Cégep du Vieux Montréal, and I would draw them in the professor's class. He'd say: 'What the hell is that? It's shit!' He didn't get it at all!"

MT: I think we were one of the last ones before things changed. If I remember correctly, it was thanks to the efforts of the ACIBD [Association des Créateurs et Intervenants de la Bande Dessinée, Association of comics professionals] and Pierre Fournier.

SIRIS: The CALQ [Conseil des arts et des lettres du Québec, provincial funding body for the arts and literature] dropped the comics category a few years later because they thought the scene was too incestuous. Everybody knew everybody. [*Laughs.*]

SO: Well, there weren't a lot of us at the time.

AL: It was always the same people getting the grants! We never got one, and it's not because we didn't try. We sent out at least ten applications!

MT: True, we sent out a lot of applications together and we never got a grant!

AL: And we had good projects. Back then, welfare was my government grant!

SIRIS: Me too! We have to mention welfare here. Almost all of us were on welfare, except Stéphane, who was making big bucks with his design firm.

SO: What? I was making big bucks?!! [*Laughs.*]

MT: When he'd be drawing his comics for *L'Organe*, I'd have to go wash his dishes to help him get things done! When the first *L'Organe* came out, I think we printed 1000 copies or more, since digital printing didn't exist yet. We had to use a rotary press.

SO: And 500 copies cost as much as 1000. The difference was $50. Once the press was running, the only thing you were paying for was the paper.

HB: And if you printed fewer copies, the unit cost was too high to make it worthwhile.

SO: That's right. A print run of 200 cost as much as a print run of 500. So the boxes were piling up at Marc's place!

HB: We all had boxes full of books piling up at home! Back then, you could get a huge apartment for $400, so it wasn't an issue. There was plenty of room for boxes!

MT: When the first issue of *L'Organe* came out, our distributor was Benjamin Presse, or Messagerie Benjamin, which doesn't exist anymore. They distributed *L'Organe* province-wide. I think we sold 200 copies in all of Quebec. Which means we had 800 left in boxes at home.

SIRIS: An "organ" library!

JC: That's when you have to start donating!

MT: The magazine (*À Suivre*), published by Casterman, had the same distributor as we did, and it sold 32 copies a month in Quebec. The market for adult or literary comics was not very developed here.

SIRIS: We were prisoners of all the old comics clichés — *Asterix, Tintin, Lucky Luke*...

HB: It's still like that!

SIRIS: Yes, I know, but it was worse. I remember when TVA [Quebec television network] showed up at a comics event. They filmed my first comic, *Baloney* (1995). You open the book and there's a two-page spread with La Poule saying: "One day I was smoking hash, the next I was shooting up..." And the guy who was holding up the book for the camera couldn't believe it. He was, like: "Whoa! This is sick!" [*Laughs.*] That was in 1995. He wouldn't give a damn today.

MT: Asterix didn't shoot up! He did have that magic potion though....

"It's hard to talk about today's underground scene because we don't know a lot about it. I know it's still out there. There are lots of people who are anti-Facebook and anti-media, and who are organizing micro-scale events you never hear about. The real hipsters don't want their events promoted on a big scale."

SIRIS: The drugs and so on — those were urban subjects. When I talk about urban comics, that's what I'm talking about. And the public wasn't ready for it.

HB: When Marc and Stéphane were on the talk show *Beau et Chaud* in 1995, Normand Brathwaite, instead of asking an intelligent question about making art, just asked, "You smoke good stuff, huh?"

MT: That was for a photo exhibition, not my comics. I answered: "I do *kuskus*, and the spices are great for inspiration." Brathwaite was speechless for a couple of seconds. *Kuskus* (pronounced couscous) was our code word for joints.... [*Laughs.*]

LPRZ: Did the alternative scene have contacts to artists outside Quebec?

AL: Before the Internet, there was a little book that published a list of all the fanzines. You'd take a chance and send your publication to someone, and that person would send back their fanzine. Everything was done by mail. In Quebec, there was no other way of knowing what other people were doing.

SIRIS: The back of every fanzine listed the addresses of other fanzines. We'd send them things and wait, and two or three weeks later we'd get a few zines in return.

SO: We organized a comics festival in 1992 and invited Swiss cartoonists from the magazine *Sauve qui peut!* (Reumann, Baladi, Kalonji...). So actually, there were some exchanges.

SIRIS: I started making contacts and speaking about other publications through *Rectangle* (a fanzine about French-language rock and comics, founded by Yvan Pellerin and Éric Thériault and

published from 1987 to 1991). I talked about *Sortez La Chienne, Mille Putois,* and *L'Organe.* And it was through *Rectangle* that I first connected with Alexandre and Simon Bossé.

MT: We sold the first *Lapin* books (published by L'Association) and the first book by Matt Konture and David B, *Le cheval blême,* at a festival at Foufounes Électriques in 1992. Siris, you're the one who put us in touch with J-C Menu. How did you meet him?

SIRIS: I met him during a trip to France with the *Rectangle* team in 1991.

HB: Denis Lord and I met the guys from L'Association in Saint-Malo in 1992. They were just getting started as well.

SIRIS: Those contacts with French cartoonists were important for us. And Simon Bossé was very close to the Americans. At the time (1990 to 1996), it was all about music and comics — they were inseparable, at least for me. Grunge music happened and comics were coming out by the shovel-load. We were really into the Americans and the alternative cartoonists from Europe.

MT: By Europe, you mean mostly France, Belgium, and Holland.

SO: And Switzerland, too.

HB: We didn't even know that manga existed!

SIRIS: We were all making our own little fanzines and we'd swap them. *Rectangle* was about French-language rock and fanzines. It was an amazing time, but it was all underground. You had to work hard to find readers.

MT: In an issue of *L'Éprouvette,* Menu talked about the avant-garde in comics, but today how would you even define underground comics?

SIRIS: It's when you put something out and it takes a long time before it has an impact on the public.

HB: Underground means things that aren't distributed through commercial channels. In music, if you're doing a show in a loft for twelve people, that's underground.

SO: Not distributed…. Is that even possible anymore? The moment you post something on the web it's out there!

JC: I don't know about that. If you put something on Facebook, nothing happens.

HB: When there's no distribution system, no real established audience, and no media coverage, it's underground.

AL: Back then, the underground scene had depth. It had rage. There was no censorship, no limits. I don't see a lot of that today.

MT: Maybe that's because there's not much of a market left for the distribution of underground culture?

SIRIS: The readership has changed, and the cartoonists have changed, too. The

Art by Hélène Brosseau

ones who were making underground comics are 50 years old now. They're working in renovation, they're laying bricks, they're doing housecleaning and washing floors…

JC: They're making websites…

HB: It's hard to talk about today's underground scene because we don't know a lot about it. I know it's still out there. There are lots of people who are anti-Facebook and anti-media, and who are organizing micro-scale events you never hear about. The real hipsters don't want their events promoted on a big scale. If you're really cool, you know about it, and if you're not, you don't. Back in the day, there'd be twenty people at a Godspeed You! Black Emperor show. It was like when the Velvet Underground played at the Factory.

MT: So when we did our first launches, and there were just ten people, that was pure underground! And sitting here right now, we're having an underground meeting! [*Laughs.*]

SIRIS: It's the old underground codgers' club.

MT: What was the main reason we wanted to make underground comics?

HB: It was about creating a community. Otherwise you were off in your corner, all alone.

MT: When you get people together who are all doing their own thing, it gives everybody a boost. It creates a family. We were talking about trajectories. Richard Suicide, who started out in the underground scene, won the Bédélys Award for best Quebec album this year (2015) for *Chroniques de Centre-Sud*, which was published by Pow Pow. What do you think about that?

Art by Alexandre Lafleur

SIRIS: It's about time, *ostie*, with his amazing talent!

MT: Siris, you're another example. You're publishing with La Pastèque now. Back in the day of the comics bookstores La Mouette rieuse and F52, in about 1998, one of the booksellers literally told me that they didn't stock Quebec comics because the work wasn't good enough. That's despite the fact that they were selling books published by L'Association, Amok, and Frigo — all the emerging comics from France that were shaking up the world of traditional comics. But there was a strong prejudice against local alternative comics.

SIRIS: Because there weren't any.

SO: Of course there were!

SIRIS: Okay, there were, but the booksellers just weren't interested in that style. They were influenced by Drawn & Quarterly and L'Association.

HB: They were more influenced by France than the US.

AL: And you could say we were more influenced by the Americans.

HB: Our stuff was too rough, too dark, too trash.

MT: It wasn't all trash. Look at Siris….

HB: Are you kidding? His work was full of hair.

He was Mister Hairy. Siris, that's what some people called your style: "hairy."

SIRIS: Yeah, but it's shaved now.

JC: In other words, if you want to make it big, it's gotta be beardless….

SO: Actually, beards are in again!

JC: That's true!

HB: Stéphane's scratchboard style is trash, too!

MT: But if you look at artists like Otto Dix and his war etchings, that was trash, too — but it was incredibly beautiful and powerful.

SO: You could say the comics we were making were difficult to read.

HB: That's why people got into them less. What we were doing was more visual than literary.

SIRIS: Like the large-format fanzine *Sortez La Chienne* (published by El Rotringo, aka Jean-Jacques Tachdjian, from 1986 to 1992; 30x42 cm format). People bashed him for it. "What the hell is this??? I feel attacked, what is it?!" They'd see an image by Valium and feel assaulted!

AL: And yet Valium was the God of the Quebec underground.

SO: We've got to mention Valium.

"I spoke with Valium recently and he was feeling totally discouraged. He said he wanted to stop making comics. He'd sent his new book around, and none of the local French publishers wanted to publish it. Even though the Los Angeles Times had just named him one of the five comics artists to watch!"

AL: He was the primary influence. When I discovered Valium, it blew my mind. The first time I saw his work was in *Rectangle*.

MT: I spoke with Valium recently and he was feeling totally discouraged. He said he wanted to stop making comics. He'd sent his new book around, and none of the local French publishers wanted to publish it. Even though the *Los Angeles Times* had just named him one of the five comics artists to watch!

SO: Back then, there weren't any publishers. They seem to be mulitplying these days, and there's an audience now, too, but it has developed around very mainstream editorial content. There are quality comics artists, except they're the only kind that succeeds. And there are comics schools today. In our day, there was no school. We came to comics via graphic design, film, or the fine arts. There wasn't a framework telling you how to make Quebec comics. I didn't even know how to draw when I started. We couldn't have cared less about comics school.

SIRIS: Valium is a cartoonist who does social commentary. He talks about society and how fucked up things are.

HB: Still, I can see how people would be shocked by Valium's drawings. He'll attack anything. Nothing is sacred. He hates everything and everybody, and nobody self-flagellates like he does. But he's our very own genius.

MT: I miss the kind of Quebecois underground comics that really shake things up. With a few brilliant exceptions, it seems like today's comics keep things simple to be more accessible.

HB: It's all about the largest common denominator, so readers don't have to rack their brains or think too hard.

JC: Isn't that the publisher's responsibility?

MT: *Chroniques du Centre-Sud* is the exact opposite. It's dense, intense, and super fun. It's a satisfying and memorable book.

HB: It sells well, but nothing like Rabagliati's *Paul* books. At the bookstore, Alexandre Fontaine Rousseau would always say: "It's not Paul, but it's not apPAULing." [*Laughs.*]

JC: But do today's cartoonists keep things simple just because they want to get published? If you take publishers out of the equation, would there be the same pressure to simplify?

HB: It can be done well. It can be very legible, efficient, and effective.

SO: The students I teach at the Cegep have the same need to create that we had at their age, but in general, I think they're much too tame, in approach and subject matter.

MT: I teach young people, too, and when you open their eyes, when you show them stories that are transgressive or wild, they really get into it.

HB: The culture you see in bookstores — official culture — is not especially disruptive or challenging. Once in a while, small publishers with a different editorial approach try things that are more experimental, but the market is so flooded with books that if you want your cartoonists to be able to make a living, you need to appeal to readers. If the work is too difficult, you automatically alienate a part of the audience and shoot yourself in the foot. It's hard to find the right balance. Of course, as a publisher, you can be more specialized, like Cornélius or La Cinquième Couche. But their books probably sell 50 copies in all — four of them in Quebec.

"Every publisher, distributor, and bookshop needs a few cash cows to pay the rent and salaries. You carry the new Asterix because it sells. As a publisher, you absolutely have to have a cash cow. Menu kept L'Association afloat with Persepolis. And those cows need to produce good milk!"

SO: When my niece opened the comics bookstore Phylactère in Quebec City, she went out of her way get unusual and original work. She held events and launches, and she worked 24/7, but she couldn't make a living off of it. Good distributors can't make a living off of it either, so they sell the new *Asterix*. If you try to carry material and books that are off the beaten path, you end up stuck with them.

HB: Every publisher, distributor, and bookshop needs a few cash cows to pay the rent and salaries. You carry the new *Asterix* because it sells. As a publisher, you absolutely have to have a cash cow. Menu kept L'Association afloat with *Persepolis*. And those cows need to produce good milk!

It's books that are more mainstream or have an unusual vantage point: for instance, a book about an Iranian woman who grew up under a dictatorship. Journalists generally don't ask themselves a lot of questions. They don't have a lot of time to write their reviews. So a book can't be difficult to summarize. If it's too bizarre or too far out, if it's hard to discuss, it won't get talked about. People will talk about something that's easier to explain in a nutshell. For instance: a) the author is a woman; b) she lived under a dictatorship; c) the subject makes good copy. Bestsellers are easy to summarize.

MT: Yes. That's why people are more likely to talk about Guy Delisle's *Jerusalem* than Joe Sacco's *Footnotes in Gaza*. We were talking before about the lack of publishers when we started out. But actually there were a few, like Les 400 coups, which published Quebec-flavoured versions of the full-colour, hardcover European standards.

AL: Basically, Les 400 coups published comics to keep the presses rolling between their more lucrative jobs.

HB: Before people started making more personal comics, we had an inferiority complex with regard to the Europeans. We tried to make a European-style product on glossy paper, without having the means or the readership. So that didn't work out too well. But then cartoonists started making books that were more representative of them, and that was more interesting.

MT: Sometimes it seems like everything goes in circles. There are more publishers today, but Quebecois comics are becoming more homogenous.

HB: Yes, that's true. People are all looking over each other's shoulders.

MT: It's like the conditions in Europe that led cartoonists at L'Association to react against the stagnant market in the early 1990s. To some extent, that's what happened in Quebec as well: we were reacting to a very homogenous landscape. Maybe that's what we need today: comics that break the mould. We're talking about underground comics here, but when I read new books, I often find myself wishing a Quebec comic would finally give me a slap in the face. Of course, there are always a few great ones that stand out.

HB: I get to read whatever I like and I see everything that comes out. I have about four new favourites every week.

MT: Are they made in Quebec?

HB: Oh, you're talking only about Quebec? I just read Samuel Cantin's new book, *Whitehorse*, and I thought it was hilarious. Two years ago, *Vil et misérable* was the book that made me really laugh. There is great product out there — that's not the problem… Oops, I said "product."

MT: You're right, Samuel Cantin's work could be considered underground in spirit — especially his last book, which I loved.

HB: *Whitehorse* is super trash. It's definitely not politically correct.

SIRIS: Do you think the storytelling is better today than it used to be?

HB: In our day, there were very articulate people too, as well as people doing more literary work. Julie Doucet was a great storyteller. It's just that people work much faster today. Sam Cantin's new book is 250 pages and he's already working on the sequel. It used to take me a year to draw 10 pages. Look at the way Alexandre worked; there wasn't a single line that was out of place. Everything was impeccable.

MT (to AL): C'mon, 200 pages! Let's go! Alexandre, you once spent an entire year of your life drawing one and a half pages! [*Laughs.*]

AL: That's because I was stoned. [*Laughs.*] And I was out in the world. I was living. [*Laughs.*] You have to have a life if you want to make comics!

JC: You need to feed your art!

AL: Exactly. You need to be experiencing things. You can't just draw. That's the other thing: we were really living back then! [*Laughs.*]

HB: These days, there's the Maison des auteurs. The cartoonists have all gotten together, they give each other cues, they help each other out. When they hit a wall, they'll ask each other for advice. That generates energy. We had a kind of clan spirit because we'd see each other at launches and do things together. But they're working within an actual group structure.

MT: We always wanted to organize a shared workspace.

HB: Yes, that's true.

AL: But comics have changed, too. Back then, we were still making traditional format books.

HB: We were making comics!

AL: How many pages was that, 24? Now, it's graphic novels that are 100 or 200 pages long. It's a whole other mentality.

HB: It's a race now. Nobody cares if a character's face doesn't always look the same. Like I said earlier, making comics has become a job.

MT: Maybe manga changed the game, or L'Association and authors like Sfar. He got readers to accept a much looser line.

AL: His line work is well suited to his kind of storytelling. To me, Sfar is more of a writer than a cartoonist. His style is almost calligraphic. His lines tell the story — they're vibrant.

HB: That guy draws five pages a day, no matter how he's feeling. After five days, he's got 25 pages.

AL: When I heard that, I told myself I'm not a cartoonist. If you want to make a living off of comics, that's what you have to do. You can't just draw one page a week. You need to be making four or five pages every week.

HB: We were illustrators more than anything.

MT: I saw Carlos Santos today at Expozine. He drew these incredible pages — they were detailed and precise — but he said they were just drafts. Everybody else was telling him he could publish them as is.

AL: He needs to get out of the house more often!

SIRIS: We've been telling him that for ten years, but he just keeps at it!

HB (to SIRIS): But you're the same! You spend much too much time doing what you're doing. It's crazy!

SIRIS: I know, I know. I don't have a lot of self-confidence, so I keep polishing things.

HB: If you were working in the studio with those people, at some point, you'd pick up the pace. Readers don't even care about details or a bit of dust on a page!

AL: Working in a studio is a good idea.

SIRIS: Yeah, but I live in Saint-Jean-sur-Richelieu! Who's going to pay for me to commute to a studio in Montreal?

HB: I understand... But working with these people who're making their goddam 250-page books would really help you.

Art by Matthew Brown

SIRIS: Right, but I'm stuck over there.

SO: Is getting published that important?

HB: It is if you want to make a living!

MT: Not just if you want to make a living, but if you don't want to starve to death. The more time you spend on a project, the more difficult it becomes to finish it.

SIRIS: And people forget about you. I've been working on my book for five years.

AL: How many books does Sfar publish in a year?

HB: At least 40!

SIRIS (to HB): If we stopped messing around, do you think we'd be able to crank things out as well?

HB: Yes. Readers don't even notice all the details.

SIRIS: Cyril Doisneau once told me that people take an average of 30 seconds to read a comics page.

HB: That's just it, Siris! The story has to flow.

MT: Siris, you just finished drawing more than 200 pages. You've got the experience — it's all inside you!

JC: How long does it take you to draw a page?

SIRIS: The pencilling takes no time at all. It's what happens next, when I scan my sketches and start reworking the whole page. Once I get onto the computer, I start moving my characters around.

HB: Oh, God!

SIRIS: I'll correct the position of a foot.

JC: That's why it takes too long!

SIRIS: If the line is bad, they'll see it, *ostie*. If there's dust on the page, I need to get rid of it. Richard Suicide is there telling me: "Forget the fucking dust!" I say they'll see it, and he answers: "No, they won't." And then I zoom in, and there's this huge detail, and I'm like, "*Câlisse!*" I really want my characters to work...

Art by Jean-Claude Amyo

AL: It's about making a living off of comics. It's that basic. Paying your rent and the bills.

SO: Right! Except if you take a month to make a page, you'll never do it in 20 minutes, because that's your rhythm — that's what works for you.

AL: It's like you're a monk in a monastery.

MT: If it takes you a month to draw page, you probably don't have a girlfriend and kids!

SIRIS: And you've got a lot of dishes to wash…

SO: Or maybe the girl-friend and the kids are why it's taking you a month!

MT: [*Laughs.*] Yes, there's that, too!

HB: Back then, we had no time constraints. We were all on welfare. You could take six months to draw a page if you wanted to. Now, you get $1000 to make a book, and the publisher wants it in time for the book fair, so you've got to get moving. If you make a page and something's not quite right, tough luck. You live with it. Siris, books have a shelf life of three months in book-stores.

JC: It's a computer problem. If you keep zooming in, you'll always see more mistakes.

SIRIS: I know. Anyway, I worked really hard on the story. That's important.

HB: Good. The story is the heart of it all.

SIRIS: If you can make a page in 20 minutes and it's good, that's great. But if it takes you a month to make a good page, that's great, too! Quali-ty has nothing to do with how much time you spend on something. A page that takes 20 min-utes can be just as bad as one that takes a month.

HB: Yes, but we're talking about the idea of tor-turing yourself to make something perfect, to the point of it not being fun anymore.

SO: You're not torturing yourself!

SIRIS: Yes, I know.

HB: And there's always more books coming out. When your three months are up, your book gets moved to the back of the shelf or returned to the distributor, and after a year it might get remain-dered. At some point, you need to stop freaking out about it.

SIRIS: But what about all those trees, *ostie!* [*Laughs.*]

"Cyril Doisneau once told me that people take an average of 30 seconds to read a comics page."

JC: True, we need to honour the trees!

HB: But of course, some books are classics and they sell all the time, and there are some good booksellers who keep good books on the shelves.

MT: Siris, you spent a lot of time on the second volume of *Vogue la valise*, but there's a qualitative difference compared to the first volume. Maybe people won't see it, but the pages look better and they're much more refined. But when you get around to drawing the biography of Jean Dallaire, you're not going to take two years to do it, are you?

SIRIS: No. I'll think of Hélène's advice, and I'll tell myself, screw the foot! If the eye is crooked, who cares? It's just Dallaire, *ostie*! The fucking pleasure! [*Laughs.*]

AL: It's true, though. The drawing isn't what matters, it's the pleasure you get making it.

HB: Siris, the more you work, the better you get. At some point, all the hard work pays off. You need to trust yourself!

AL: I once spent a whole month on a single drawing, eight hours a day. After that, I told myself never again!

JC: Is that why you don't like my drawings?

AL: I've always admired your super-fluid style.

JC: But that's just it: I wasn't thinking about it too much.

AL: No, but were you having fun?

JC: Yes. I wasn't controlling anything.

HB: Right, and that pleasure really comes across in the work!

SIRIS: You learned your lesson!

JC: It's either that or you don't have a kid. It's one or the other. [*Laughs.*]

MT: Oldsters, any advice for the new generation? [*Laughs.*]

JC: It's the same advice, whether you're young or old.

MT: And what is it?

JC: Don't worry too much!

AL: To hell with everything, just do it for yourself. It'll either become a hobby, or it'll become a job.

MT: My girlfriend says that my comics are just a hobby. [*Laughs.*]

AL: Do you make a living off of them?

MT: Well… I'm teaching thanks to the time I put into comics.

AL: I'm talking about your comics, not your teaching. That's something else.

MT: I guess you could say that my comics are my occasional Christmas bonus.

AL: A little $1000, once in a while.

HB: Marc didn't study to become a teacher. His comics and his experience are the reason he's teaching.

JC: So comics aren't your profession….

MT: I should mention that I get grants from time to time, too. Those are like really big Christmas bonuses.

SO: Still, there's the question of profession. It's been, what, 30 years? 25 years? If that's not a profession, I don't know what is!

MT: Thanks, Stéphane!

SO: It's a nice profession. Even if the money doesn't come in the way it should, it's still a profession.

HB: A profession is something you do to make a living.

SIRIS: We're craftspeople who just spend our lives tinkering around.

MT: If we'd been born in another country, like Japan, Belgium, or France, we might be making a living off of comics.

HB: To be honest, the thing that mattered most to us back then was our freedom!

AL: That's what nourishes a really great story. If you're not free to experience things, how are you going to create a story that resonates?

SO: You're not drawing while you're experiencing things.

HB: The comics that sell these days are reportage comics. Cartoonists are going out and experiencing things so they can make a book about it. But the results are kind of uninspired, because you've got some random person going out to randomly experience some random thing.

SO: Is it because they don't know how to tell story?

AL: Or because the experiences they're having are boring?

HB: Not necessarily. It's because they're so formulaic. It's the big trend. In our time, it was autobiographies. Some pretty boring stories got told, but there was also very interesting stuff. I wouldn't want to live with Joe Matt, but that guy

L'Organe magazine, art by Julie Doucet, 1988

sure is interesting in his books! If you travel and you spend a month somewhere, have you really assimilated anything? If you're not a journalist...

MT: Hélène, it's about sensibility. Artists are sensitive. They pick up on things and they're more interested in the people they meet than someone who's more self-centered.

HB: I'm just saying that's the trend right now, so you get all these cartoonists who'll give documentary-style reporting a try for three weeks.

MT: When I was on the jury for a grant, there were applicants who wanted money to go somewhere, do something, experience something, and then make a book about it. They were asking for money to go experience something.

HB: The worst application I ever saw was from a guy who wanted a grant to examine his own life. He wanted to revisit his childhood, track down his teachers, and ask them what he was like as a kid. Where was this guy during his own life? It made no sense! [*Laughs.*]

MT: And then there were the people who came to comics with the idea that they were going to make the next *Asterix*. They figured they'd sell 100,000 copies in Quebec and get rich. And they'd publish with a big print run and lots of marketing, and then they'd give up because it didn't work out.

JC: Are there still people doing that?

MT: Yes. At TCAF, there was a cartoonist who had put out a European-style album. He had these giant banners in front of his table and everything. It must have cost him $5000 just to print it, and he was gone the next year.

JC: Does anybody still make work that's as popular and successful as *Asterix*?

MT: *Les Nombrils* [by Quebec cartoonists Delaf and Dubuc, translated into English as *The Bellybuttons*]!

HB: In bookstores, you get hits like Michel Rabagliati's *Paul* books, *Asterix*, and *Les Légendaires* [by French cartoonist Sobral, translated into English as *The Legendaries*]. They sell like crazy!

Mille Putois #3, art by Simon Bossé

JC: *Les Légendaires*!!! *Ostie*, is that his head, his eye? I can't tell what's what! There are four or five characters, and you can't tell them apart!

SIRIS: What is the future? There is no future!

HB: Having lived through a part of the history of Quebec comics as a bookseller, from Les 400 coups and alternative comics to the emergence of independent publishers and everything, I think it's been an amazing evolution. It's been interesting to see how this whole phenomenon has developed. I often hear young cartoonists say they're sorry to have missed out on what we experienced. [*Laughter all around.*]

SIRIS: Would they rather be struggling? Do they want to be on welfare?

HB: When we tell our old stories or they hear about those days, they think it sounds interesting, like there there was a feeling of freedom in the air.

SIRIS: We had a kind of freedom, that's for sure.

AL: What I find interesting about that period is the diversity. All the artists were doing something different.

SIRIS: That's true. You could tell them apart by their style.

AL: These days, when I go to events like Expozine, a lot of the work looks alike.

SIRIS: Next time, Marc, you should interview some of the hairy youngsters, like Iris and Zviane.

JC: I'd like to wrap up by thanking my mom and dad, because without them, I might not have learned how to draw. That's it!

MT: One last question. Jean-Claude, will you ever make comics again?

JC: I'm making one right now.

"I often hear young cartoonists say they're sorry to have missed out on what we experienced."

SIRIS: Yeaaaah!

MT: What about you, Hélène?

HB: Definitely not.

SIRIS: Oh no! (Begins to cry.)

MT: That's too bad. What will you do instead?

HB: Some day, I'll make silkscreened stuffed animals with Stéphane.

MT: Will you keep doing sculpture?

HB: Maybe. For the moment, I'm having fun learning to play the ukulele.

MT: And you, Stéphane?

SO: No, not comics.

MT: But you're still making books and prints, and doing other projects like the typography for *Trip* books. You never really stopped.

SO: It's storytelling, but not with comics. I don't draw enough in any case. I'd be making a panel a week, too. What hasn't changed is my desire to create. But I want to do other things, too: go biking, travel, make prints....

SIRIS: He wants to live! He's smart — he's living, *crisse*.

SO: You bet!

MT: Stéphane is running a new collective, so that's another thing he's doing. He has other people working for him.

SO: I'm still creating, but the medium isn't comics anymore. I got into comics by accident.

SIRIS: Marc is the one who dragged you into comics!

SO: Actually, the thing I liked at the beginning was that I knew nothing about it. We just decided to make comics one day, and it was like, "Let's go!" It wouldn't be the same anymore. There are people who are so good that when I see them, I just tell myself: "Whoa, I'm nowhere near that level."

HB: It's interesting. Like Siris said, his passions were music and comics. Alexandre is putting more time into painting these days. Jean-Claude, you say you want to get back into comics, but in the meantime, you've been drawing and making music. Basically, we all got into comics by accident.

SO: Not Siris!

MT: Not me, either.

SO: Back when Marc and I met, it was a good pretext for doing a creative project as a group. We got to know Siris, Simon Bossé, Richard Suicide, Caro Caron, G.B. Edwin, Matthew Brown, and all those people.

MT: And we still hang out and have fun together!

SO: Right. And personally, I think there are other ways of making books. That's what interested me.

MT: And you're still making books. You're making them with your students and on your own.

SO: Yes, but not comics. It's still narrative, though.

MT: And you, Alexandre? Will you go back to making comics? Or would you rather do something else?

AL: I'm not closed to the idea. I have something in mind. But if I do it, it will only be for fun.

MT: Alexandre, you're a bit like Stéphane now, doing graphic design.

AL: For me, comics were always a school for learning how to draw and learning about art and self-expression. That's comics for me. If you want to learn how to draw, there's nothing like comics.

SIRIS: Damn right.

AL: If you want to tell a story using images, and you're not making movies or whatever, comics let you do it on your own. You're the cameraman, the director, the set designer... you're God, *crisse*! You're building a universe, and it's cool! It's an amazing training ground. After, you can go do anything you like. [*Laughs.*]

JC: Like washing dishes!

AL: Like washing dishes. I'm teaching now, and I really like it. I can teach a course about character building, collage, anything. Comics taught me so many things, like brush techniques and different drawing techniques.

SO: It's funny, before I was hired by Cégep du Vieux Montréal, people would tell me that comics were a dead end. But when I applied to teach and showed my portfolio, professors like Alain Cardinal looked at my comics and said: "The students are going to love this." And so they

hired me because of the comics in my portfolio. (Stéphane is a coordinator in the department of graphic design at the Cégep du Vieux Montréal.)

AL: That's what it's all about: getting the students excited!

SIRIS: You don't get teachers like that every day!

SO: Sometimes it can feel like comics don't lead anywhere, or you don't know where it's all taking you, but it does get you somewhere.

JC: You two young guys, FREDC and LPRZ, do you still want to make comics after hearing all this?

FREDC: It's really about the pleasure of learning, of expressing what's inside you, without knowing where it's going to lead. Maybe you don't want to limit yourself to one medium, or maybe you want to stick with it and never give up.

AL: I stayed in comics for a long time because it was the medium I was familiar with, but you shouldn't be afraid of exploring other mediums, too.

FREDC: That's how it's been for me, even though I'm younger. I've done animation, photography, and sculpture. I ended up in comics because I wanted to get back to animation, but I wasn't ready to dive in again. Ultimately, as an artist, you evolve and keep learning — it's a way of moving forward. And then maybe you start teaching at some point because you want to share that passion with other people. It's about exploring and finding out what you've got inside. I think that's what makes a difference.

MT: Siris, want to wrap this up?

SIRIS: I'm gonna be making comics till the day I die! ✐

Art by Al + Flag

Art by Stéphane Olivier from *Mac Tin Tac*

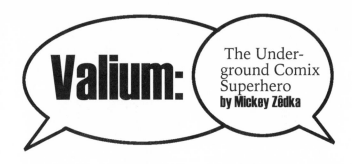

Valium: The Underground Comix Superhero
by Mickey Zêdka

Originally published in:

TRIP #9, 2016

Translation by Rupert Bottenberg

Artist, illustrator and comic creator Patrick Henley, aka Henriette Valium, is undeniably among the key figures at the heart of the Montreal underground comix movement.

Born on May 4, 1959 in Montreal, Canada, Henley began his career as a cartoonist in the early 1980s, drawing inspiration from the seedier corners of his city and of his own life, depicting grotesque characters drawn out of a realm of hallucinations and delirium.

A pioneer in graphic arts and a grand master of deviant imagery, Valium's perverse, provocative and unorthodox style has kept him at odds with the conventional comic book industry. In truth, Valium's work is hard to pin down, unclassifiable, as complicated as it is complex.

It's true that Valium is recalcitrant and difficult. He is a renegade, an indomitable creator who has devoted himself to his work without concession. His is an expansive body of work, constantly surprising and innovative, always pushing the limits. He has always operated at the margins of the comic art establishment, even its rambunctious alternative element. Nevertheless, his work has become a reference point.

Since his earliest efforts, Valium has earned the recognition and admiration of his peers, attracted the attention of aficionados, and fostered a small but dedicated international following.

There is no question that Valium's work has greatly contributed to the evolution of comics in Quebec and elsewhere. Its impact in the fields of comics and graphic arts has echoed well beyond Quebec's borders.

Valium creates his books without compromise. And it is exactly that, perhaps, that his fans admire most! He reveals himself to the public unfiltered, castigating himself with the revelation of his faults and fixations — a veritable exercise in self-abnegation.

For this reason, the work of Valium is more than just comics. It is a journey into a parallel universe of neuroses and deviation, an orgiastic mass of grotesque images, monstrosities and maledictions. Amen!

ICEBERG

VOS YEUX TREMPENT DEDANS

No 5   99¢

Dans ce numéro: Paulette Hachure,
Anémie de Pain, Henriette Valium,
Charlotte Béton, Violette Bristol, Ginette Plume-Pinceau,
Dolorĕs , Ringo la Balafre et plusieurs autres

Yes, Valium is undeniably a deviant. He has abandoned the sacred precepts of the comic book, and his works have continually transgressed, infringed and defied. His violations of the norm are manifold: linguistic, graphic, sexual, ideological....

If Valium makes everything perverse, it is because in his opinion, "making art" is a deviation in itself. This understanding has marked him as a true master of the "deviant arts".

Valium: The Art of Deviance

Alternative comics, also referred to as independents emerged in the early 1980s, following the underground movement of the late 1960s and early 1970s.

Emblematic creators of underground comics are Americans Robert Crumb, Gilbert Shelton, Art Spiegelman, and more recently Daniel Clowes, Craig Thompson and Chris Ware. It is necessary, though, to distinguish these cartoonists from those who devote themselves to graphic art, silkscreening, and other deviant forms, without compromise or censorship.

The undisputed pioneers and masters in the latter domain are most certainly Pascal Doury, Placid & Muzo, Marc Caro, and Henriette Valium. These artists in the margins were the first to steer comics firmly and frankly into the arts. In addition, Henriette Valium was Quebec's first underground comic book artist to expand his efforts well beyond the comic strip.

In the universe of French-language European comics, we tend to differentiate between underground comics, which mainly represents the world of comic fanzines (small press chapbooks, minicomics, graphzines, one-man-zines...), and alternative comics, which favour the "micro-edition (...) between artisanal publishing and deluxe fanzine."

As early as 1981, Henriette Valium delved into the creation of the "one-man-zine" with his publication *Iceberg*. This is what we call "self-production" and "self-publishing."

Self-publishing is often artisanal, the author assuming the tasks of printing, cutting and binding their books. Valium's silkscreened and largely self-published albums are works of art in their own right — true collectors' items. The books of Henriette Valium have always evolved in this way, with the intention of being a comic and a work of art at the same time.

Still, in the francophone sphere, "graph'art" exists mainly through zines that circulate in the underground. The tradition of graph'zines as such began with the punk DIY movement in the mid-1970s. In France, this movement was first represented by the Bazooka collective and the zine *Peltex* (published in two series, from 1980 to 1991).

Following the example of avant-garde agitators, the most diverse social, political and cultural movements — those with numerous networks, artists' collectives, associations, and micro-groups — create great quantities of fanzines, because many independent artists create and self-publish their own works.

Comic books and fanzines have proven themselves to be the free press par excellence. We can fill them up with our ideas: literary, graphic, even cinematographic. If we examine the marginalized thought and creation of each epoch, we can see that it is also the place of knowledge claiming its independence and its freedom, and a mode of expression chosen by the authors of independent comics.

Henriette Valium is the very first Quebec artist to represent this movement, and so he is its pioneer and guiding light. Valium explores, digs and innovates to illuminate the way, and this gave birth to a real movement, a rising hunger for unusual comics and DIY zines.

In his wake followed comic artists like Julie Doucet, Siris, Richard Suicide and a variety of comic collectives. So to a number of small, independent publishing houses — and also, a craze for silkscreening that radiated around the world, in Quebec with Henriette Valium and Simon Bossé, and in Europe with, among others, Pakito Bolino and his troupe of graphic designers.

In the mid-eighties, with cartoonists Pascal Doury, Muzo, Marc Caro and Henriette Valium, Blitzo Schwartzo, Philippe Gerbaud, Stéphane Blanquet, Philippe Lagautrière, Y5/P5, Charlie Schlingo, Bertrand Lecointre, Jean-François Caritte, Frédéric Poincelet, Pakito Bolino and other talents from the edge, the comic strip joined the universe of graph'zines, and gave rise to the emergent "deviant" comic book.

In the United States, this movement was associated with "anti-comics" and is represented by the publication *Raw*.

This underground movement inspired groups like L'Association, with Lewis Trondheim, Jean-Christophe Menu, David B., Stanislas, Matt Konture,

Mokeit van Linden and Patrick Killoffer. And subsequently, independent publishing houses such as Artefact, Futuropolis, Fremok, Ego comme X, Cornélius and les Requins Marteaux allowed a renewal of the comic form, which has led many major publishers to imitate their approaches.

This goes to show the depth of the influence that the work of Valium and his companions has had in the community of the graphic arts.

The innovation is at multiple levels: the eccentric configuration of the page, the deconstruction, deformation, superimposition and subversion of the image, the exploding of the basic panel and demolition of established norms; raw language, experimental vocabulary, scathing humour, punk attitude, trash style — and an intense attention to detail…

In Quebec, we find his influence, among others, in the comic strips of Richard Suicide or Caro Caron (the distinctive Quebec jargon and invented vocabulary, and the raw, confrontational themes and expressions). In this sense, Valium is to comics what Plume Latraverse is to pop music.

Still, though... Valium is above all guilty of having diabolically diverted the comic to areas never yet explored. Through his work, there emerges a quasi-militant drive to affirm the value and diversity of comics. This vindication of the comic as an art in its own right is expressed in Valium's ability to forge links with other fields of practice.

He thus helped to liberate the comic strip from its limitations, connecting it to the noblest artistic activities, in particular to literature and to the fine arts, and to the health and viability of art in general.

Valium has made paintings, collages, sculptures, and art objects of all kinds — clocks, games, playing cards, and more. He has also made videos, and several musical recordings. Valium's prolific body of work is overflowing with originality, ingenuity, and surprises! Moreover, it truly isn't recognized and appreciated to the extent that it should be.

Obviously, exploring the universe of Valium comes down to a willingness to step through the looking glass and plunge headlong into a parallel world where decrepitude reigns.

It must be known that Henriette has built his work as a labyrinth, where riddles and jokes are the guardians at the threshold.

The Quest for the Graphic Grail

Over the years, Valium's drawings and collages have been scattered throughout numerous anthologies, fanzines, his own publications and various collaborations, making it difficult to find any complete chronology of his work.

Valium began in 1981 with the zine *Vagorbine 14*, his first self-published title.

His work first appeared under the pseudonym Henriette Valium in the self-produced zine *Iceberg* (1984).

One can uncover Valium's first incursions into the world of comics through various compilations and fanzines, like *Motel, Rectangle, The Dart, Stamp Axe,* and *Tchiize.*

1001 Adventures...

After disseminating his artwork across a variety of independent zines and journals, the crucial moment finally arrived for Valium's first album: a collection of his stories created in the 1980s, at last compiled into a self-published anthology, entirely screenprinted by Valium himself.

This first album, *1000 Rectums, c't'un album*, was released in 1987 and marked the consecration of Valium as a must-read comic artist in the Montreal underground. The book presents a number of themes and characters that populate and inform the unique universe of the author. Among others, Valium introduces characters who will become his most recognizable, such as his alter-ego Pattou, the enigmatic Mr. Iceberg, and the diabolical scientist Doc Lekron.

"It must be known that Henriette has built his work as a labyrinth, where riddles and jokes are the guardians at the threshold."

The stories, often a single page, revolve around Valium's familiar themes: sickness, decrepitude, addiction, sexual deviance, neurosis and social decline in general.

While the artwork is marked by a powerful penchant for punk aesthetics, *1000 Rectums, c't'un album* does not yet display the complex and violent graphic excess that will characterize Valium's publications to come....

That said, it can be said that *1000 Rectums, c't'un album* is the book that cements Valium's place among the masters of underground comics, but also and above all it is the book which announces his reorienting towards a new approach, increasingly obsessed with graphic innovation.

At the beginning of the 1990s, Henriette Valium surprised readers once again by making an album of punk rock songs, the eponymous *Valium et le Dépressifs* (Valium: voice, Coco: guitar, Jules: bass, Bowell: drums), which includes such titles as "C'est un monstre," "Les Angloïdes," and "Chu malade."

Unjustly ignored at the time, the album deserves only praise. One of the rare Quebecois albums of punk-rock-noise with industrial flavour, mixing ironic lyrics, tasty, catchy riffs and solid composition. Despite somewhat poor production quality, the record is certainly one of the best of its kind to have been produced in Quebec in the early 90s (the album was completely re-mastered in 2015).

The brief adventure of Valium et le Dépressifs lasted from 1990 to 1993. The band left behind this unique album and memories of remarkable performances.

After this incursion into the world of punk-rock-industrial music, Valium continued to make other musical creations, solo efforts under various pseudonyms, collections of sound pieces that certainly have affinities with his graphic universe. These peculiar recordings explored the

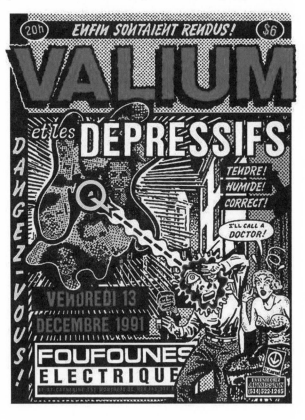

realm of *musique concrète*, and can be described as ambient industrial music acting as soundtracks. This collection of music can be appended to Valium's pictorial art, and is among the very rare works of industrial music in Quebec.

During the 90s, in parallel with this brief foray into punk rock, Henriette Valium began connect-

lide: bizarre living organisms of doubtful provenance, anomalies, comical strangeness, distorted objects, corrupted, putrefied matter.... We hear noises, rumours, shrieks and sobbing. We smell the odours. We are nauseated and disoriented, but nonetheless we cackle with disgusted delight!

Valium embarked on *Primitive crétin!* without considering whether his plan was to make comics, or art, or something else.... Valium undertakes more formal experiments with collage, bringing his art towards ever more elaborate, sophisticated and horrifying forms. It is inevitable — Valium does Valium, obsessively.

With *Primitive crétin!*, Valium began in earnest his journey in the unseemly universe of "decomposition," something already hinted at in his earliest works — and already exploited in work published in *Chacal puant*, between 1992-1995. This is decomposition of the image, in every sense of the word — a foul parade of characters affected by disease and deformity. This is the work that will lead to the era of Mutants, starting in 2001.

For all these reasons, *Primitive crétin!* marks an important turning point in Valium's career.

ing with European and American publishers. Impatient with the lack of concrete results, though, he decided to self-produce a screen-printed album in a final push that led to the creation of the oversized, self-published *Primitive crétin!* (1993).

Primitive crétin! is probably Valium's most recognized work to date. It is a collection of absurd and incoherent stories that revisits the themes and characters of his previous books, with the added bonus of new characters, notables being the Gant boxing family and Tiplouplou.

The most remarkable aspect of this album lies in the elaborate illustrations — astonishing bursts of punk-trash-surrealist intensity. It is from this book forward that Valium's work becomes an alchemical marriage between comic strip and graph'art.

Every page in the book is a world in itself, in which the incongruous and the indecent col-

While enjoying numerous collaborations with independent fanzines throughout Europe and North America, such as *Zero Zero* (which led to the American reprint of *Primitive crétin!* In 1996 by Fantagraphics), Valium was already back at his drawing table, concocting a new work, something that would surpass his previous efforts. It was a project that would require no less than six years of work.

Constantly Mutating...

At the turn of the third millennium, Valium's madness metastasized and he took up the challenge of surpassing himself in excess, in dementia, degradation and careful attention to detail...

The year 2000 was marked by the publication of the mythical book *Cœur de Maman*. Again, it was

"Every page in the book is a world in itself, in which the incongruous and the indecent collide: bizarre living organisms of doubtful provenance, anomalies, comical strangeness, distorted objects, corrupted, putrefied matter... We hear noises, rumours, shrieks and sobbing. We smell the odours."

a large-format, screenprinted, self-produced and self-published comic book.

Cœur de Maman picks up where *Primitive crétin!* left off — all of Valium's distinctive characters materialize again, more neurotic and disfigured than ever, in the middle of pages overflowing with hallucinatory graphic detail. A truly awesome book, and perhaps also the most touching. Because under this pile of provocative drawings hides true sensitivity and honest reflection....

Cœur de Maman tells the bizarre story of a monstrous and oversized mother's heart. Within, Valium discusses topics such as violence, addiction, alcohol, sex and science.

Ever More Brown

In the spring of 2007, the French publisher L'Association released the first complete anthology of Valium's comics.

Almost at the same time, Le Dernier Cri worked toward a deluxe edition that would include L'Association's anthology, an audio CD and a comprehensive collection of Valium's drawings and paintings.

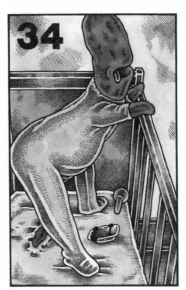

from *Mutants*

It was also in 2007 that Valium locked himself away to work assiduously on a new book, promising to surpass all precedents — the phenomenal *La Princesse Brune!*

La Princesse Brune is a "phenomenal" work. It was Valium's first collection with colour plates, and

his most refined, most dreamlike and most extreme work to date. This unusual book reveals a veritable orgy of drawings, skillfully intertwined details, shattering page layouts, sordid scenarios — and of course, madness bordering on genius (or vice versa).

This book is one of the zeniths in the history of art, graphics and the comic strip. One is struck dumb when confronted by these pages overflowing with breathtaking prowess.

It is no longer a question of placidly reading a comic panel by panel, but rather of deciphering each drawing, detail by detail. And one never ceases to be surprised by the jokes hidden here and there, or a grotesque detail that adds to the grotesquery of the whole.

In this book, Valium's hallucinatory illustrations drag the reader into subversive, immersive environments that are virtually impossible to absorb at a glance. Images that appear to us like geographical terrains, undecipherable treasure maps of a crazy world run off its rails.

Yes. It is also like a mad diagram of a world both internal and external, a world made of delusion, blasphemy, outbursts, heartrending cries, anxiety, anguish...

The complexity of the illustrations, their opulence, their excess, their extravagance, combined with the hypertrophy or atrophy of the alienated characters crawling amid them, amplify the horror of this grotesque, chaotic, apocalyptic universe.

To create these prodigious images, Valium had to work for several months on each of the pages. A truly monastic effort! With this book, Valium's meticulous technique has become the cornerstone of his practice.

Therefore, for Valium, designing and producing such a book was a long and arduous process that took up to six years of work.

It is now clear to what extent attention to detail and graphic mastery has become in Valium's work, and this is undoubtedly an element that makes the difference in his unorthodox comic art. It is this form of obsessive disorder that leads him to maniacally create these overflowing pages.... All this in order to divert boredom, to divert torment, to divert vice.... A great festival of jubilant deviance! Because with Valium, the comic book itself becomes a mutant, a sleazy whore raising debauchery to the rank of art!

This is precisely what I call "deviant comics," just as we speak today of deviant art. Everything that does not conform, all that is indecent.

In a word, I would say that Valium always grasped the art of making art without ever pretending to make art. That's it — that's the art of deviance.

Hurtling Headlong Into Art

It's facile to say that Henriette Valium is a "comic artist." In my opinion, it's a little reductive. To me, Valium is an artist, an artist who is a comic artist, but above all a full-fledged artist who has explored multiple fields of the visual arts, music, writing, and more. Now, in my opinion, the work of Valium is a whole. And as they say, "everything is in everything."

From his beginnings in the field of comics, at the time of *Obu International* in the early 1980s, Valium was already creating collages, mangled images, and serigraphs. He developed a very personal style which had strong connections with his

work as a cartoonist, but at the same time was inspired more by advertising, and was even more laden with shocking images, disturbing, provocative allusions, and defiance of censorship.

During the 90s Valium earned his living mainly by designing and screenprinting posters for various bars and rock groups in Montreal (such as Café Campus and Les Foufounes Électriques).

During this period of the deviant 90s, many of his posters were pasted on walls throughout Montreal, for countless shows by iconic local and international bands. Valium's posters were certainly part of the underground landscape in Montreal, one of its special flavours. These large, colourful, silkscreened posters were immediately recognizable.

I suspect that Valium has incorporated much of this work into his overall practice. It is perhaps due to his work designing posters that he broke the rules of comics to make art. Certainly, poster design forced him to conceive images closer to graphic art than to comics, and this forced him to constantly renew himself and constantly innovate in the field.

Poster design has surely had an impact on his work, something I think distinguishes it from that of other cartoonists. In addition, it allowed Valium to do screenprinting, which has become his medium of choice. And indeed, his work in the field of screenprinting is recognized by artists around the world, for Valium is the godfather of "silkscreen punk."

Millennial Master of the Image

The artist Pakito Bolino, who learned the most sophisticated screenprinting techniques, has stated that it was Valium who made everything switch. He says that what allowed him to create his own studio was the discovery of Henriette Valium in the cold country of Canada, of what he calls "punk techniques."

"It is now clear to what extent attention to detail and graphic mastery has become in Valium's work, and this is undoubtedly an element that makes the difference in his unorthodox comic art."

from *Primitive Cretin*

Subsequently, in 1993, he founded with his accomplice Caroline Sury Le Dernier Cri, a publishing house dedicated to the dissemination of the works of artists from the underground world of Paris and beyond, including: Valium, Kérozen, Keiti Ota and others.

Le Dernier Cri created graph-zines, a hybrid of the artist's monograph and the fanzine tradition. Le Dernier Cri, which produces books by screen-printed artists, posters, collective collections, videos and music albums, provided a great home for the work of Valium.

It is a question of "formula". Valium's comic books are confusing at first because they do not tell a story linearly, each box can be read independently of the next. It is like a quilt in patchwork... it is a dismissal, chewed and half-digested, a dirty and raw visual world that offers itself to us, whether we like it or not.

This particular style, this "formula" where comic strips are deconstructed and become a source of inspiration for the graphic arts, is the domain of Valium and will be a model for the "formula" adopted by Le Dernier Cri and other independent publishing houses such as United Dead Artists.

In a way, the "deviant" work of Valium was a reference for this new concept of graph-art punk-trash, from comic book transmuted into art. And, obviously, he was a source of inspiration for several illustrator artists and "deviant" cartoonists of this new generation.

In the mid-nineties, Valium became increasingly involved in the trafficking of images, collages, modifications and transmutations....

Among the most interesting collages of this period are the series of "Curés Malades" (1994) and "La Prison Anale des Frères Rouges" (1996). It was with great sarcasm and derision that Valium was inspired to paint a critical portrait of the fatal influence of the Roman Catholic Apostolic Church on the history of Quebec and the damage it caused. Sweet vengeance!

In the same year, Valium also completed "Le Survivant", an impressive painting inspired by a family photograph by Joseph Goebbels. This painting was exhibited at Galerie Clark in Montreal with "Les Curés Malades" and several other paintings and objets d'art. This exhibition marked the beginning of his recognition as a full-fledged artist — not just as a cartoonist.

Taking into account the horrors of history, we understand that the work of Valium is a caricature of our sick society. It is with this critical state of mind that he realized his series entitled "Our Elite" (1997).

At the turn of the 3rd millennium, Valium experimented more and more with collage, sculpture, integrating work with computers into his comics and silkscreen printing; among others, a series of illustrations entitled "Les Héritiers du Rêve" (2002) and the little books *Mutants I* (2002) and *Mutants II* (2003).

Valium continued his work on mutants, later in 2013, with *Mutants III*, a card game made in homage to Hans Bellmer, which consists of unusual collages, pornographic anomalies, and monstrous amalgams, mainly made by computer.

First Aid

In the years preceding the release of the *Mutants III* card game, Valium produced many works, paintings, collages and large format silkscreen prints. Most of them have been reproduced in fascimiles published by Le Dernier Cri, for example, *First Aid* which brings together a series of silkscreened works.

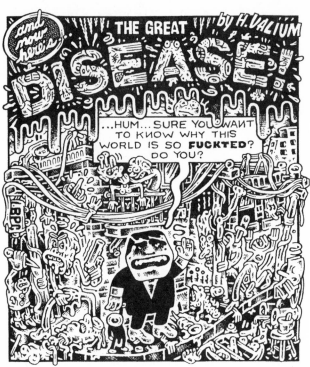

from *Primitive Cretin*

2012 was a big year for Valium. His last comic strip, finished in 2005, (published in 2007) was the *Princess Brune* and then, on the comic side, nothing....

Meanwhile, when Valium pauses, to rest from making a comic, he paints paintings, he meditates by making collages and silkscreens, he fills a vacuum by making sculptures, he relaxes.

So when Valium takes a break from comics, he finds himself with extra work, and he passes them on to Bolino, who publishes them immediately with Le Dernier Cri.

In 2012, with his series of *Mutants*, and his series *First Aid*, he momentarily forgot that he is a cartoonist and he convinced us that he is a specialist of the image. Therefore, in 2012, he deserved to be finally exhibited in art galleries in Europe and the United States.

Valium and Music

"I created the kind of sounds I like to hear when I draw."
— Henriette Valium

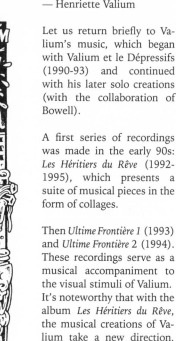

Let us return briefly to Valium's music, which began with Valium et le Dépressifs (1990-93) and continued with his later solo creations (with the collaboration of Bowell).

A first series of recordings was made in the early 90s: *Les Héritiers du Rêve* (1992-1995), which presents a suite of musical pieces in the form of collages.

Then *Ultime Frontière 1* (1993) and *Ultime Frontière* 2 (1994). These recordings serve as a musical accompaniment to the visual stimuli of Valium. It's noteworthy that with the album *Les Héritiers du Rêve*, the musical creations of Valium take a new direction. If Valium et le Dépressifs offered us songs in the tradition of punk rock, Valium's solo work changed direction and explored new realms of sound. He produced music with descriptive atmospheres, similar to *musique concrète* or the scores for radio plays.

Obviously, there are not many fans of this kind of music, and I imagine that is the reason why Valium did not bother to dwell extensively on this aspect of his work. But then, this music is obviously not intended for a wide audience.

After a long pause, Valium returned to music in the early 2000s, after the release of his book *Cœur de Maman*, and it was no doubt in a very particular state of mind that he realized *L'Exil* (2002) and *Le Naufrage* (2004), albums of thematic music

"(with) Curés Malades (1994) and La Prison Anale des Frères Rouges (1996) … Valium was inspired to paint a critical portrait of the fatal influence of the Roman Catholic Apostolic Church on the history of Quebec and the damage it caused."

that confront the listener with distressing atmospheres, in the vein of industrial noise.

Then came three albums on which Valium shows greater seriousness than he suggests, revealing a composer who commands a sense that "everything Valium touches becomes art." First, *Le Projet Tosh* (2007), an album of 26 short, very evocative soundtracks. Certainly eccentric, but rather accessible, these 26 aural miniatures are true tiny masterpieces of the genre.

Then, Valium concocted *Olympus mons primal innocentis* (2008), which is in the same vein as *Le Projet Tosh*, and would make a good science fiction soundtrack. These two albums of ambient music are comparable to that of groups like Lustmord, Zoviet France or Coil.

If you are a fan of industrial noise music, or a real music lover, *Le Projet Tosh* and *Olympus mons primal innocentis* are two essential albums for your collection.

Then came *Guantanamort* (2009), a thematic album of sound collages, arguably more in the spirit of the comics and visual universe of Valium. Again, the pieces are very close to music for a radio play.

More recently, Valium presented *In the House of the Weef* (2013), an invitation to a journey into a post-apocalyptic future. There are the disturbing underwater atmospheres, the sense of being trapped in a vacuum, in a test tube somewhere in a laboratory, plugged into a machine, fed intravenously, in a place full of lugubrious echoes, at the mercy of our own nightmares, our own imagination... Without exaggeration, *In the House of the Weef* is among the best albums of "dark ambient" music out there, meriting constant replays.

In short, even if the musical work of Valium does not address a large audience, it really deserves the attention of lovers of this kind of music.

Valium's music had not really been properly released and distributed until 2015 when Valium completely remastered all his musical albums. These new editions will be available on his website.

Champion Without a Palace

In the fall of 2015, after nearly eight years of work, Valium wrapped up his latest book, *Le Palais dé Champions* [eventually published in English as *The Palace of Champions*, Conundrum 2016].

I can assure you that I have never seen anything like it! This book, once again, managed to surpass all the others, and provides the strongest proof yet of Valium's hallucinatory graphic prowess.

119

The Palace of Champions is unquestionably the album of a champion. Each image is a stunning tableau, worth every one of the proverbial thousand words. Every page is a veritable explosion of little marvels! Hilarious stories that operate like little games, like mazes to confound, to perplex, and to reward the dedicated with unexpected twists and turns. Everything is executed in a manner intended to amaze. It is the opposite of restraint, the opposite of minimalism, the opposite of the measured.... Rich in delightful excess, it is a work in which everything is trash but perfectly controlled, the lines, the colours, the patterns repeated, deformed, intertwining and colliding....

It's Valium, but unlike anything seen before.

In devouring this album with my eyes, I had the impression of gazing at the illuminations of a master craftsman of the Middle Ages in the grip of delirium.

Without exaggeration, this album is a zenith. Stupefying, hilarious... and beautiful.

Interview with an Undesirable

When you encounter Valium at home, it's like arriving at the entrance of Ali Baba's cave. You find yourself in front of a garage, in an alley, a kind of bunker, but with a certain style.

Valium has painted his bunker yellow and I can tell you that his humble dwelling is quite welcoming.

Valium lives there in his den, in voluntary simplicity... not to say destitution. Valium seems to follow a regime of austerity.

Anyway, his home is inviting, and Valium himself is a person so welcoming and full of tales to tell that one often forgets why one is there to begin with.

Valium knows how to make one forget the purpose of their visit. He knows how to make one forget the time. In his company, time passes quickly, for there is not a second lacking a joke, an anecdote or a marvel arriving out of nowhere, as if by magic.

Yes. One wonders if Valium might not be some sort of magician, finally.

Valium's home is a repository of original works, often oversized, such prodigious work, almost superhuman, almost supernatural, that it induces vertigo. It is magic. It is undeniably overwhelming. Even someone who does not care for the themes that Valium addresses cannot fail to admit that these are masterpieces! Faced with the original, physical works, that magic is all the more potent. One immediately recognizes that this is an accomplishment without any comparison, a pantagruelian corpus resulting from a gargantuan effort!

Valium's work left me speechless.

Besides, I have nothing more to say.

Let's take advantage of this opportunity to let Valium speak for himself a little.... ●

Henriette Valium

Interview by Mickey Zêdka

Originally published in:

TRIP #9, 2016

Translation by
Rupert Bottenberg

Mickey Zêdka: Okay, for starters, we'll go with the easy questions. What made you want to start drawing, and get into making comics?

Henriette Valium: Whoa, Mickey, man! Okay, I'll try to reply without going overboard but if I forget something, don't give me shit about it… and don't take my word for gold, I'm the type who exaggerates all the time, just to get attention. Nobody really gave me the urge to draw, it showed up by itself early on, kinda like epilepsy, teen acne and chronic allergies. I think I was born with it. Maybe also to fill my time, I was never really big into TV. Plus, paper and pens were — and still are — a cheap and easily accessible medium. So I've been drawing since I was in diapers. Comics came later in my teens — probably after I'd read Hergé's *Crabe aux pinces d'or* 150,000 times! I did my first comic when I was 17. It was the full-colour story of a turd that talked. It was four or five pages, if I recall.

MZ: What were your earliest influences, the comic artists that made their mark on you, and inspired you?

HV: The formula for my creativity is the following: in the mixmaster of a permanent obsessive with a confessional imagination, add one-quarter Hergé, one-quarter Crumb, one-quarter Willem and one-quarter Jacovitti. Into this mix, pour any alcohol, of at least 5.7%, some acid and occasionally fresh mushrooms. Plus some copying from here and there, sprinkle with existential anxiety, stew in melancholy and — Ta-dah! Obviously that's just the beginning, it gets more complicated later on.

MZ: Talk a bit about getting started in the comics domain, and in self-publishing.

HV: Already in our early twenties, it was quickly becoming clear, to myself and some of my college peers, that the door to official publishing would remain closed to us forever, so me and Normand Hamel (aka Charlotte Béton), started with *Vajorbine 14*, in 1982 or 83. I worked at a print shop at the time, which made the task and costs easier. So we ended up with badly photocopied 8.5x11s, folded in half. It was the first issue of *Iceberg* (five issues, 1984-86), with Thibeau de Corta (Violette Bristol), Paul Rossini, Diane Obomsawin, Denis Lord (Rose Beef), and several others whom I've unfortunately forgotten. *Iceberg*, which in our quixotic imaginations was supposed to sink *Titanic*, *Croc* magazine's comics offshoot. It outlived it, anyway! After that, I kept on screwing around with Bruno Guay and *Motel* (six issues, 1986-89, with Hilton, Bing, Pratt etc.), and then finally I put an end to this mess by self-publishing my own books in oversized format, printed with water-based silkscreening, in the early 1990s. This was after repetitive, chronic rejection from publishing houses of any category or nationality, in France, U.S. or Quebec. I don't know how many goddamn letters and packages I sent at that time… I would have given anything for just a response from *Raw* or L'Association! It goes without saying that these things are now collector's items, and there are even some I don't have a copy of myself!

MZ: When we look at your comics, we immediately recognize the particular Valium universe, one that's "very typically Quebecois." Your work is "local" and intimately linked to Quebec, especially Montreal, its language, its culture. Do you consider your work a reflection of Quebec society? Or of society in general?

HV: Well, okay, the fallow ground where my comics sprouted is the backyard of some ghetto housing in Hochelaga-Maisonneuve, I'll give you that. On the other hand, it's hard for me to reduce my comics to the single dimension of being Quebecois, even if that sounds pretentious. My work is underground and the underground is kind of the same everywhere — welfare, government cheques, marginalization and so on. It's often the portrait of a counterculture that exists the same way elsewhere, regardless of language or local culture. For example, Bertrand Boisvert (R.I.P.) took my books with him to a squat in Poland, and even if the kids there did not understand the written words, they immediately recognized the universe depicted there. Apparently, they were fighting each other to read them, or at least look at the pictures! So I was a star in the Polish squats in 1997! More recently, I had a *Valium's Greatest Hits* book published by Insulin Addict… in Macedonia!

MZ: The fact that you put yourself in your comics necessarily places you in the role of witness

and narrator. Could one consider your work, in this sense, to be autobiographical?

HV: Hmmm… good question. Okay, I think that maybe there is always autobiography in art, but maybe I'm wrong. My second comic — the first that wasn't destroyed — in *Vajorbine 14* was essentially total crap and autobiographical. Later things evolved, but Pattou was and is my alter ego, putting aside all the times I've done self-portraits. In any case it's more striking in my new book, which is in part autobiographical stories, or stories inspired by events that happened to me. And in this book there's not one instance of ass-fucking! But that doesn't stop the majority of publishers from ignoring me. In the past, to be honest, I never really reflected on that question. I know that at the beginning I wanted to do a bit like Crumb, the self-portraits and self-loathing. I quickly associated that with the underground, for me it was part of the genre. It's perhaps also an unconscious way of marking my territory, and of telling the reader: "Be careful where you step, you rotten little moron, you're in my world now, you shitbag!" Or like a dog that goes around the alley, pissing on every utility post, before crawling into his hutch and eating his bowl of snacks — his welfare, his little monthly gift.

MZ: Are these nasty, apocalyptic stories you're telling criticizing society? Is this a satire, a caricature of society?

HV: Yeah, obviously there's a lot of criticism, veiled or not, of the ultra/maximum/mega/total crazy world in which we're obliged to live. I corked it with my forthcoming book — I don't think there's a single page without two towers getting smashed by planes…. But I still believe that even if I lived for 3,500 years, drawing constantly, I would never be able to portray a billionth of a billionth of the immensity of the ultra/maximum/mega/total mess of humans being ultra/maximum/mega/total idiots.

MZ: Your comics are populated with singular characters. I'm curious to know how you came up with them? Your alter ego, Pattou? The enigmatic Mr. Iceberg? The legendary Doctor Lekron? Tiplouplou? The Boxing Glove Family?

HV: Pattou is my alter ego, already there in my earliest comics. As I was finishing college, at the beginning, I was drawing him wearing a black rectangular hat with a ribbon. Iceberg came lat-

"The biggest pain in the ass is to feel useless and despised, often by one's own family. To get turned down for my 150th grant request because it does not fit with the goals and policies of the establishment ... ask yourself what it's worth to be a genius when you live in a garage at the corner of Hochelaga and Joliette."

er, he was a comic-book variation of a picture I'd made of Klaus Barbie in the early 80s. I found it so spaced out that I later decided to add him in all over the place in my comics, as a kind of idiotic, impotent bystander. I even created a feminine version as a logo for Foufs, where I worked, but they didn't want it. I think that he has become over time a metaphor for perpetual, permanent, immobile and infinite general bullshit. Then, in the early 90s, I needed a crazy scientist to torture Pattou — anally, among other things — so Lekron pops up in *Primitive Cretin*. At first, his skull was open and you could see his brains, but I quickly closed it up because of the smell. For others, it's dictated by the needs and ideas of the moment, some that I should maybe revive, you never know. Tipouplou is cool, a root-creature fond of tubes.... Denis Wolf, a music producer and publisher, bought the rights to use the Paper Bag Family, around 1996, to do some animation, but I'm still waiting and have seen nothing to date. Anecdote: my former landlord on Ontario St. is Lekron's spitting image, physically and psychologically, and I came across an *Allo-Police* issue with an article on a murderer in the US, and it was Iceberg in the flesh, glasses, suit and tie, everything! That was so crazy that I kept the photo to make a collage, which can be seen in *Prison anale des Frères rouges*.... Reality crushes fiction, without a doubt.

MZ: To me, it's obvious that your characters exist somewhere. And speaking of your inspirations — given that provocative, disturbing work and scatological humour are a priority for you, you must surely encounter obstacles with publishers because of it. What are your relationships with publishers like?

HV: The commercial publication of Valium has always been problematic, and it leapt out at me even more with the attempts related to my last book, not to mention that print editions are in peril because of the Internet. With my fantasies of the 48-page, Tintin-style hardcover album, I feel more and more like a dinosaur, worn out, obsolete and endangered! And then I wonder, when I look at what is done in comics today, if the underground still wants to say something. Everything is so cute, nice, lick-ass, shit, non-racist, non-deviant, eternal pollyanna suckiness, bending over to take it in the ass with the deepest indifference. My last book took me nearly eight years, I sent it to Quebec, French and American publishers, and in the majority of cases I did not even receive an e-mail in return!

MZ: My friend, you're an old dinosaur, on his way to extinction! You're going to end up in a museum. [*Laughs.*] So we can infer you've had to deal with censorship?

HV: Yes, at the beginning with *Croc* and *Titanic*, I had a rather complicated and opaque story, "La Malette de Plastique" — four pages each month. At the beginning, they made me remove some syringes and hide a couple of pairs of tits that were too obvious, but the honeymoon didn't last. Let's say that when they kicked me out, I wanted to get the hell out anyway... Afterwards I realized that, for my physical, me.ntal and psychological balance, in short/medium/long/total term, I could never again — and this was imperative — let some fucking asshole impose some line of conduct on my sacrosanct, pure and inviolable creativity. It was that or instantly go insane. And the business of licking ass, bending over without lubrication — others do that better than me. To each his specialty, as Willem would say.

MZ: Which stage of creation is the most exciting for you?

HV: In comics, the initial pencils are most exultant part, because that's the moment when an idea you have in your head, one that's maybe even been there for years, comes to life on paper.

MZ: And which stage do you enjoy the least?

HV: The shitty part is when you've finished a book and not only is it rejected everywhere, but that in spite of 35 years in the field and a certain amount of fame, some publishers can't even be bothered to answer... but I'm just flapping my gums here!

MZ: Do you have other passions aside from comics? If you didn't do comics, what would you do with your time? What other line of work could you see yourself in?

HV: I paint and make music — or rather, musical collages. Also, with my son, who is an actor, I've started to write a TV series. I don't know what it will lead to but we're having fun, and I'm actually reconnecting with the passions of my youth because I performed and wrote theatre as a teen. But honestly, if I didn't have my art, I think I would have become a professional derelict.

MZ: Theatre?! I can just imagine it... Valium in the role of a drunk vagrant! [*Laughs.*] No kidding, I could see you in a Beckett play, but the "Waiting for the Jackpot" version. [*Laughs.*] Okay, now, a bit of professionalism, please. Let's continue with the interview. What are the most difficult stages, the biggest obstacles you face in the production of your work?

HV: The biggest pain in the ass is to feel useless and despised, often by one's own family. To get turned down for my 150th grant request because it does not fit with the goals and policies of the establishment, and to see for years this endless parade of whiners, idiots, suckers, hasbeens and never-weres, incompetents, hypocrites and slackers receiving money and accolades for their sad, empty artistic trinkets (but that's not everyone, of course!). Ask yourself what it's worth to be a genius when you live in a garage at the corner of Hochelaga and Joliette.

The Arts...

MZ: Your attention to detail, the complexity of your illustrations brings your work closer and closer to fine arts. I often wonder if Valium is aware that he is much more than a simple cartoonist. You create almost as much work in other media — sculptures, collages, music, etc, — as you do comics. I also consider your comics works of art in themselves. Your work has had a very strong, very considerable influence on contemporary arts, art-zines, graph-art, comics and underground arts. Would it be fair to say that your work straddles the realms of comics and fine arts?

from *Curé Malade*

HV: Interesting remark. My next book [*The Palace of Champions*] is largely inspired by medieval illuminations, and is much closer to Bosch than to Gotlib! Those who know my work know that over the years, I have developed two distinct styles, one in comics and the other in art, but at present, given the problems related to publishing the comics, I am in the process of combining the two styles and making sort of comic paintings — much like the triptych of Bosch — and even taking advantage of the occasion to settle the recurring problem of language once and for all by inventing a blatantly false language, a kind of Latin-Esperanto-French-Spanish-Chinese-sounding universal tongue! For example, I'm sure "prout!" means fart in all known languages of the universe! I'm going to compile all-encompassing words like "krack," "plott," "sniff," and "twipp," and smear them all over panels with pictograms, nice and easy to understand for all the future generations of idiots to come!

MZ: So you agree that you constantly transform and reinvent the comic strip in order to find the most universal, essential and representative platform for your ideas. But I have to say that because of that, you make "art." Have you ever thought of embarking in "the Arts," with a capital A, and presenting yourself with the more honourable title of "artist"?

HV: Ha! How marvelous is the poet! No, not really. But I'm in the arts with a big A! In fact, it's quite the opposite, it's Official Art that rejected me, that spat me out, really, or even better vomited me up, or super-better-than-that re-regurgitated me and re- re-vomited! In fact, Official Art and I self-vomit on each other through reciprocal self-regurgitation which continues automatically. On the other hand, around 1983, Hamel and I received a grant from the Canada Council for the Arts, and then another time I received a half-grant split in two with someone else, from the Council of Arts of Quebec, around 1990, thanks to the kindness of Denis Lord, the little bugger who was on the jury! And I have already exhibited at the Montreal Museum of Contemporary Art, in 1983, as part of "Entre la Magie et la Panique." Once, I was invited to dinner as part of an interview for a serious art magazine whose name I forget, and it was the shittiest supper of my last 150 lives! Everyone had 150 sticks up their ass! But because I do not know how to behave at the table, I have never been invited again to the banquet.

MZ: In my opinion, your work really deserves to be exhibited in art galleries, and shared with a wider audience! I wonder what prevents that.... For you, to exhibit in an art gallery, what does that imply?

HV: What blocks me, in my opinion, is the nature of our society and the buy-and-sell system on the

one hand, the lack of resources and individuals like myself on the other. For me, art and money is like water and oil, you can mix them well but they always ends up separating. Here, the gallery owners do not have time to wait, it's necessary to sell to pay the rent, and because it's a small market in a small, timidly conservative society, they will promote the inconsequential painter with the local flavour of the moment, and try to snuff out whatever comes up that is better and that could possibly threaten their tiny little micro-business. Not to mention the horde of people who get into the arts for the personal advancement of themselves and their clique, without any relevant questioning about the value of the artistic product offered. We've come to subsidizing tap-dance shows at the casino, or light-shows on buildings put on by moving companies! This means that the system of loans and bursaries in art has long become completely corrupt, poisoned from the inside, obsolete and outdated. It would be possible, as in Sweden or Norway, to establish a status for artists with funding and national recognition, but still, there, the choices to be made would end up bringing back the same bullshit as before! In the States, the opposite happens, it's this incessant race to be doing whatever is hot, but you gotta be a superficial American for that to work, because for them nothing exists outside the USA. That's why many of the painters here are exiled to L.A. or New York, to sell and make money, but once there they quickly change their style to the flashy, in-vogue thing of the moment. And then those dirty words come up: selling art. And then there are cases like that of Valium. I do not paint to sell, to accumulate stuff or prestige, nor to impress the galleries, but with a reflex of basic survival and obedience to a chronic obsessive-compulsive disorder. My equation is simple: if I do not paint or draw, I will jump off the next bridge I pass. Which makes me hardly bankable in the mechanism of buying and selling art, at least in the short term. There is always patronage, which is generally weak and conservative in Quebec. Still, I have had the luck to be supported — I want to mention it here — by Robert Poulin, who keeps my head above water every month, and I really appreciate it. He must continually justify his decisions to his entourage. And then comes the matter of the evil Internet. The web has democratized image and sound, but at the same time completely devalued artistic product. Today, everyone can produce sound or image, so an image or a song is no longer worth anything! I myself have tons of downloaded concerts and movies.

126

"I detest that little prick Picasso. I regard him to be an unscrupulous opportunist copycat whose genius was to make everyone believe that he was a genius, and I consider it to be the greatest swindle in the history of mankind. But look, I feel people's teeth grinding, fists clenched and snarling all around me, so I'll stop – I'm not equipped for fighting in the forest."

And what is culture now? It's an uninterrupted succession of small-screen vignettes, animated or not, on the tablets and phones of these Ritalin kids with a maximum attention span of thirty seconds! Everything is formatted for shittiest quality and reduced to the level of a cultural sewer.

MZ: You've told me that one of your favourite artists is George Grosz, and that did not surprise me because there are indeed similarities in your work. Are there other artists with whom you feel affinities? Who are your favourite artists?

HV: On the fucking top of the hill, Hanz Belmer and God Van Gogh. But also, many others that I have not the guts to name out loud because I'm secretly ashamed of my choices — actually, any painting or comic that looks good and has something to say. I detest that little prick Picasso. I regard him to be an unscrupulous opportunist copycat whose genius was to make everyone believe that he was a genius, and I consider it to be the greatest swindle in the history of mankind. But look, I feel people's teeth grinding, fists clenched and snarling all around me, so I'll stop — I'm not equipped for fighting in the forest.

MZ: Besides painting, you also make sculptures and art objects of all kinds. Do you ever plan to do an exhibition of these artworks? A retrospective that would give the public an overview of your work?

HV: No, I don't think I could organize any exhibition of my works in the short, medium or long term. I simply do not have the means or the motivation, much less for a career retrospective! First, it would require a fairly large space, and second, a lot of money, or maybe a cancer diagnosis. On the other hand, I will probably launch the French version of my book, if Blanquet publishes it as he promised me.

MZ: Nowadays, do you consider yourself a comic artist or a fine artist?

HV: I consider myself a "bédariste" or an "artebédien," take your pick!

MZ: Let's talk a bit about cinema. Does film have a place in your work? Does it influence your way of writing comics?

HV: Yes, I think unconsciously cinema influences my comics. In fact, comics are films on paper. Composing a panel or a page using points of view similar to what can be seen in movies — fisheye, low-angle, etc. — can often have surprising results.

MZ: You must surely be interested in cartoons and animated films! I don't know if you've given it any thought, but is cinema a medium that interests you? Are you interested in making cartoons?

HV: Yes, yes, and yes. The gods of animation for me are the Fleischer brothers and their old *Popeye* cartoons of the 1930s! Those guys invented everything! I have versions that have been cleaned on computer, they're a pure wonder! For my part, I shot an animated film as a teen, with a friend, Daniel Faucon. His father worked as a cameraman at Channel 10 and his basement was equipped with Super 8 cameras, tripods, lights and everything! I watched it again recently, let's say that it won't revolutionize the seventh art, but at the time, we had a lot of fun. Animation, I'm afraid, will remain a missed opportunity for me because I don't have eight lives. Already, I do music collages, and that's extremely work-intensive, so I imagine that with animation, it's even worse. But I have Flash on my computer and maybe one of these days I'll try it out. I indulge the fantasy of making Ultra-Con and Coconette live in small, animated vignettes, like one or two minutes, but I'm hesitant about embarking on such a huge task. I also have some ideas for films that I really should write one day. Already, in the short term, I have to redesign my website (henriettevalium.com), it's completely obsolete, set myself up on Paypal and try to sell prints of my art, then become a multi-billionaire, and finally fuck off to Mars with some uninhibited girls and a bag of transgenic Hells Angels pot....

Music...

MZ: Some of your fans know that you made an album in the early 90s, *Valium et les dépressifs*, but most of them don't know that you have also made many other recordings. The scope and quality of your musical work is truly impressive. Although it is marginal in its style and approach, in the form of "soundtracks," it really should be better known. There is an audience for this music. One gets the impression that you made these recordings for your own personal pleasure... Do you intend to make them available?

HV: Yes, you're right, at the beginning I started musical collages just to scratch an itch, with little effort at distribution. I've started to take the music I do more seriously. I'll try to put excerpts on YouTube, then see if I can't hustle my albums on iTunes. If I do, it will have to be under the heading Laure Phelin, which is my musical name now. I'm currently making mp4s with movie bits, making visual collages to go with the music collages, so that it's not too dull to watch/hear. My style, for those who are interested, is called "dark ambient" — I found this out just the other day, searching on YouTube. I came across stuff similar to what I do under this heading — Kammarheit, Atrium Carceri, Biosphere. But really, thank you for talking about my having a musical "oeuvre," it's more than I'd ask for.

MZ: I'm a fan of industrial noise music, and I think your musical work really needs to be discovered, especially since there is very little of this kind of music in Quebec. Few people know that you've made so much music. And it would be a serious omission not to talk about it, because I consider it really part of your work, a kind of appendix to the rest of your creations — for example, *Les Héritiers du Rêve*. So let's talk a bit about your music. What ideas and inspirations inform your recordings? Do they have any connection to the rest of your work? Do you consider your music as being off to the side of your pictorial work?

HV: No, the music goes with the images and the reverse is just as true. Right after my career as a magnificent solo rock singer with Valium et les dépressifs, I started to make analog noise – this was before I had a computer. I made two records of this kind with Pakito Bolino, *Ultime Frontière* and *La Dimension du Mal*, without thinking too much about the results or having a precise musical goal, leaving room for lots of improvisation — music similar to Coil or to Throbbing Gristle, if you want. Then, with my first computer, I started by editing my first analog recordings — *L'éxil, Les Héritiers du Rêve* with Bowells on certain parts — and little by little, I realized the potential of this machine, so I became more interested in musical collages potentially accompanying an exhibition of my paintings. It was in this spirit that *Le projet Tosh* and *Olympus Mons/Primal Innocentis* were created. Then I based my musical creations more on my reality, a particularly painful separation having given birth in the rage and dishonour of *Le Naufrage* and the news of the fake attack on the Twin Towers on 9/11 leading to *Guantanamort*. There was also *In the House of the Weef*, a collection of collages that had sat on my shelves and were mixed in a hurry, because of having to move suddenly for the 157th time. Currently, I'm working on *Olympus Mons/Terminal Culpabilia*, a concept album in three stages: climbing, cresting and then descending the immense mountain of our collective madness.

Politics... and Spirituality...

MZ: Do you consider your comics to be political acts, even revolutionary?

HV: Ha ha ha! Shit, you're high, Mickey! But in fact, my last book pushes some messages here and there, but from there to talking about revolutionary acts — I don't think so, no! In my opinion, the only genuine political and social revolution that humanity is going to experience is the appalling environmental mess that is currently right in front of our noses.... The shit is about to hit the fan!

MZ: You often address thorny, even psychotic themes, delving into taboos, blasphemy, sacrilege, which rubs up against pornography, things that provoke and shock.... Is it a way for you to attack all conventions, all dogmas and ideologies? What's the idea?

HV: Maybe in the beginning, the provocation was to distinguish myself from the general conformity around me, by emulation of masters like Bellmer or Grosz, or to push further the seeds planted by Crumb or Willem. But I wonder if this is really a conscious process, in the sense that whenever I have pictorial or scripting choices before me, I always choose the worst for general decorum and the best for my obscure obsessions.

MZ: You often use the swastika motif in your artwork. Are you worried about being associated with the Nazi movement, with racist ideology or the Illuminati or some esoteric movement? Why do you often refer to swastikas?

HV: First, good ol' Valium, he's like Captain Haddock, there's nothing he's afraid of! Second, you make a serious mistake in your choice of words, my dear little Mickey Zêdka. What I use are not the Nazis' twisted crosses but swastikas, which are very different, even if the symbol is of the same nature. The swastika is a symbol as old as humanity, all societies have produced them, even the Jews, and they're found in caves that date back to prehis-

toric times. One often forgets to mention that besides the Shoah, the Second World War produced several other abominations, including the refinement of the propaganda machine begun under Mussolini and the perversion of the symbol by Adolf and his Nazis, who unfortunately chose it as their logo. But if I go back to my comics, obviously I use the swastika (right or left, no matter) knowing very well the semiotic discomfort that these two small black intertwined lines can cause in the closed-off, pure and chaste spirit of the good bourgeois of Blainville. Also, there is a certain perceptible movement on the web for the rehabilitation of the swastika, and I am a very great supporter of it. Anecdote: one time, a big black guy, after reading my comics, asked me if I was racist. I replied no, since I hate everyone equally.

MZ: The portrait of society you depict in your comics is really jaded and apocalyptic. Is it because you consider society itself to be jaded and apocalyptic? Are you seeking to denounce something more specific? In your comic strips, you often depict the human condition, the poverty, the disillusionment in the midst of a sick, alienated world where cruelty reigns, or the stupidity of an insane world made of garbage. I would say that your stories often speak of the "human condition," of the decrepitude of the world... So I tell myself that you are trying to describe a world of decrepitude to make us realize that we are destroying our world and that this is the source of all the problems, all the defeats, the source of violence, addiction, madness and poverty.... What do you say? Do you portray degradation because

"Maybe at the beginning, the provocation was to distinguish myself from the general conformity around me, by emulation of masters like Bellmer or Grosz, or to push further the seeds planted by Crumb or Willem. But I wonder if this is really a conscious process, in the sense that whenever I have pictorial or scripting choices before me, I always choose the worst for general decorum and the best for my obscure obsessions."

you dream of a better world? Are you worried about the global political situation? Are you worried about the environmental situation? How do you see the future?

HV: Shit, man! You really blew it out of your ass with that one! I believe that humanity is ending the ancient epoch of its history, characterized by the end of the incestuous fractal clan pyramid, culminating in a fabulous and probably irreversible ecological and environmental catastrophe, the biggest winner being China, which managed to mix the last two systems, capitalism and communism, and culminate in a social organization whose name remains to be defined (something sort of like *1984* by George Orwell), where coarse and servile masses work as slave-citizens in prison factories for the well-being of a few hungry pigs to the detriment of all decent and elementary social and ecological benchmarks (I would advise you to see the documentary *Manufactured Landscapes*). I say fractal because at all levels of existence, this pyramid is of the same nature as under the Mesopotamians and has not changed since antiquity, money being the base element of all this conflict. The concept of incest from the clan angle is not necessarily a sexual act, but the submission and obedience of the individual before the clan leader and his acolytes in exchange for any material protections and favours. This situation leads to two facts: the tacit and accommodating compromise of the other members of the clan, knowing very well what kind of submission and advantages it is about, and the ostracism of the "refractory" individual.... The outcome is, for the first time in the history of humanity, that man retreats before his own weapons (1963, Bay of Pigs), and the computer, a technological advance that becomes synonymous with setback:

we unlearn how to write, how to play. You no longer need to know how to calculate, draw or play music.

What's right in front of our noses, in my opinion, is between 10,000 and 15,000 years of blackout, although it might seem exaggerated. When the stretched elastic snaps back, we're going to have to learn to walk again (you have to watch the movie *The Road*). It will happen exactly like what happened in Europe after the fall of Rome at the hands of the Vandals, in 440 AD I believe, but this time on a global scale, and the planet will vomit us out. It was not until Napoleon III and the laying of the sewers in Paris that the level of public hygiene returned to the standards of ancient Rome — almost 1,400 years! Industrialization has taken our elementary knowledge of communal survival hostage and it is slowly choking and dying. Who knows how to manage agriculture now? Tanning the leather and sewing a boot? Growing a carrot? Repairing fishing nets or building a boat? Forging metal? All that, my grandparents knew....

Darwin was right about everything except humans. I think we are not an animal but a disease, a planetary cancer. And I have never seen a living organism with cancer spontaneously cure itself! We fuck around with the thermostat! Pollution and ecological degradation is a 400-million-ton train without a driver going 400,000 kilometres per hour to hit a titanium wall of indifference 400,000 feet thick! Everything is made sick by humans. The grass is sick, the flies are sick, the clouds, the sand, the ashes are sick!

MZ: In your opinion, what role should artists have in society? Since artists, like you, want to be free, and not have to make compromises in their work, how do you make a society of paid workers accept that you also deserve a place in society? What would you like to change for artists? What would your first request be to politicians? If you were Prime Minister, what are the first changes you would make? What is your message to humanity?

HV: We need to stop thinking in terms of compensation and Prime Ministers, and put away the goddamn Monopoly game, damn it. Then comes the problem of the gregarious nature of humans, our mentalities, received wisdom and so on. Gregariousness is a paradox in which the individual goes all out to belong to the group while thinking only of his own interests, so that the combined action of individuals determines the behaviour of the group, which in turn influences the behavior of the group's members. Thus, most people will prefer to maintain their place in a familiar situation, one which often disadvantages or even annihilates them, over the agency and freedom of a new, unprecedented and potentially unstable situation in the short term — which makes societies by nature conservative. The role of politicians in this is to maintain at all costs the status quo, to ensure that the little everyman gets his ass on up Monday morning and continues to operate the oppressive but reassuringly familiar collective machine. We are conditioned. Take the idea of anarchy. For 101 per cent of people, anarchy is synonymous with chaos, ruin and war. But this is quite false! Anarchy is simply a utopia, the absence of power, and there is nothing in it that tells us that the absence of power must necessarily lead to chaos, panic, or war! It is the clan education — conceived and dispensed by the clan — which has conditioned us for centuries to think so! Here the notion of clan must be seen in a global way — state, family, company etc. Take austerity. Another beautiful piece of bullshit! Not only are there resources and money, but there have never been so many resources and so much money, there has never been so much waste of resources and money! Billions and billions of dollars sleep in tax shelters or get spent on the war-wagon while it's difficult to give a shower to an old man in a hospital...

MZ: You took almost eight years to make your last book (which is equivalent to about 1,200 hours of work per page). I also know that it will be published first in English. I think it's a sign that your work has become international. I know you designed this last album simultaneously in English and French. Did you have the feeling that you might not find a publisher in French? I know it has become difficult to publish comics. Do you have a message for Quebec publishers, who are uneasy about your books?

HV: Message to Quebec publishers: "*Foculentrum pactabolo centrabilis!*" It's funny, I thought about it recently and what's happened is exactly the opposite of what I expected. I thought that the French edition of *Palais des Champions* was going to be a pure formality, and I'd be obliged to fight with English-speaking publishers, but the reverse happened. October 2016 is the date for Conundrum Press and I really look forward to seeing my baby in the flesh, even in English.

And finally...

MZ: What would you like to say to your fans? What would you like to let them know about you?

HV: Big news to me, I have admirers?! Just joking. I would tell them that everything I have done up to now I have done under duress, that it is not my fault, that because of drugs and alcohol I lost control of myself and that, to earn forgiveness, I will use what remains of my talent and lucidity to illustrate the Holy Bible in black and white on eggshell-yellow Arches paper! ●

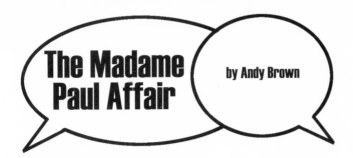

The Madame Paul Affair

by Andy Brown

Originally published in:

The Montreal Review of Books, Spring 2001

The publication of *The Madame Paul Affair* marks a turning point in the career of internationally acclaimed Montreal comic artist Julie Doucet. Her new graphic novel is Doucet's first book not reprinted from her popular comics series *Dirty Plotte*, which featured often controversial stories of menstruation, mutilation fantasies, and sex dreams.

Doucet initially self-published *Dirty Plotte* as cut-and-paste mini-comics before getting her big break in 1990, when she was picked up by Montreal's own Drawn & Quarterly, a house internationally respected for its commitment to literary comics. One of the few women recognized in the medium, Doucet was one of D&Q's first signings, and the only native Montrealer.

As a writer and artist Doucet's coming of age came in the last three issues of *Dirty Plotte*, in which she serialized the darkly autobiographical *My New York Diary*. (D&Q published the graphic novel's English version, which won the 2000 Firecracker Alternative Book Award.) *Diary* chronicles Doucet's move to New York, where she passes her days in a cramped apartment trying to work on her comic (which, in a postmodern twist, we now hold in our hands) but ends up taking too many drugs, resulting in increasingly frequent epileptic seizures. It also documents her rise to "fame" and her possessive boyfriend's increasing jealousy. Doucet's characteristic drawing style — marked by darkly inked, densely filled panels — is perfectly suited to the claustrophobic narrative, and the dialogue is written in a realistic French-inflected English.

From New York Doucet moved to Seattle, then Berlin, before returning to Montreal, where *Madame Paul* is set. "I love Montreal, I have no regrets about coming back," says the normally press-shy Doucet. "It's a big city but not too big, it's easygoing and not expensive, but there's not too much you can do in the comics community here so you need to send stuff away to get published. People get their act together in Berlin and New York, they're not just waiting. Another problem here is that it's all boys. I used to feel comfortable with a boy crowd but not anymore."

"I've finished with *Dirty Plotte*," Doucet continues, "because it's quite a lot of work, and not that much money. I went to a newspaper to propose a comic strip [*The Madame Paul Affair* was initially serialized in French-language Montreal weekly *ici*] because I only had to draw a small page and it would be out the next week. For once it was regular pay and good money."

This new "comic-serial" represents a move from strict autobiography to autobiographical fiction. Doucet uses many tropes of the mystery genre and the narrative seems more consciously structured. "I wrote the whole thing before I started (drawing). It's more fiction and that's not something I'm used to but I needed to do something other than autobiography. People complained when it was in the newspaper because there was not enough action. It's much better as a book."

The book begins with Julie moving into a cramped rooming house in Montreal's notorious East End. The title character is a jovial woman who wants to set Julie up with her nephew, the landlord. Over the next few months Julie becomes involved in disturbing events in the building: the ex-con upstairs throws himself through the window after trashing his apartment, while another neighbour attempts suicide. Meanwhile Madame Paul has disappeared. A series of shady nephews come looking for their aunt and the sto-

THE MADAME PAUL AFFAIR

20

PREVIOUSLY: MADAME PAUL LEFT SOME MAIL BEHIND HER. AMONGST THEM, A $600 CHECK FROM HER NEPHEW. JULIE AND SOPHIE WOULD LIKE TO KNOW MORE ABOUT THE OLD LADY.

© j.doucet

from *The Madame Paul Affair*. Image courtesy Drawn & Quarterly

ry gradually unfolds. Julie is forced to move into Madame Paul's apartment so the new landlord can renovate. When she discovers a Poe-esque trap door leading into a secret basement, parallels to Polanski become acute; imagine Nancy Drew starring in *The Tenant*. This is classic genre storytelling made fresh through the medium of the graphic novel.

The French versions of Doucet's books are usually put out by L'Association, one of the top publishers of alternative comics in France. Although they will be releasing Doucet's book later this year, it was first published in French by L'Oie de Cravan, a local small press which usually publishes poetry. Inspired by the surrealist movement in France, Benoît Chaput formed L'Oie in 1991 to publish the poetry he loved. His definition of poetry, however, is very broad: "My idea is to publish stuff that I feel is poetic, which is not necessarily limited to poetry." Chaput collected the *ici* strips into a book and published *L'Affaire Madame Paul* in a beautiful handprinted edition.

Chaput launched the book at Angoulême, France's largest festival of mainstream and alternative comics. "I'm fairly new to the world of comics," he says, "so it allowed me to see that world. Julie was invited by the festival. I think being with Julie opened many doors." Doucet's international reputation is substantial; many of her books are published in Europe, where the comics medium is respected as a legitimate art form. (In fact, *Madame Paul* just came out in German in the Swiss magazine *Strapazin*.) Says Chaput of his experience at the festival, "I knew Julie was known and respected in the States as a comic artist but it was shocking to see how popular she is in Europe. At the signing she did I immediately had to close the line because there were too many people. They would point and whisper, 'I think that's Julie Doucet.' I think in Montreal she doesn't have that aura."

Doucet views the experience in a different light. "For me Angoulême is always crazy. This time I had a new book so everybody was after me. It was very stressful."

L'Association's publication of *L'Affaire Madame Paul* also represents a significant turning point for the acceptance of *joual* in Quebec comics. "When I translated my first books from English to French L'Association complained it was too Québécois," Doucet recalls. "But I said I didn't want to change it, and eventually they said it was okay."

Chaput agrees. "It's her most Quebecois in a long time. I feel something has been lost in the translation to English. When L'Association saw how popular my Quebecois version of this book was at Angoulême, that people liked it that way even if they didn't always understand, they published it like that, which was quite new for them."

The unique publishing history of *The Madame Paul Affair* adds an interesting backdrop to what is essentially a beautifully crafted and entertaining book. Perhaps even more significant, however, is Doucet's claim that it is the end of an era for her. "I'm out of it," she says. "I'm not into comics anymore. *Madame Paul* is my last comic."

Although this news will greatly disappoint her dedicated fans around the globe, they will be comforted to know that Doucet has started *Sophie Punt*, a new series of self-published limited edition silk-screened minis filled with non-narrative illustrations. They bring Doucet full circle to the days when the publication of her work was still in her own hands. ●

POSTSCRIPT, 2017

Since Julie Doucet is such a trailblazer for alternative comics, not just in Quebec but internationally as well, we thought it was important to check in with her to get an update on her feelings toward *The Madame Paul Affair*. Right after she declared in this article that she was finished making comics, Drawn & Quarterly released her book of drawings *Long Time Relationship* (2001) which contained the work from her self-published minis *Sophie Punt* #1, #2, and #34, as well as the linocuts from her L'Oie de Cravan title *Melek* (2002). When I asked her (via email) if *The Madame Paul Affair* was a turning point in her career this is how she responded:

"I wouldn't say it was a turning point. I was then already tired of drawing comics. The serial comic-strip was something different, potentially exciting, that could keep me interested in the comic form. I quite liked the serial way of working... having to produce in a very regular schedule, just enough pressure and intensity... but I was not super satisfied with the end result. For one thing, towards the end of the story the newspaper changed editors and he was not too thrilled about the comic-strip idea (and the pay that came with it) and forced me to wrap up the story earlier than planned. I drew the proper ending for the printed book. I was trying to quit autobiography, but just couldn't do it.... I tried fiction but to me I couldn't quite pull it off, not knowing where else to go next... I just quit. Going back to autobiography was just not an option. It seemed too easy. I needed a new challenge. But I have to say, in *Madame Paul* my comic drawing style was at its best." 🗨

darn

self-portrait of the author.

Nov. 29, 1998

from *Long Time Relationship*

135

Art by Jean-Pierre Chausigaud

THE MONTREAL COMIX SCENE

Design by Olivier / Boulerice
Text and Photography by Marc Tessier

When solitudes unite,
A personal history
1987 — 2003

ontreal 1983. I moved here to study film and photography. In those days, French Quebec was feeling the post-depression syndrome caused by the loss of the YES side in the 1980 referendum. Political instability and friction between provincial and federal parties created a depressed economy while two separate cultural identities (the English and the French) lived side by side across a language divide.

In 1987 I began writing comics. At that time, publishing options were severely limited by the few conservative outlets that existed. Cartoonists with artistic ambitions were ostracized. In order to survive the times comic book people needed to get creative.

In the nineties a new generation of artists began appreciating comics based on the visual merit of the art itself. Language became less of an issue as more people became bilingual. The lack of publishers became an incentive, challenging writers and artists, French and English, to work together for the first time creating a self-publishing grass roots movement which came to be known as **The Montreal Comix Scene.**

If you're looking to settle somewhere to write and draw comics, Montreal is one of the most beautiful places in the world. The quality of life is excellent, people are friendly and rents are cheap. It's easy to find parttime jobs and work on your magnum opus. The downside is you can be at it for twenty years and still be as poor as the new guy or gal arriving in town full of hopes and dreams. The homegrown market for comics is growing but is still very small. You might get a book published but you won't make a fortune. After a while those who can't stand the poverty or the lack of recognition either move on or go crazy (and I mean that literally). Those that stay have a real love and passion for the possibilities of narrative art. They're not interested in a fling; they're willing to commit until the very end. It's these Montrealers **who have kept the scene alive.**

Above, Jean-Claude Amyot with a view of downtown Montreal

To make ends meet comic book artists work as musicians, makeup artists, graphic designers, booksellers, teachers or photographers. Having a life outside of comics renews and recharges our creative juices. Of course, there is always hope that a living could be earned from comics (and a few have made it) but most are content with the pleasure they get from drawing their quota of pages every year.

Turning back the clock

French people in Quebec have always bought lots of bandes dessinées (mostly well known European exports like **Astérix**, **Tintin** and **Lucky Luke**) but rarely are they aware that books by local authors exist. Homegrown comics only started getting reviews in alternative newspapers in the early nineties, a big victory since previously reviewers had been adamant, insisting cartoonists would never be featured until they were distributed across Quebec or Canada.

After a rich period of experimenting in the late sixties\early seventies (as exemplified by the work of André Montpetit and André Philibert); in 1979 a little revolution began with the launch of **Croc** magazine. A humor publication in the **Mad** vein, **Croc** gave a new generation of authors like Rémy Simard, Caroline Mérola, Gaboury, Réal Godbout, Pierre Fournier, Claude Cloutier and Jean-Paul Eid, among others, a chance to be published regularly. **Croc** soon expanded by creating the first magazine entirely devoted to Québécois BD and thus **Titanic** came to port.

In the first issues of **Titanic** the infamous Henriette Valium provided pages but his stories were deemed too fucked-up and he was swiftly shown the door. Valium would retaliate with the first issue of **Iceberg** (get it? Titanic? Iceberg?) showcasing artists rejected by **Titanic**. Ironically, after two years, **Titanic** went under while **Iceberg** thrived for more than a decade, under the leadership of Thibaud de Corta, publishing alternative artists like Luis Neves, Tali, Grégoire Bouchard, Obom, Cedric Loth, Rose Beef, Reno and a few others still active today.

Origins of the Scene

Around the mid-eighties, with **Croc** going strong, the independent scene got a boost. Yves Millet put out a magazine called **Tchize**, which welcomed all styles of comics (Julie Doucet's first pages were published here). Millet also began producing self-bound books in limited print runs. His publishing house was called Éditions du Phylactère and he gave a lot of French artists their first shot. Years later Millet launched Zone Convective, which was bought out in 1997 by local publishing conglomerate 400 coups. Since then, Zone Convective has truly become a serious publisher of quality contemporary adult comics with books like the Cyclope anthologies, Luis Neves's **"Les Chemins Silencieux"**, and French translations of Chester Brown. Yves Millet is also the owner of Fichtre!; the only Montreal comic book store with an extensive section devoted to local authors.

Neves

Hélène Brosseau

Apart from being an incredible colourist and sculptor, Hélène has produced beautiful scratchboard comic pages. Working at Fichtre! since it opened seven years ago, Hélène has organized countless group exhibits and recently co-edited the last two Cyclopes anthologies.

Rose Beef (Denis Lord)

A master of collages, Mr. Beef uses photos and old Marvel comics to produce post-modern strips filled with the zest of bitter irony. He's also a journalist and the comics reviewer for the prestigious French language daily **Le Devoir**.

Henriette Valium

As the nineties began, a new humour magazine called **Safarir** (a rip-off of **Cracked** and **Mad**) gave **Croc** a run for its money and **Croc** soon began its decline. Meanwhile alternative and underground comics were on the upswing. Like their American counterparts of the seventies, they were raunchy, personal, and groundbreaking explorations of form and content. After publishing **Iceberg**, Valium began to produce and distribute his own books by silkscreening gorgeous colour covers and photocopying (and later silkscreening) the pages inside. True to the punk ethos, Valium became the first independent artist, flipping the bird to the few traditional publishers that existed and went on to create a little revolution (all artists of note that followed "post-Valium" tried their hands at self-publishing). Highly respected among comic book artists, Valium is regarded as the godfather of the alternative scene in Montreal. When I photographed him in the basement of his house where he does his silkscreening; he told me about his projects in the pipeline (a huge painting, a color comic book, a web site and a new music CD). This man crackles with an incredible energy that has kept him going through thick and thin. Because his work deals with controversial and disturbing subjects such as death, disease and sex, Valium continues to traumatize the *bourgeoisie*. When the contemporary art world in Quebec finally comes to recognize comics as a medium of merit and depth, Valium is poised to gain recognition as a major artist.

Siris

While Valium and Julie Doucet inspired a whole generation of artists to self-publish, Siris began to pull the scene together one person at a time. Siris studied at the Cégep du Vieux Montréal. There he met Éric Thériault and helped him with **Krypton** (1986-1987), an anthology magazine showcasing emerging talents like Richard Suicide, Thierry Labrosse, Luc Giard, Costela, Marie Dumas and Jean-Marc Saint-Denis. In 1990, Siris got a job on a government program putting out a free magazine called **Rectangle**. He had a couple of pages in every issue talking up a storm about French and English local comics. Siris has a good eye. He'd spot future luminaries like Jean-Pierre Chansigaud, Simon Bossé and Alexandre Lafleur just as they were emerging and encouragingly praise them in his column. When you walked down Ontario Street with him, every thirty paces he would stop to say hello to somebody. He knew them all: musicians, painters, poets and comic book artists and everybody knew him. Siris brought people together.

Julie Doucet

Doucet is another trailblazer that set the local scene on fire. In 1988, Julie self-published her 1st issue of **Dirty Plotte**. Her goal was to print an issue every month for as long as she could (a feat no one here had done before). For a couple of years she pulled it off, all the while getting bolder, trying different sizes and varying the design. Her minis were her best promotion. She stopped doing them when Chris Oliveros of Drawn & Quarterly offered to publish her. From then on, Julie's reputation grew exponentially. She was the first break out star from the Montreal scene.

In 1992, while living in Seattle, she was invited to be the president of honour at The Seventh International Festival of Bandes Dessinées in Montreal. In its previous incarnations, the Festival had rolled out the red carpet for Europeans while local artists were often relegated to the back room. This time the organizers made a ground-breaking decision to feature Quebecois artists. During the festival, the media buzzed about Julie and the local comix community. Julie's triumph here and abroad recharged her contemporaries' batteries.

His own comic art is unique; his layouts bristle with invention yet to most, it's the man himself who's an inspiration. He gives his time relentlessly. He is both the Mom and the Pop that hold the family together. His legwork forged lasting links between French and English. Without Siris the Montreal comix scene would not stand as united as it is now. Two years ago Siris moved to the countryside to work on *Vogue la valise*, his new graphic novel.

Chansigaud

A mural by Siris on St-Urbain

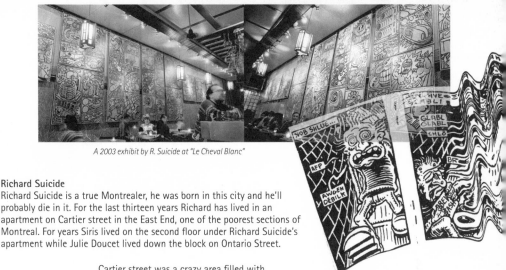

A 2003 exhibit by R. Suicide at "Le Cheval Blanc"

Richard Suicide

Richard Suicide is a true Montrealer, he was born in this city and he'll probably die in it. For the last thirteen years Richard has lived in an apartment on Cartier street in the East End, one of the poorest sections of Montreal. For years Siris lived on the second floor under Richard Suicide's apartment while Julie Doucet lived down the block on Ontario Street.

Cartier street was a crazy area filled with drunks, addicts and prostitutes of every sexual denomination. The downstairs neighbour was an old garbage picker. He made alcohol from potatoes and spoke gibberish that only Richard could decipher. For a couple of years, the ground floor apartment was a crack house. Richard would relish the local atmosphere as fodder for his stories. All he had to do to get ideas was to sit on his balcony and watch the theatre of life unfold up and down the street. Today the neighbourhood has changed, families with kids have moved in while the rest of the crazy urban fauna has dispersed. A survivor, Richard still lives on Cartier, dividing his time between comics, painting and working as an animator.

A writer and artist with a savage wit, his humorous comics documenting his neighbourhood are an amazing testimony of life in the East End. Apart from being a kick-ass painter, Richard is a prolific artist amassing an impressive body of comics, yet to be collected. His dialogues and supreme sense of the absurd have brought Richard acclaim as one of the best writers of comics in Montreal.

Caro Caron

From Montreal to New Orleans, Madrid and New York, Caro has traveled all over while earning her living as a makeup artist and painter. For years, she's also lived in the East End of Montreal. She self-published **King Can Comix** in 1999 and has appeared in various anthologies. Her witty and raunchy comics have resulted in hilarity and controversy.

Martin Lemm

Martin Lemm worked in a copy shop and pushed the envelope, experimenting with different coloured toners to achieve silkscreen effects for his **Zen Zen Shit** books.

The Photocopy Revolution (1988–1995)

In the late eighties, a revolution grumbled deep in the bowels of Montreal. Photocopying technology became affordable and could finally reproduce pure blacks. Suddenly it was viable for artists to print their own comics, sell it at a book launch, cover the printing costs in one night and make a little money. Over two years, the independent scene exploded with artists like Matthew Brown, Luc Giard, Éric Thériault, The Bacha cousins, Chantale Doyle, Marc Bell, Gavin McInnis, Rodz and Martin Lemm. Soon every alternative artist in Montreal was self-publishing. Joining the scene became simple, you just had to disseminate your book into the few good shops that everyone went to, and voilà! You'd accessed the Montreal underground!

Simon Bossé

In 1990 Simon Bossé published **Mille Putois #1**, welcomed new partner Alexandre Lafleur and then published #2. At the time, **Mille Putois** became the best selling mini-comic in Montreal with a print run of 250 copies. It often sold out within a month. **Mille Putois** was the underground's second big hit after Julie Doucet's minis. Simon and Alexandre were young (early twenties) yet both showed a mastery of the medium that few could match. A lot of people still remember **Mille Putois**; it struck a chord that still reverberates today. Influenced by Valium and the new wave of high quality silkscreened books coming out of Europe, Simon Bossé began experimenting with his own silkscreening techniques. A recent exhibit of his posters and comix art at Le Cheval Blanc showed a beautiful array of images masterfully designed, drawn and printed. Last year Simon completed **Intestine** a wordless graphic novel published by L'Oie de Cravan.

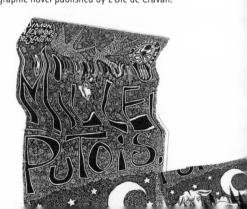

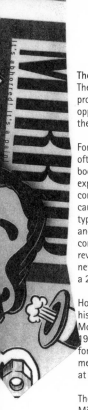

The English Artists

The English, being a minority in a French province, had even less publishing opportunities. Like their French counterparts they joined the Photocopy Revolution.

For a long time, Rick Trembles and Valium were often mentioned in the same breath. His amazing book **Sugar Diet #2**, containing the most explicit exploration of personal sexual mores I'd ever come across, was published in 1992. His book caused a big stir. Of course there were other types of stories showcasing Rick's truly distinctive and original graphic style. Today Rick has a comic page called "**Motion Picture Purgatory**", reviewing movies for the weekly alternative newspaper the **Mirror**. He's currently pitching a 200 page collection of his best reviews.

Howard Chackowicz, earned his keep by showing his art outside the province. He was the first Montrealer to be published by Fantagraphics in 1991, illustrating scripts by Dennis P. Eichhorn for **Real Stuff** and **Real Smut**. To make ends meet, Howard taught comics for seven years at the Saidye Bronfman Centre for the Arts.

The veteran of the English comix scene is Bernie Mireault, best known for his series **The Jam**. Bernie is a truly nice guy who helps his cartoonist colleagues get exposure whenever he can. For example, in **The Jam**, Rupert Bottenberg and the Bacha cousins illustrated back up features.

At the French comic book events Bernie, Rick, Howard and Rupert would show up with their own books and minis to mingle. Siris would introduce everybody and soon the two communities began to merge. In 1992, Rupert Bottenberg created the first of the renowned "Montreal Comix Jams". French and English artists jammed in a bar or at an art gallery on the same comic pages in front of a crowd while bands played; it was a huge success.

When Rupert became music editor for the **Mirror**, he coordinated two yearly issues illustrated with drawings and comics by local artists from both sides of the track.

The Art Connection

In 1992, a shift occurred. Art/comics events were organized in galleries rather than bookshops. This facilitated exchanges while attracting the gallery's regular crowd who knew nothing about the Montreal Comix Scene. That was the point, to reach a new audience. These launches were a success and the comix scene began to attract attention in art circles. **La Fou Art**, a giant three-day extravaganza featuring all artistic disciplines, incorporated comics because of its growing reputation as a force to be reckoned with. An exhibit was set up and eight new comics were launched on opening night. Quebec magazine **Esse** declared the comics component of **La Fou Art** the most successful.

In 1995 the Montreal scene peaked with its biggest event/book launch ever called "Our Times Need Violence" (a quote from Henry Miller relating to artistic violence more than senseless brutality). Planned months in advance, with the help of the whole comix community, it featured the unveiling of a record breaking eighteen new self-published comics. The event created a buzz that has yet to be duplicated. The launch generated over two thousand dollars in profits (which is a lot considering most of these books went for as low as fifty cents to a couple of bucks each).

The place was packed with huge line-ups down St-Denis street, waiting to get in. Photographers, sculptors and painters provided original artwork to decorate La Piaule, the two-story bar. This was a "happening" in the best sense of the word. It marked the apex of the Montreal Photocopy Revolution! The public was awakening to the incredible energy, talent and teamwork deployed by comic book authors. In other fields, artists began to acknowledge that one of the most thriving artistic communities in Montreal was the comix scene.

Doucet and friends, 1992

Gogo Guy and two acolytes, 1987

Gogo Guy Publications

In 1987, Stéphane Olivier and I founded Gogo Guy Publications (and in 1992, Alexandre Lafleur joined us at the helm after leaving **Mille Putois**). Gogo Guy's mandate was to explore the notion of comics as a valid means of artistic expression. Some of the most successful book launch/art events in galleries were initiated and organized by members of the Gogo Guy collective, often with the help of Siris and Simon Bossé.

Mr Swiz

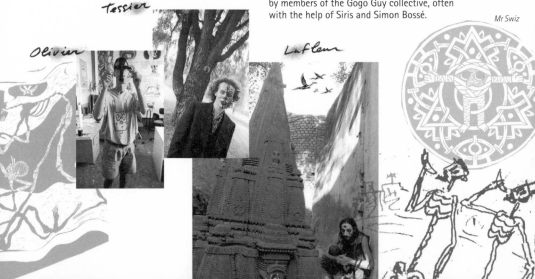

Tessier

Olivier

Lafleur

Written and published in English by Francophone artists, **Mac Tin Tac** (five issues from 1991 to 1995) became the repository of Gogo Guy's graphics and narrative experiments. Gogo sought out the best local artists and asked them to contribute to the ongoing adventures of **Mac Tin Tac**. With each issue, the crew improved the look of the book with superior printing and sharper design (winning top prizes in design competitions). The last issue brought together painters, sculptors, photographers and comic book artists from Quebec, the US and Europe (like Blanquet and Helge Reumann). The overall quality of the Gogo Guy books raised the bar and forced everybody in Montreal to stand up and adapt.

Gogo Guy recruited talented artists like Jean-Claude Amyot, Jean-Pierre Chansigaud, Al+Flag, Marc Richard and Hélène Brosseau. Others like Martin Lemm, Gilles Boulerice, Richard Suicide, Matthew Brown, Siris and Simon Bossé also published comics under the Gogo Guy banner. At the end of 1995, Gogo Guy unofficially disbanded. Olivier began work on a graphic novel with Gilles Boulerice (**Le clairon** which they completed in 2003) while Alexandre Lafleur and I performed street theatre based on rituals associated with Native American shamanism. In 1995 we traveled to India to work on **The Theatre of Cruelty**, later published in 1997 by Fantagraphics Books.

Douglas

Rastelli

Martel

Perron

The Scene's Supporters

Le Cheval Blanc is a regular watering hole for artists. So much so that Le Cheval began to hire artists for its staff (Siris has worked there and Simon Bossé has just been rehired). Frank Martel and Gigi Perron are in charge of booking exhibits and artistic events at the Cheval. Frank is a witty musician, poet and writer with a few CDs under his belt. Gigi is a painter of great acclaim whose shows always sell out (a truly rare occurrence in Montreal), she is also the author of two comic books published by L'Oie de Cravan. Apart from organizing amazing exhibits, Le Cheval Blanc has a soft spot for comics; it has hosted and sponsored over a hundred comic books events! The English equivalent of Le Cheval is Casa Del Popolo on St-Laurent Street. Hosting a Comix Jam monthly (co-ordinated by Max Douglas), the Casa also harbours the first Distroboto (three more are on the way). Invented by **Fish Piss** publisher Louis Rastelli, it's an old converted cigarette distributor in which you slip in a couple of dollars, pull a lever and get small chapbooks and original art by the likes of Julie Doucet, Billy Mavreas, Dominique Pétrin, Leyla Majeri and Guy Boutin. The Casa is the cool place to launch local comics and alternative books by English authors.

Oliveros

Jetté

Marc Jetté

A local expert on the scene, his interests cover a whole range of comic books and BD. In the pages of his magazine **Jean Nendur** (begun in 1994), Marc illustrates stories and writes articles. His well-documented profiles of local artists have also recently appeared in the monthly **MensuHell** published by Francis Hervieux.

Local Publishers

Today, Montreal boasts some mighty fine publishers, the most famous being Chris Oliveros of Drawn & Quarterly. In 1988 Chris worked on a government program which financed an anthology of local comics called **Core**. Two years later, he ventured out on his own and founded Drawn & Quarterly. His first books featured Julie Doucet and ex-Montrealer Chester Brown. With a unique flair for modern visual literature, Chris Oliveros has grown into one of the most respected publishers of comics, reaping worldwide acclaim.

La Pastèque, headed by Frédéric Gauthier and Martin Brault, created a bang in 1998 with Spoutnik (an anthology) and **Paul à la Campagne** by local author Michel Rabagliati (the English translation published in 2001 by Drawn & Quarterly won Michel a Harvey Award for Best New Talent). Close in spirit to the editorial choices of Chris Oliveros, Frédéric and Martin favour alternative European authors and locals like Réal Godbout and Rémy Simard. They have endeavored to unearth forgotten Quebec authors like Jacques Gagnier and Albert Chartier and publish new compilations of their work. High quality design and content have been the launching pad for La Pastèque's meteoric rise on both sides of the Atlantic.

Brault

Gauthier

L'OIE DE CRAVAN

Rabagliati

Influenced by the original Dadaist and Surrealist books (small hand-bound print runs), Benoit Chaput founded L'Oie de Cravan. His first publications were formal experiments and featured poetry and illustrations by various local authors. Benoit is a meticulous publisher, motivated by passion more than profit. In the last few years he began publishing graphic novels (some with silkscreen covers) by Obom, Gigi Perron, Julie Doucet, Jeff Ladouceur, Geneviève Castrée and Simon Bossé. Benoit's books feel like they've been individually crafted, striking a beautiful balance between an "objet d'art" and printed matter.

Paul à la campagne

Chaput

Brown

Writer and graphic designer Andy Brown runs Conundrum Press. Andy began by publishing chapbooks of poetry. With time he got bolder, mixing text and graphics, producing stories by local authors and spokenword artists. Andy entered the comix fold by publishing Howard Chackowicz. He then followed suit with **The Overlords of Glee** by local luminary and Bunny philosopher Billy Mavreas and most recently, the **Cyclops** anthology. Andy is a courageous individual that periodically sets his aspirations aside in order to provide an outlet for others.

With virtually no money to be made, publishing in Montreal is often a clear sacrifice of one's free time. So let's be frank, the Montreal scene exists because of the selflessness of generous souls. People like Andy Brown, Benoit Chaput and all the other comix artists/ philanthropists have my utmost respect.

Jamie Salomon is another patron publisher. After co-producing **The Overlords of Glee** and **Image Gun**, Jamie's now working on English translations of Valium's work and a career-spanning book by Rick Trembles. I first met Jamie through Rupert Bottenberg back when they were roommates. Jamie has one of the most extensive private collection of American underground and alternative comics in Montreal.

Salomon

Éric Braün is a well-known artist publishing his strips in local newspapers and compiling them as books for Zone Convective. Éric has always been interested in the hardcore elements of comics: sex, drugs, humour and very graphic mayhem. Since the early nineties, he's self-published six issues of **106 U** (a french play on words meaning "No Escape"). With the fifth issue it morphed into an international outlet for wordless comics and extreme visions. Over the years Éric has forged lasting links with artists here and abroad helping to put Montreal on the map. He's known for the inventive packaging of his books (a metal cover that weighed close to ten pounds and another with fake fur and teeth). The latest issue of **106 U** will sport an original latex wraparound cover designed by Rick Trembles.

Dominique Desbiens is the founder of **Exil**, an anthology of comics featuring science fiction, fantasy and horror stories. Begun in 1993, every issue features a host of Montreal artists either with a classic European style or known for their alternative work. Dominique initiated a co-operative approach to publishing. Every artist invests a minimal fee per page, becoming a full partner-publisher. After printing, each gets a quantity of books covering his share. To recuperate their investment, the artist needs to sell a few books to make his return. Dominique is also a mural artist; his work can be seen all over the Plateau Mt-Royal area.

Mavreas

Desbiens

Jimmy Beaulieu is a dynamo and a colossus. After moving to Montreal from Quebec City, within a few years, Jimmy boosted the Montreal comix scene. In 2000, he founded mécanique générale; an imprint dedicated to publishing his own work plus the comics of Sébastien Trahan, Luc Giard, Leif Tand, Benoit Joly and PhlppGrrd. The imprint was soon bought out by 400 coups, which enabled Jimmy to create a collection of smaller books with a distinctive voice. Not satisfied with the slow pace of a big publisher, Beaulieu created the Colosse imprint, publishing on his own a plethora of mini-comics by other artists.

Jimmy's own work is amazing (especially **Résine de Synthèse**). With honesty and a hint of compassion, he mixes incisive autobiography with reflections on everyday life.

Leif Tande

Philippe Girard

Luc Giard

...Let's conclude
The Photocopy Revolution brought acclaim and visibility to the Montreal scene. As demos, the comics had served their purpose. From 1996 on, more local artists were published in Europe and the United States. In Montreal, as the nineties drew to a close, new publishers began to scoop up local talents while creators like Éric Braün, Dominique Desbiens and Jimmy Beaulieu stayed on as part-time publishers. Today, all the artists in this essay are drawing away, tackling longer narratives. The work is daring, sophisticated and mature.

Ironically, the independence that the Parti Québécois sought for Quebec in 1980, was achieved on a smaller scale by French and English cartoonists working together.

The Montreal scene is not a school of one thought, Montreal is a school still thriving because it celebrates diversity and unites solitudes.

— Marc Tessier: October 15th, 2003 (updated September 2017)

Éric Thériault

Marc Tessier & Stéphane Olivier would like to dedicate part of this book (The Montreal Comix Scene article) to Gilles Boulerice (G.B. Edwin), 1957-2017. His many talents and vision will be missed.

Art by Éric Thériault

149

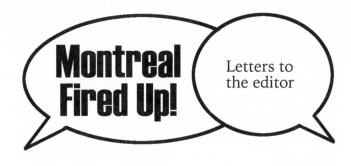

Montreal Fired Up!

Letters to the editor

Originally published in:

The Comics Journal #274
February, 2006

Ed. note: The original essay by Tessier (pp. 137-148) was updated in 2017 for this publication and therefore the letters here may refer to comments which Tessier has now revised.

PART ONE

Dear Gary Groth, et al,

As members of the Montreal comics scene, the bowdlerization of Quebec's cultural history is not something we wish to find in the pages of *The Comics Journal*. Unfortunately, this has occurred with "The Montreal Comix Scene" as published in your Special Edition 2005. Although we are in favour of attention being paid to local talent and comics-related activities, considering the inflation, excision and disinformation in Marc Tessier's piece, we must respond and point out the following.

Barely into the first paragraph, a first hint of bizarre revisionism surfaces. Tessier refers to "the slim loss of separatists in the 1980 referendum." Actually, the sovereign option then lost by a wide margin. The "slim loss" occurred in the 1995 referendum.

Tessier states that "Nothing truly groundbreaking would come from local publishers until *Croc* magazine was launched in 1979." Yet some of Quebec's finest experimental comics, such as *Oror 70* and *L'infecticide*, predate 1979. Refer to Georges Raby's landmark article in *Culture vivante* #22 (Ministère des affaires culturelles du Québec, 1971). Before 1979 lies a rich history that stretches from thousands of strips, magazines and books to audacious underground collectives. The first use of adult-oriented comics, complete with word balloons, has been traced to a political poster dated 1792, as detailed by Michel Viau in *MensuHell* #45 (August 2003).

Tessier identifies *Titanic* as "the first magazine entirely devoted to Quebecois BD." Quebec comics historian Jacques Samson in his *Mémoire* sur la situation de la bande dessinée au Québec et au Canada (ACIBD, 1991) estimates the predecessors of *Titanic* at about 40. The Quebec comics repertory *BDQ* (Mille-iles, 1999) describes an earlier publication, *L'écran*, as the "first professional magazine entirely devoted to Quebec comics." (Please note that this quote and all future French quotes in the present text are translated into English b the authors.)

Even *The Comics Journal* has previously described *Titanic* not as a "first" but in terms of its ambition as a comics periodical "to rival those coming from Europe." That news item from issue 181 also offers a clear view of Valium's notorious *Iceberg* cover, free of the disfigurement to which it is subjected in "The Montreal Comix Scene." For 12 pages, the luxurious paper and printing lavished upon the Special Edition uncharacteristically provide only cropped, distorted and altered visuals, a subtle warning that the text contains similar manipulations.

Concerning Montreal's alternative weekly *The Mirror*, it does not have "a print run of about 300,000." One brief phone call to their offices would have provided the correct figure: 70,000.

We're told, in bold type yet, that The Photocopy Revolution occurred in 1990-1995. "In the early 90s (...) photocopying technology became affordable" and how fast did the prices come down to a viable level? "Suddenly!" This revelation brings up some interesting questions. What did a photocopy cost prior to 1990? What did Jay Kennedy really mean by "newave comix" in his 1982 *Official Underground and Newave Comix Price Guide*? And how to explain the small press and mini-comix showcase in the entrance hall of Montreal's Fifth International Festival of Comics in 1989, meaning in effect that an exhibition and some related events occurred before the revolution which spawned them?

Looking beyond the Photocopy Revolution, Tessier spots a new revolution in its infancy, comics in art galleries! We're told that "the comix scene began to attract attention in art circles" and that events "incorporated comics because of its growing reputation as a force to be reckoned with." Apparently, he wasn't around for the exhibition "La bande dessinée québécoise" at the Montreal Museum of Contemporary Art in 1976, a show which also traveled to the Canadian Cultural Center in Paris and to the third edition of the Angoulême Festival. Or how about the 1996 retrospective in Quebec's premier museological institution, the Musée du Québec, twice held over for a 46-week duration, complete with Valium's giant serigraph masterwork laid open in a transparent case like some pre-Columbian artifact, his page entitled "Comicks?" (see *Zero Zero* #10) on an adjacent wall, framed with chemically inert board behind shatterproof plexiglass and further protected by constant temperature and humidity. It was worth attending the opening cocktail to witness esteemed museum director John R. Porter's miraculous transformation into erudite comics scholar brilliantly ad-libbing on the astounding artistic merits of comics. Perhaps the time will even come when Quebec's oldest and most prestigious arts magazine, *Vie des Arts*, will greet comics as *le neuvième art* unless of course they already did so; in their Fall 1972 issue.

To explain briefly: Thanks to intellectual influence from France, the recognition of comics as art has been the easiest of all the struggles within Quebec. Media coverage has been mixed but increasingly forthcoming since the mid-70s. Nowadays, the quantity and variety of comics criticism produced locally can only be envied in the rest of North America. The most difficult hurdle has been the general public's lack of curiosity, herd mentality and conformist taste. On May 1, 2005, Quebec's leading newsmagazine, *L'actualité*, published the results of its readers' poll for the top 100 books of all time. The lists (50 from Quebec, 50 foreign) contained only a single work of comic art: *Garfield*. To woo the art world is to tackle the easy end of the spectrum, an ego trip unlikely to yield concrete results since there are more public art shows in Quebec than private art collectors. Talking comics in a trendy bar or art gallery may be novel to some, but before presenting it as an unprecedented event in *The Comics Journal*, envision people waiting in line to see a cartoonist's one-man show at the Montreal Museum of Fine Arts, which is what Robert Lapalme achieved in the early 60s. Lapalme capitalized on this success to create the International Salon of Cartoons, a Montreal event that lasted several months every year for 25 years, produced massive catalogs that peaked at over 1,000 pages, attracted astonishing numbers of visitors (over one million a year in its heyday) and ceaselessly promoted comics as art (Quebec's Albert Chartier was honoured with a special exhibition in 1985 and Cartoonist of the Year titleholders include Hogarth, Schultz, Quino, Pratt and Eisner). So when Tessier waxes ecstatic over "a giant three-day extravaganza" or informs us that "In 1995 the Montreal scene peaked with its biggest event/book launch ever" which "created a buzz that has yet to be duplicated," there's a problem of perspective. And please define buzz, second man on the moon, former Kitchen Sink title, or *paradis artificiel*?

Regarding Montreal's Seventh International Festival of Comics, we're told that during this 1992 event, "the media buzzed about Julie and the local comix community." Here's our chance to figure out what buzz really means. In the big daily *La Presse*, as elsewhere, Julie Doucet provided the main commentary on our beloved community. Here's what she had to say (Oct. 22 1992): "When I was in Montreal and told people about what was happening to me, nobody had a clue what I was talking about and so I left." More buzzing awaits the buzz researcher in Montreal's intellectual newspaper *Le Devoir* (Oct. 24): "I moved to New York. An old dream. The opportunities here are zero, everybody knows that. Over there, I received so much encouragement whereas here, next to nothing, that it all seemed so natural." Not buzzing yet? One more major article appeared in the cultural weekly *Voir* (Oct. 22): "the market is so limited here, you have no idea! [...] I love comic books but Quebec seems allergic to that format. I think that explains in part the lack of interest for the new comics." For more straightforward observations about the Montreal scene, forget Special Edition obfuscation and check out Doucet's candid comments on local collaborators, booksellers and publishers ("He's someone I'd like to see under the wheels of a truck") in her interview for *The Comics Journal* #141.

Tessier also informs *Journal* readers that "In its previous incarnations, the Festival had rolled out the red carpet for Europeans while local artists were relegated to the back room."Au contraire. In his summary of Quebec comics history published in *Panorama de la littérature québécoise contemporaine* (Guérin, 1997), Jacques Samson highlights the key role that the earlier Festivals played in the evolution of the Quebec comics scene. Historian Mira Falardeau makes a similar assessment in *La bande dessinée au Québec* (Boréal, 1994) and points out that for the fourth Festival, the European role was virtually nil. An examination of the catalogs for the first four Festivals, which peaked at 100 pages, will instantly convince anyone that these events were, first and foremost, a Quebec showcase. The fifth Festival produced no catalog but a 16-page program in which Europeans occupy two-thirds of one interior page and the bottom half of another. Finally, for the sixth Festival, the Guest of Honour was Quebec's Pierre Fournier who was awarded the Albert Chartier trophy, a $750 cash prize and a retrospective exhibition at the University of Montreal. Next to that, Julie Doucet got crumbs: an improvised exhibition in a bar, regarding which the aforementioned feature in *La Presse* quipped, "bring your lighters if you want to see something."

Concerning this 1992 Festival, Tessier declares that "the organizers made a groundbreaking decision to feature Quebecois artists." Having just maligned the organizers of the six previous Festivals by misrepresenting their work, wouldn't it be nice if he named the organizers of the seventh one, since he thinks so highly of them? It would also be more ethical, since one of those organizers was Marc Tessier. In fact, the *Voir* article quoted above refers to him as organizer (singular) and as the one who chose Doucet to be Guest of Honour. Amusingly, when Tessier writes "she was invited to be president of honour," his fantasies of Angoulême betray him. Montreal named a guest of honour. Angoulême votes a president.

To Tessier's credit, he did expend considerable efforts to generate the "buzz" on Julie Doucet quoted above, and to do so prior to Festival activities featuring her. An examination of the two-colour ledger program of the Festival (widely distributed and inserted as an *Iceberg* centrefold) illustrates his devotion. Out of the nine events scheduled, two feature Doucet and by an amazing coincidence, both are paired up with another event, the launch of Tessier's *Mac Tin Tac*.

Which may explain why some people mistakenly believed he was the sole organizer.

The minutes for the May 10, 1993, General Assembly of the ACIBD, the association responsible for the Festival, contradict Tessier's claim that a "groundbreaking decision" was taken to feature homegrown talent rather than rolling out "the red carpet for Europeans." President Jean Lacombe opens the proceedings with a statement devoid of ambiguity: "due to the modest budget, we could not invite European artists." Tessier was one of the 13 voting members present and voiced no objection to the President's assessment. Granted, *The Comics Journal* is a much better forum for some clever post-Festival spin.

Beyond the mainstream press, a McGill University student newspaper noted that the Festival having reached its seventh edition is a sign of vitality, henceforth promising to become a yearly event. Which begs the question, if the seventh Festival was the groundbreaking buzz Tessier describes, then why was it the last hurrah? Because: Montreal's Seventh International Festival of Comics was a Gordian knot of metastatic malfeasance which not only sabotaged its own future but plunged the ACIBD into disgraceful agony, its funding severed by outraged government officials. Michael Dean's article on past associations of comics professionals in *The Comics Journal* #262 would have been enriched by a sidebar on the ACIBD, since its accomplishments between 1986 and 1992 were enviable next to American efforts. For over a decade now, Montreal artists have had to do without the spotlight and opportunities provided by its founding artist-run Festival and without the lobbying and services of the ACIBD. This twin loss, much like the disappearance of Lapalme's Salon, is a tragic dilapidation of heritage, next to which Tessier's metaphor about "recharged... batteries" is not very electrifying.

Given Tessier praises as seminal an event in which he had a hand, one may suspect that the art happenings which he is so fond of may also bear his fingerprints. Doesn't mentioning an event was "Planned months in advance" suggest possible involvement? A little connect-the-dots process reveals that, in this case at least, Tessier is hiding in plain sight. After identifying himself as co-founder of Gogo Guy Publications, two sentences later he attributes "successful book launch art events" to "members of the Gogo Guy Collective." It's like a prose version of Where's Waldo?

This is followed by some self-congratulations over the *Mac Tin Tac* series. If *The Comics Journal* is field-testing a policy of hiring writers to pen reviews of their own work, this may explain the growing page count. We read that the "overall quality of the Gogo Guy books raised the bar and forced everybody in Montreal to stand up and take notice." Such an assessment borders on delusional. Many fine productions preceded *Mac Tin Tac* and there is no new minimal standard for local comics publishing. What kind of "bar" is he talking about and would "everybody in Montreal" agree to having witnessed its elevation? If instead of standing and noticing, everybody in Montreal had bought the book, then whoopee.

Upon scrutiny, it appears the raised bar served to batten down the hatches. "At the end of 1995, Gogo Guy unofficially disbanded." Just a minute, weren't we told that in 1995, "the Montreal scene peaked with its biggest event/book launch ever" that "created a buzz that has yet to be duplicated" and "generated over two thousand dollars in profit"? Since connecting the dots points to Gogo Guy behind that event, why follow success with harakiri? And why does the repertory BDCR (p. 27) list a Gogo Guy publication as dated 1997? Are we being served the authentic lowdown or some doctored hype?

The longest of three sentences devoted to Howard Chackowicz reads as follows: "In 1991, he was the first Montrealer to be published by Fantagraphics, illustrating scripts by Dennis P. Eichhorn for *Real Stuff* and *Real Smut*." In fact, his first contribution to these books was in *Real Smut* #3 dated December 1992 (not 1991). Even within the confines of Eichhorn's books, Chackowicz was preceded by Julie Doucet in *Real Stuff* #6 (April 1992). And thanks to a Fantagraphics indicia error, both were preceded by Éric Thériault in *Real Stuff* #11, dated February 1992 (but no, that should read February 1993). The first Montrealer published by Fantagraphics may possibly be Jacques Boivin, whose *Melody* illustrations for the Swimsuit Specials began in *Amazing Heroes* #164 dated May 1, 1989. For more accuracy, we could query the publisher but it looks like Fantagraphics' private historian is on vacation.

We are informed that *"Mille Putois* was the underground's second big hit after Julie Doucet's minis." Now if a teenage fanboy wrote in his zine that *Spawn* was a "big hit," that would be awesome. Unfortunately, this is *The Comics Journal*. Doucet's

success was due to plugs and reviews in publications such as *Factsheet Five*, which allowed her to sell much of her 150-copy print runs through the mail, trade with cartoonists worldwide and contact alternative publishers. Locally, only a handful of sharp-eyed afficionados followed her work. Given that the term "big hit" is problematic, we may nevertheless wonder: were there any successful or significant minis by Montrealers before *Dirty Plotte* or *Mille Putois*?

Dale Luciano's "Newave Comics Survey" in *The Comics Journal* #96 refers to one of the undersigned as a "talented Canadian artist" whose second minicomic is quoted as "possibly the most successful selling mini of all time." So it appears a Montrealer held the world record for best-selling mini during a few years, at least until eclipsed by Scott McCloud and Matt Feazell's lightning bolt, *Zot!* #10 1/2. A few years later, Hal Hargit's "Small Press World" survey of Montreal in *Amazing Heroes* #177 (March, 1990) is one of numerous articles which mention Sylvie Rancourt's self-published comics. Two 500-copy editions of her first photocopied zine and 500 copies of her second one, almost entirely sold in Montreal bars, were followed by six 5000 copy offset editions for Quebec newsstand distribution. After a 1987 minicomic, Rancourt and Boivin became the only Quebecois to ever create a series for one of the original underground comix publishers.

By 1992, Robert Boyd encapsulated the Montreal comics scene with a five-sentence description in *The Comics Journal* #154 that is more compelling than 12 pages in the Special Edition 2005. Boyd's cogent assessment frames a laudatory 800-word review of "One of the most prolific young Montreal cartoonists" who is absent from said 12 pages. There's a reason why Tessier's article contains no references or footnotes. Facts are irrelevant to his purpose, which shines most brightly through the next item.

And so Hélène Brosseau is credited for having "co-edited the last two *Cyclopes* anthologies." This anthology is the only title in the text to receive three mentions. Tessier fails to disclose his role as the other co-editor on these two books, as well as that of editor for the first anthology (cannily described as "quality contemporary adult comics"). In order to discover his central role, one must turn to the Conundrum Press advertisement in the back pages of the Special

Edition, where Tessier gets top billing. This ad is also revealing in another fashion: The list of contributors to *Cyclops* is almost a roll call of the cartoonists featured in "The Montreal Comix Scene." The few discrepancies are easily explained. The pattern is rather obvious: The main criterion for being part of the "Montreal Comix Scene" is to have been successfully courted for a Tessier project.

In the critics' corner, dozens of locals have written about comics and some of those with the most notable accomplishments aren't mentioned by Tessier. The three who have found their way into his article (Jetté, Lord, Bottenberg) form a diverse group with few traits in common. Except all three have written at length promoting Tessier's work and collaborated on his projects.

Regarding Montreal publisher La Pastèque, we learn that "High quality design and content" launched their "meteoric rise." O brave new world that has such publishers in it, whose refined judgment rapidly translates into sales. The missing key information here is that within Quebec, La Pastèque's sales were next to nil until its co-publisher Martin Brault was hired as chief comics buyer for Quebec's largest bookstore chain, Renaud-Bray, whose 26 stores control over 25% of the market. Nowadays it is not uncommon to be greeted at Renaud-Bray by colossal pyramids of books majestically crowned by La Pastèque's fine offerings, first as you step into the store, again as you round a strategic corner such as the cash register, then towards the centre of the store and finally, on top of a table in front of the graphic novel bins. It's quite heartwarming to finally see homegrown comics get the exposure so long yearned for. Renaud-Bray's main sales and promotion tool is their attribution of "Coup de coeur," an in-house seal of approval with which La Pastèque's books get stickered at a rate which would make any small publisher stop bellyaching about not getting on the shelves. Amazing what dividends may be reaped from attention to editorial (and other) details.

Imagine a Fantagraphics editor being hired as main graphic novel buyer for the largest bookstore chain in North America. Wait for results then add a journalist to report that Fantagraphics increasing sales are due to their fine paper quality. Beautiful. But that would be doing things the Canadian way.

Tessier estimates that "the Montreal scene exists because of the selflessness of generous souls." Due to lack of financial reward, Montrealers who "have a real love and passion for the possibilities of narrative art... have kept the scene alive." This paints a very romantic picture but is it on the level? Since the ACIBD lobbied the government to obtain the recognition of comics as a separate art form with specific requirements, the amount of financial aid provided to comics has increased considerably in the past fifteen years. Various branches at each level of government provide a wide variety of financial aid for the creation of comics, travel expenses, publishing, etc. In this area, Tessier is an established master, having obtained no less than three grants just for the first two *Cyclope* anthologies and having participated in numerous government-funded activities such as trips to Belgium and France ("armed with a fistful of government dosh" as Rupert Bottenberg put it in the *Mirror*, Feb. 10, 2000) or the 1992 Festival previously discussed, which was made possible by over $50,000 from government programs.

It is hypocritical to pose as a pioneer bringing comics to the art world and to prophesize about some future era in which "the contemporary art world in Quebec finally comes to recognize comics as a medium of merit and depth" when it is precisely that contemporary art world's funding establishment which has provided for his costliest undertakings. Once the Olivier/Tessier *Mac Tin Tac* series generated a grant, Tessier learned from the experience: "I always thought that if I had done *Mac Tin Tac* in French it would be easier to get grants from the Quebec government" he explained in the 25th anniversary issue of *Matrix*, a local literary magazine which has itself survived thanks to a combination of municipal, provincial and federal generosity. This is not a taboo subject. When projects are tailored to seduce the purses of power, isn't the integrity of the artist in danger of compromise? With anthology projects, an additional level of power relationships further complicates matters, requiring political skills and tactics (such as getting a vanitous article published in a prestigious magazine of criticism).

A successful grant application typically suggests many more that failed. Line Gamache has produced a lovely minicomic about the artist's life as a ceaseless pursuit of grants and the inevitable refusals (*Peut-être à la Saint-Glin-Glin*, 1996). What's a struggling artist to do? "Everybody's on welfare. I know some people who have stayed on it for fifteen years," as Julie Doucet tactfully put it in Juno Books' *Dangerous Drawings* (1997). "I received an arts grant from the government, and that's how I got off welfare." None of this is acknowledged in Tessier's Montreal: "It's easy to find part-time jobs," he writes. "To make ends meet, comic book artists work as musicians, makeup artists, graphic designers, booksellers, teachers or photographers." This detailed list smacks of public relations. The reader is being distracted with a trivial enumeration that expels marginality and cloaks sycophancy. Behold, a respectable group has recuperated the creation of subversive art.

Tessier's platitudinous conclusion that "Montreal is a school still thriving" (huh?) "because it celebrates diversity and unites solitudes" reads like crafty formula recycled from grant applications, where a politically correct posture is preferable to undisguised ignorance and arrogance.

Outsiders may question how it is that Marc Tessier has been able to avoid strong critical opposition for over fifteen years. Too easygoing and preoccupied with fun, eh? Partly. The Montreal comics scene is a discontinuous scattering of individualized idiosyncrasies, associating capriciously according to temporarily pooled resources. Within this context, Tessier's activities have touched relatively small groups, But on March 4, 2002, he accessed a larger audience than usual when the site bdquebec.qc.ca hosted one of his opinion pieces. Bookseller Francois Mayeux then undertook the debunking of Tessier's intellectual smoke and mirrors with his own opinion piece entitled "One viewpoint may hide another." As the messageboards began to entertain speculation about Tessier's past shenanigans, Mayeux altered his focus midstream to quell the rumours. He bemoaned the fact that Montreal has seen too many hustlers seeking to exploit the scene for their own purposes and suggested that Tessier seize the opportunity to come clean. Tessier failed to respond. Or so it seemed.... At about this time, he started work on his Special Edition piece which does contain two (indirect) responses. The first is that François Mayeux is quite absent from "The Montreal Comix Scene," despite his unparalleled contribution to the promotion of comics in Quebec over the past twenty years. The second is that rather than owning up to his past, Tessier used the hospitality of the *Journal* to rewrite history.

Nevertheless, there are no vendettas against Marc Tessier. His graphic novel *The Theatre of Cruelty*, as illustrated by Alexandre Lafleur, is a rich visionary journey deserving wider recognition than it has garnered to date. Tessier's photojournalistic take on the Angoulême Festival in *The Comics Journal* is original and entertaining. Nor are there outstanding gripes against any of the individuals selected by Tessier for "The Montreal Comix Scene." Given the forum and the circumstances, being included or excluded is equivalently honorable.

As recently as *The Comics Journal* #265, Michael Dean described the amateurish lower end of comics journalism, "the fan's uncritical celebration of his or her subject." Tessier's stream of imprecise formulation, inappropriate metaphors and unwarranted hyperbole should not even have satisfied an Eros proofreader. The few occasions when the text leaves clichéd exuberance to attempt expressing fact or idea, it is difficult to believe that no frowns crossed editorial brows.

Instead, Fantagraphics has promoted this article as "a major survey of the Montreal comics scene, with profiles of all the major participants" and the only clue given to the revisionism and nepotism that pervade it comes from the subtitle "When solitudes unite, A personal history." Is this a "personal" version of "history"? If so, the narrator is strangely absent from the text. First person singular appears a total of eight times and only once as it relates to involvement in the comics scene (the defunct Gogo Guy Publications). The word "we" appears exactly once out of nearly 4300 words. By comparison, Tessier's photo-report on Angoulême, at only 1400 words, uses first person singular twenty-four times, a tenfold greater frequency. Which may explain why that report on France is more credible: Tessier explains his choices and takes responsibility for his opinions,

Tessier is not incapable of being candid. His introduction to the first *Cyclope* anthology (Zone Convective, 2000) begins with the admission: "ever since my first publication I have yearned for recognition, that magical word whose utterance would support the act of creation by untying the purse strings of the State and of publishers." He goes on to name his other yearnings, the "ivory towers" of the art establishment and the desire to produce freely "without money and ego at the centre of my creation." Now that qualifies as "personal history." *The Comics Journal* Special Edition deserved better than the concoction it ended up with.

Hopefully we are correct in assuming that Fantagraphics agreed to publish a 12-page feature on Montreal based upon the evaluation that our city harbours a notable variety of worthwhile talents. The five additional colour pages by local cartoonists delivered a fine but too small sampling of the reservoir of sensibilities Montreal offers. In keeping with Valium's intricate labyrinths of visceral tubing, may we have demonstrated that Montreal is even more convoluted and fertile than previously imagined.

— Jacques Boivin, Éric Thériault, Rick Gagnon, Francis Hervieux, Jane Tremblay, Kurt Beaulieu, Leanne Franson

PART TWO

> "One thing I have to say about Montreal comic artists is that they're not so strong on conventional storytelling. The story seems to be an excuse to have a bunch of illustrations of ugly, disturbing sado-masochistic people sexually penetrating each other with lots of phallic symbols and bodily fluids in the background."

— Peter Bagge, interviewed in the Montreal *Voice* (May, 1995)

It saddens us that Marc Tessier's article, "The Montreal Comix Scene, When Solitudes Unite: A Personal History" does little to dispel this dim view that the Montreal comics scene is long on inaccessible artiness and short on solid narrative. Peter Bagge's narrow viewpoint has the excuse of coming from another city, another country, where his exposure to the broader spectrum of Montreal's offerings is likely very limited.

What's Tessier's excuse? Most of this Montrealer's piece focuses on his personal friends and associates whose esoteric comic-book output has been less than prolific and treated as a sideline to their other artistic endeavors. Where, we ask, are so many of the prominent figures of the Montreal scene in his article? Do their accomplishments in the medium pale simply because they are not personally acquainted with Mr. Tessier? Their glaring omission renders any serious discussion

of Montreal comic artists moot, and exposes Tessier's piece as no more than a sampler of a city's output that is much more diverse, in both style and longevity, than he would have us believe.

"The Montreal Comix Scene, When Solitudes Unite: A Personal History" is, it seems, far too personal to serve anyone as a true history of the last thirty years of the Montreal comics scene. As a group of cartoonists, publishers and comic historians, we would like to take this opportunity to offer a few notes on what has been omitted, particularly what's happening now and where it evolved from.

Let's get things moving with an item that is barely noted by Tessier (and for its historical articles, not even its comics!): *MensuHell*, a monthly zine that actually is monthly and has been published almost continuously since 1999. It was founded by Steve Requin first as an outlet for his questionable humour; then he opened its pages to various contributors. When Steve happened upon a copy of *Rectangle*, a zine from the late 80s, he read therein that the goal of that zine was to be published almost every month, even if it meant an issue four pages long. Adopting that philosophy, *MensuHell* has been presenting around 40 pages of comics each time out. Among past and present regulars, one finds Jack Ruttan, Michel Lacombe, Kurt Beaulieu, Jane Tremblay, Rick Gagnon, Sirkowski, André Poliquin, Michèle Laframboise, Jacques Boivin, etc... along with valuable and informative articles on Quebec comics by historians Michel Viau and Marc Jetté. *MensuHell*'s editorship changed when founding publisher Steve Requin decided he'd done (more than) his part. Francis Hervieux took over the reins at issue #35 and issue #70 hit the stands in September, 2005. No mean feat of endurance, considering the high mortality rate in the zine business....

Most of the *MensuHell* regulars can be found every month at the local Comic Jam. Founded in its actual form by Rupert Bottenberg in 1993 (other types of live improv jam have existed since 1986), it's been revived by artist and promoter Salgood Sam, who modernized the idea, adding a website, a zine and an online forum for regulars. It's attended, on the last Wednesday of each month, by a mixed group of anglophones and francophones. Aside from the *MensuHell* gang, one can encounter Bernie Mireault, Howard Chackowicz, Sherwin Tjia, Rick Trembles, Billy Mavreas, Peter Ferguson, Jeff LeBlanc, MARR, Shane Simmons,

Tim Moerman, Éric Thériault. The last five, with their benevolent dictator, Rick Gagnon, are a splinter group specializing in a micro-managed species of jam, published annually in the *What the F**"?* mini. Nom d'un Chien is a new group of artists, that have been putting out some excellent zines and getting themselves published here and there, and making noteworthy contributions to the Comic Jams.

Safarir is more or less Quebec's version of *Cracked* or *Mad*. Published since 1987, it passed the 200th issue milestone recently. The magazine shifted its base to Montreal, from its original home of Quebec City in 2001, and has since adopted a number of local artists in its staff: Dany Lavoie, Frefon, Jean-Paul Eid, Éric Allard, Denis Lord, Sayman, Jérome Mercier and Steve Requin. There's a very active studio in the east end of the city, where a batch of creators are producing a mix of work-for-hire and indie material. Yanick Paquette just finished work on *Terra Obscura*, co-scripted by some bloke named Alan Moore; Michel Lacombe and Éric Thériault are also doing work-for-hire (for Dark Horse and DC Comics, for instance) when not working on their indie books *One Bloody Year* and *Veena*, respectively; Serge Lapointe is a busy inker and Frefon does some *Safarir* art, among other things.

Several other local artists are producing work for mainstream comics: Louis Lachance, Gabriel Morrissette, Azad, Salgood Sam, Karl Kerschl, Clement Sauvé and Djezer among others. Major European publisher Soleil publishes two locals: Thierry Labrosse draws *Morea*, an adventure series, and François Lapierre writes and draws *Sagah Nah*.

Tessier also underplays the importance of what came before his time. *Croc, Titanic, Iceberg* and *Safarir* get name-checked, but their actual importance is swept under the rug, leaving in its place the illusion that Tessier's scene is an earth-shaking accomplishment without precedent or peer, the beginning of a complete turnaround in the importance of comics in Montreal. In fact, it follows a full century of comics history, and similar scenes existed in the 60s and 70s.

Several factors helped spark the "scene" explosion in the 90s. Alternative-underground comics have existed in town since the early 70s. One of its pioneers, Jacques Boivin, published locally and kept in touch with American publishers. Boivin was one of the first to be published in the United States in comic-book format (*Love Fantasy, The Complete Fluffhead*). His series, *Melody*, is a visual adaptation of Sylvie Rancourt's real life story. She was an exotic dancer and also the first woman to self-publish locally, back in 1985. Starting in 1988, *Melody* was published by Kitchen Sink Press, where Boivin did 10 issues and a trade collection, followed by *Melody On Stage* at Eros Comix in 2001.

Éric Thériault and Grégoire Bouchard founded *Krypton* in 1985. The genres of art and stories favoured straddled realistic and stylized art, alternative comix and science fiction emulating early *Métal Hurlant* [*Heavy Metal*]. The sci-fi content is easily found, but look past it, and there're roots of more personal and unusual work. Over the years, a group of friends formed, becoming the early nucleus of the "underground" of the 90s: Richard Suicide, Siris, Luc Giard, Jean Costella, Olivier, Morissette.... Later on, most of the group moved on to *Rectangle*, started by Yvan Pellerin and Éric Thériault, a zine with a slightly different focus, viewing itself as a cultural magazine and covering the rock music scene along with the local comic scene. Valium and Julie Doucet soon joined the group. From there, the influence of *Factsheet Five* and local punk zines and DIY culture jumpstarted a minicomic avalanche. That was on the French side in the 80s.

On the English side, creators such as Mark Shainblum and Gabriel Morrissette focused on the American market and self-published such books as *Northguard* and *Mackenzie Queen* through their Matrix imprint; Bernie Mireault was first published there, going on to create 15 issues of *The Jam*. *Northguard* had a second life at Caliber Press and Canada Post issued a stamp featuring Northguard's partner, Fleur de Lys, to celebrate the centennial of comics in 1995.

Even in the mid-90s, an era more fully covered in Tessier's article, others are left out because they don't fit the author's tidy portrait. Most of his choices are very much in the tradition of the multimedia artists doing not only comics but also painting, sculpture, silkscreening, music... but there were others that considered comics a valid art form in itself, one that did not need to latch on to other media to justify and elevate an artist's worth.

The majority of Tessier's chosen are close friends and collaborators of his, having worked together on many projects and going through the same schools, notably the Cégep du Vieux Montréal and UQAM university. Let's not forget that every scene has its loners, dissenters and sidelined participants. Some of these include Sophie Cossette, who did *Sweet Smell of Sick Sex* and several covers for *Screw* magazine; Kurt Beaulieu, very active on the international Mail Art circuit since moving to Montreal in the early 90s; and Martin Dupras with his *Kiss Me Quick* and his *Cheapo* album.

Leanne Franson created an impressive 41 issues of her ongoing minicomic *Liliane, Bi-Dyke*, as well as contributing to various anthologies internationally such as *Action Girl, Dyke's Delight, Boy Trouble* and *Dyke Strippers*. Two trade paperbacks of her work were published by Slab-O-Concrete (UK) and she recently self-published a third, as well as having an ongoing daily webcomic since the spring of 2004. Luc Giard also gets short-changed by the article. He deserves better, as he's had as much influence locally as some of the big names like Valium or Doucet.

And what about such notables as Shane Simmons? He produced numerous printings of 13 issues of his very popular *Angry Comics*, not including its offshoots *The Squalids, The Couch Potatoes*, etc. He was published in the US (and beyond) by Eternity Comics, Slave Labor Graphics, and even Aardvark-Vanaheim. A German edition of his *The Long and Unlearned Life of Roland Gethers* did very well in the Fatherland.

Sherwin Tjia is the kind of multimedia artist Tessier should like, but he wasn't mentioned. He is the author of the darkly witty *Pedigree Girls* comic strip, a tour de force wherein all the strips are created using the same drawing of the two girls. Insomniac Press published a handsome collection of a few hundred of the strips. He also exhibited paintings, published poetry and written short stories. He's currently working on a graphic novel [*The Hipless Boy*, Conundrum, 2009], among many other things.

James Lemay, active since the early 80s, published a handful of issues of *Spectrum* (with co-writer Bradley Doucet) in the 90s and went on to specialize in erotic comics; his work appears regularly in several publications to this day: *Québec Erotique* (who issued a couple of full-colour collections of his strip *Les p'tites vites de Brigitte*), *Photo Police* and more.

La Trak was a freewheeling satirical newspaper with a large print run that featured a lot of cartoons, comics and humorous pieces. Sophie Cossette, Kurt Beaulieu, Quesnel and Jean-Pierre Chansigaud reached a wider readership there.

Another cultural newspaper that went big and did much to promote Montreal comics at the same time was *Vice Magazine*. It began as *The Montreal Voice* in 1994, with cartoonist Gavin McInnes as one of the founders. He'd published several issues of *Pervert Comics* and would later co-create *Pip and Norton* with Dave Cooper. Rick Trembles, visiting Montrealer Marc Bell and others, placed strips in *Vice*.

The traditional comic-book format, using the distribution system set up by the American direct market, did inspire a lot of creators to self-publish from the 80s right up to the present. From Matrix in 1984 to La Pasteque these days, lots could be written about publishers like Frank Rosa with Scarlet Rose Productions (*Variations On The Theme*), Jordan Raphael with Graphic Cartel (*Newbies Eclectica*), Void Comics and *The Other Side* with artists Michel Lacombe and Yanick Paquette.

A second "underground" generation came up in the mid-90s: Swiz, Quesnel, Guim, Geneviève Castrée, Bonhomme, Julien Bakvis, Rodz, Carlos Santos and others who were in some cases influenced by pioneers like Valium, Doucet and Trembles. They self-published and collaborated on scads of minicomics such as *Mr. Swiz, Guillotine, Foetus* and *Mucus de Puce*. Several of them would later publish regularly in *MensuHell* and/or carry on with their own minicomics.

Held since 2002, the Montreal Expozine is an annual event that gathers various publishers from Montreal, from the humblest self-publishers to Drawn & Quarterly. Not limited to comics, this fair also features literature, poetry, political zines, posters... and it gets bigger every year! The 2004 edition included people from the rest of Canada and the States.

Let's finish this by correcting some factual (as opposed to philosophical) inaccuracies that crept up in Mr. Tessier's piece. Rick Trembles is mentioned as being "published in 1992, his book caused a big stir." Trembles actually began doing comics around 1979 with Surfin' Bird. With his band the American Devices, he's one of the original musicians of the punk explosion of the 70s, having played since 1979. Sort of our Canadian John Holstrom. He's had non-stop artistic activity since then. He was also the first Montrealer to be published in *Weirdo*, under Peter Bagge's tutelage, in issue 11.

Iceberg did not actually "thrive for more than a decade." It began life as a minicomic; six issues were published around 1983-1985 by Tibo De Corta and Valium, followed by a second run with a different crew, published in magazine format from 1990 to 1994.

"Homegrown comics only started getting reviewed in alternative newspapers in the early 90s" is true only in the sense that alternative newspapers, in their current form, did not exist in Montreal for very long before that time. Mainstream newspapers had followed comics activities from a distance since the 70s.

Today, the scene is still as active as ever. The grizzled vets (not the ones you might think) are still at it, while new talents offer hope for the future. Their enthusiasm is contagious, and they just keep on coming, seemingly out of nowhere. Might be an untapped form of energy for the future.

— *Éric Thériault, Rick Gagnon, Kurt Beaulieu. Supported by: Francis Hervieux, Sebastien Frechette (aka Sirkowski), Jane Tremblay, Jeff LeBlanc, Tim Moerman, Shane Simmons, James Lemay, Bradley Doucet, Gabriel Morrissette*

MARC TESSIER REPLIES:

Firstly, thank you for the wealth of information that has been contributed on the history of comics in Quebec. Mistakes have been drawn to my attention regarding my photo-essay "The Montreal Comix Scene: When Solitudes Unite, a personal history 1987-2003."

Indeed, the print run of the Montreal *Mirror* is not 300,000. The first comic issue was published on January 1, 1998. It advertised its print run at 80,000 (not 77,000 as was erroneously redressed) and its readership at 259,000.

When the first referendum to separate Quebec from the rest of Canada was held in 1980, final results were 40.44% for the 'Yes' and 59.56% for the "No". While the 1995 results were 50.58% for the 'No' and 49.42% for the 'Yes'.

Although the aforementioned letters brought to light some interesting facts, they also lend a great deal to fiction. The writers delude themselves — portraying themselves as conspiracy theosophists and crusaders for truth, justice and the Canadian way. In doing so they disparage my personal perspective with slanderous accusations. This also needs to be addressed.

My pitch to Fantagraphics was to publish a photo essay on the Montreal Comix Scene (essentially chronicling how the French and English, underground/alternative authors banded together between 1987 and 1995 to form a community).

I was qualified to produce this essay, because I lived in the frontline of this movement. I was educated in communication and visual arts (film and photography). My interests lie in modern arts specializing in narrative arts such as *bandes dessinées*, graphic novels and photography. As the letter to the editor points out, I have edited numerous anthologies and collective series; co-founded a publishing company; organized and executed special events; published numerous graphic novels as co-author; and have written several articles and manifestos.

The photo-essay was meant to be a portrait of the era in which I am fortunate to bear witness. The community I belong to is a unique blend of English and French language and diverse cultures. A community that has come together in recent years and formed a voice that has brought local, national, and international critical acclaim to a maligned art form.

The photo-essay was meant to attest to the achievements of a group of individuals that I feel should not be glossed over. It was never my intention to imply that these individuals were the only influences in Quebec and Montreal that should go down in the history books!

I based my selection of individuals on two criteria. First and foremost, these persons must have worked to build a community by promoting others and bringing people together.

My second criterion was to pick artists whose work and recognition in Montreal and abroad have been an inspiration and a driving force to this community. Furthermore, I have chosen to conscientiously highlight the work of creators who labour to fashion a mature and personal artistic vision.

I can only presume from the defamatory tone of the letters that the writers misinterpreted the nature of the essay. They assumed it set the stage for the entire gamut of work published by Montreal artists — which is absurd and reprehensible to even consider that it could be covered in a mere 12 pages!

The letters, full of false accusations, are filled with quotes taken out of context to prop up their rhetoric. Among other things, it implies that the collective book launch "Notre Époque a besoin de violence" referred to in my article, pales in comparison to what Robert Lapalme had achieved in the early 60s.

One letter starts by quoting Peter Bagge of Voice (p.5, Local Comics, May, 1995) leading us to conclude that Bagge believes that Montreal locals produce works of "inaccessible artiness" — and that my essay reinforces this point of view. Yet Mr. Bagge's last sentence was purposefully omitted. He says: "I have to admit however, the level of talent coming from that city is abnormally high."

Of course the letters neglect to mention that on the very same page of the same issue of Voice, Bernie Mireault, author of The Jam, also writes about the 1995 book launch:

> So, we begin to hear the high, clear, undiluted voices of some amazing storytellers and we have only begun to grasp the vast potential of this viciously underrated art form. Comic art is an important new medium and Montreal is a major centre of comic book activity! You should be proud. People might not be too hip to it now, but the art coming out of Montreal is its most potent cultural export and it's already put this city on the map for thousands of people all over the world.

On the same event Denis Lord comments in Lecture (May, 1995):

> On May 2, At La Piaule, a launch of underground comic books took place. How many comics? Fifteen my dear, and a few in Bukowski's tongue. Never seen before! Gigantesque, extremely big! Through a concentrated effort between all those involved and an aggressive promotion, it turned out to be an unbelievable success. The press and TV crews were there including serious bandes

dessinées authors. The public was lining up outside the bar, any big publisher dreams of such a turnout!

In La Presse (May 3, 1995), Jocelyne Lepage quotes noted comic historian Jacques Samson about the Piaule comic book launch:

> This is a new generation of authors. They're spontaneous. The mainstream doesn't interest them. They find the French market insufficient and they're open to English and International movements. What they do is more individualist and very personal.

Lepage goes on to say: "For a few years now, alternative comics in Montreal have been particularly dynamic and are taking a bigger and bigger place among what is published. It's a form of expression often closer to poetry or autobiographical writings than traditional bande dessinée."

The accomplishments of past artists should not be used to diminish the work of those still struggling today. The people behind these letters bend facts and yield numbers in the name of servicing their hidden agenda. In the process credibility is lost and damage is done. These frustrated individuals fling about libelous allegations, particularly regarding the Seventh and last International Festival of Bande Dessinée of Montreal.

Let me start by acknowledging the importance of the Fournier and Godbout team. Their contribution to the history of comics in Quebec is indisputable. Pierre Fournier had a major part in lobbying the government to fund comic book artists. Recently La Pastèque has begun reprinting their entire oeuvre. The Croc artists were an inspiration — but their generation was not the focus of my piece.

That part of my article on the 1992 Seventh International Festival speaks of local alternative comic talent, small publishers and the likes (essentially the next wave). Marc de Roussan, a respected journalist specializing in Quebec comics, writes in Continuum (October 26, 1992) talking about the preceding Sixth Festival:

> During the last festival that L'ACIBD organized in the spring of 1991, we saw a parade of European authors like Schuiten, Peeters and Yann. This display of stars did not bring in the crowds. The small press, composed for the most parts

of fanzines, was put aside.

Journalist Jocelyne Lepage writes in the daily *La Presse* (October 22, 1992):

> It seems that the Seventh International Festival of Bande Dessinée of Montreal who at last leaves the University of Montreal to wind up in local bars downtown; has fallen into the hands of the radical faction of cartoonists. A sign it seems, that it is off the path beaten by *Croc* and *Safarir* that you can find the most exciting things in the wonderful world of comics.

One of the letters alludes, with half-truths and hearsay, to facts and events that bring into question my ethics in regards to my involvement with this edition of the Festival. Let me take this opportunity to set the record straight.

The president of the Seventh edition of the Festival, Jean-Marc Urbain's first choice for guest of honour was Fred from France, celebrated author of *Philémon*. He agreed to come but insisted on a specific hotel and certain conditions that the festival simply could not afford. Basically, the festival could only pay for his plane ticket. How can that be when the letter writers have just revealed that the Festival's budget was a whopping $50,000??? In fact, this $50,000 budget was a government subsidy with the specific mandate to allow the ACIBD (a non-profit organization created to help Montreal cartoonists) to employ four full-time people for a six month period. The money left to operate and organize an eight day festival was peanuts. To replace Fred, I proposed Julie Doucet as guest of honour. She agreed. The Festival paid for her ticket and she stayed at friends.

In the letter, you ridicule the buzz that the festival generated and deny that it electrified the scene. Now picture this: a festival director that can only work half days on the project (more on that later), one graphic artist (Siris), one secretary, and one publicist (me) starting at the end of August. With a tiny operating budget and two months to prepare an eight day international festival, how were we going to pull this off?

The solution was to involve the whole Montreal comics community and have them contribute in anyway they could (helping to build and set-up exhibits, providing transportation and lodging, etc...) Not all, but most who answered the call were underground or alternative artists. This way, we wound up with more than 25 volunteers. They all worked hard as hell. The last few weeks were 18-hour days. The end result turned out to be an amazing opportunity for the comics community to work together, networking and socializing with fellow cartoonists. The spotlight was turned on a new generation of artists all of whom deserved it because they were willing to invest their time and effort into a festival that at last recognized their existence and contributions.

Remember, this came at a time when L'Association took matters into their own hands and created a movement of independent artists/publishers reacting against a lack of vision, diversity and publishing opportunities. The Festival highlighted this by importing, for the first time in Quebec, the first publications by L'Association (including *Lapin*, and the first books by David B. and Matt Konture). European alternative artists like Helge Reumann, Alex Baladi and Kalonji came to the festival courtesy of their publisher (who footed the bill for the plane tickets). This seventh edition of the Festival was a passing of the flame.

On to the metastatic malfeasance of which I am accused. When the grant for the seventh edition was received, time was of the essence and the president of the ACIBD, noted cartoonist Jean Lacombe, scrambled to find somebody with enough experience to helm the project. For the second year in a row. Jean-Marc Urbain stepped up to the plate... with one condition: He needed to keep his permanent job. His solution was to come in the afternoon. Mr. Lacombe agreed, mostly because he had no other options and no one else showed interest in the position. Here lies the conundrum: these grants aim to provide work experience to people on social security. A director for this kind of project is needed full-time. The secretary who was hired couldn't care less about comics; she was there to receive training and the director's role was to provide it (which under the circumstances, he could not). This led to conflicts between them, culminating in her telling the government official in charge of the project of the situation. This is when the shit hit the fan. Jean-Marc Urbain was fired, he had to pay back part of his salary, funding was cut and the ACIBD had to hire a new director and pay for his salary without government funding — crippling the association. From that point on, L'ACIBD was unable to recuperate its loss.

At that time, I was vice-president, not a salaried position of the ACIBD. I applied for the position of publicist, filling out the necessary forms but was told that my wife made 50 bucks more than the monthly limit so I was not eligible. Alexandre Lafleur was on social security and was eligible. Together we worked out an agreement where we would split his salary and I would do the office work while he worked on setting up the exhibits for the festival. Let's be clear, half a salary was not a lot of money, it was like being on social security. I didn't mind. At the time working on a comic festival was a dream job.

After the project was over a member of the board of directors of the ACIBD recommended that its members divide the deficit — approximately $2,000 each. After half a salary for six months, I was flat broke. I'd worked my ass off and at this point I had had my fill. I objected to the motion. Another president and staff were voted in but the new team could not save the association. L'ACIBD died (and so did SCABD, another association representing cartoonists in Quebec City. Without subsidies or volunteers non-profit organizations simply can't survive).

Ten years later, I wrote an opinion piece for the website BDQuébec discussing the artistic merit of certain Quebec cartoonists and why quality not quantity should be considered when appraising their work. My text invited discussions and an exchange of ideas. François Mayeux, a respected local expert on *bande dessinée*, was fed false information about me. Mr. Mayeux was shocked and proceeded to report that I might have filled my pockets with money from the association by refusing to pay back the deficit, I single-handedly toppled the ACIBD. After this came out, at a book launch for Michel Rabagliati, I met Éric Thériault (one of the writers of the letters) and he reminded me that he was on the ACIBD board at the same time and was also asked to pay back part of the deficit. Because he had limited financial resources, like me, he declined to pay. Since he regularly visited the BDQuébec website, Éric Thériault could have gone online and disclosed this information but he chose to remain silent.

As for accusing me of failing to respond to François Mayeux, the fact of the matter is that I communicated directly with Mayeux and explained what had happened. He urged me to come out with this information and I declined because the people involved had suffered enough

shame for their bad decisions. There were personal consequences for all involved.

I have since appeared on panels and met and enjoyed talking with Francois Mayeux and I hold no bitterness toward Mr. Mayeux, only respect.

The other unfounded accusations, which state that I compromised the quality of my work to attain subsidies is completely unacceptable and utterly absurd. I've worked hard at applying for funding so that I can pay the artists that I work with.

In the case of *Cyclops*, as with every collective I have been involved with, I don't pick artists because they're my friends, I seek them out because their stories and art astounds me. To produce a *Cyclops* book from idea to print, it means one to two years of personal involvement. A grant for a group project is equally divided among its members. If we receive $20,000 and we're a team of 20, each gets a $1000 cheque (it works out to $100 a page). My only salary is the money I get for my own pages.

Even my own quotes are tailored to support the letter writer's crackpot views. Here it is: "I always thought that if I had done *Mac Tin Tac* in French, it would be easier to get grants from the Quebec government." Later on the letter adds: "When projects are tailored to seduce the purses of power, isn't the integrity of the artist in danger of compromise?"

Here is my full quote from the *Matrix* issue: "There is a strange attitude towards publishing English comics in Quebec. I always thought that if I had done *Mac Tin Tac* in French, it would be easier to get grants from the Quebec government. Since it was in English it became part of another culture." The letter subverts a quote of mine in which I talk about the experience of being French and producing English work. We are talking about integrity here, but whose?

One of the letters implies that Julie Doucet's harsh quotes are about the Montreal scene that I reported on. I disagree; they're about the publishing scene. How do I know? Around that time, I worked with Julie Doucet. As I've said in my essay, in the early 90s, traditional publishers of comics in Montreal were few and none were interested in anything remotely alternative like Doucet's work.

You slight Julie Doucet's achievements by saying that they were due to plugs and reviews and that, locally, only a handful of sharp-eyed aficionados bought her minis. As a group of comic historians, how can you make that claim? Hélène Fleury, who used to be editor in chef of *Croc* writes in *Clin d'Oeil* (#196, October 1996): "When we talk about a successful fanzine we're talking about 50 copies sold in Montreal and 20 in Quebec City!"

Of her first minicomics, Julie Doucet published 125 copies, then 150 and 200 towards the end and they were all amazing and gorgeous comix. By the time she was picked up by D&Q, she had self-published at least 15 minis. In the same *Matrix* article quoted from earlier, Simon Bossé talks about his silkscreen mini by Julie Doucet (that he published), stating he sold out 1000 copies and had orders for two hundred more. The letter writers imply that Sylvie Rancourt was a bigger success than Doucet or Bossé because she had sold 500 hundred copies each of her two minis in Montreal bars. Jack Ruttan in the *Mirror* says (October 21, 1991): "One vocation nearly as despised as cartooning (but usually better paying) is exotic dancing. Perhaps it isn't so strange to find a stripper who dances on tables, then sells comic books of her life story to the patrons."

This is a little tidbit the letter writers neglected to mention. Yes, Sylvie Rancourt comics have merit, but she wasn't involved in building a community, was she?

My assessment that the Montreal comic scene began to attract attention in art circles is ridiculed. One letter states, "Apparently, he wasn't around for the exhibition "La bande dessinée québécoise" at the Montreal Museum of Contemporary Art in 1976, a show which also traveled to the Canadian Cultural Center in Paris and to the third edition of the Angoulême Festival."

Hey, I was 14 years old!

The other exhibition in Quebec City organized by Mira Falardeau in 1996 did include Valium and even, gosh, *Mac Tin Tac*. This exhibit was an historic overview; it did not cover in detail the events chronicled in my essay.

Keith Marchand, art critic for the *Mirror* wrote for the August 14, 1997 issue about the Montreal exhibit of alternative and underground comix artists BD: Bande à part: "Contrary to popular opinion, comics are not unsophisticated illustrations paired with amateurish text. With careful planning and thought, the urbanity, wit and pacing of comics may be a necessary shot in the arm to the stodgy world of contemporary art."

Hear, hear! Too bad Mr. Marchand's opinion must be invalidated since he also did not see the 1976 exhibit.

I don't know what Leanne Franson and Jacques Boivin's signatures are doing at the bottom of these letters, I understand their indignation if they thought this article was about the comic book artists of Montreal and felt excluded. It was never my intention to slight their accomplishments. To the others who signed these letters, you claim to have no vendetta against me, yet you accuse me of excision and disinformation, of undisguised ignorance and arrogance, of imprecise formulation, inappropriate metaphors and unwarranted hyperbole. Have you read your own letters?

You have circulated one of your letters to Montreal cartoonists, asking them to sign it and they refused. Since this Special Edition of the *Journal* came out, one of you has twice gone to Howard Chackowicz's place of employment and verbally assaulted him in front of the store's patrons for being included in my essay. Now, Howard Chackowicz is a true gentleman, nominated for a Harvey Award in 1993. Like few others, he has been extremely generous both in his time and efforts to help his fellow Montreal cartoonists. He deserves to be in the essay.

You act like thugs.

By continuing to deny the achievements of others in order to elevate your own, you only serve to ostracize yourselves even more from your peers.

In Montreal, many, many people have done an extraordinary deed. Across differences and barriers they have built a community and fostered a climate of exchange, tolerance, openness and artistic creativity while producing amazing comix. To have a city host such an amazing community of artists is a rare gift that should be acknowledged and celebrated. ●

POSTSCRIPT 2017:

When Andy Brown suggested republishing the original article (in *The Comics Journal* Special Edition No 5, 2005) and the letters and my reaction to them (published in *The Comics Journal #274*, February, 2006), I was a bit dubious. I was proud of the original article, mainly a photo essay that I worked on for months to book the artists and publishers in order to take their portraits. So, I voiced my concern to Andy Brown that this should not be done in order to stir up another controversy. But Andy saw the whole thing differently! He convinced me that the article, the letters and my reply were chock full of information on the history of Quebec comics and that it needed to see the light again. After some reflection, I agreed with Andy. To provide the other parties with a voice so as to not recreate that sentiment of exclusion, I asked Éric Thériault, one of the writers from the original letters, to also write a postscript.

I had not read the original letters and articles since they came out more than twelve years ago. The controversy and backlash had left me with a bitter taste and quite shaken. It took me more than a decade to make peace with most of the artists, writers and publishers who wrote those replies. So my first thought upon reading the whole thing again was that they were right in pointing out my mistakes. If I had worked with an experienced editor, she or he would also have singled out those mistakes (some of which I fixed for the Conundrum reprint). On the other end, I was happily surprised to note that most of the artists that I had chosen to spotlight in 2003 are still active, even more highly regarded, and have won awards and acclaim for their work. If I had the power to update the original essay, the article would include the Montreal Comic Jams of the times, *MensuHell*, Éric Thériault and the creation of *Krypton* magazine and I would add more contemporary voices that have since popped-up, like the rise of Pow Pow Press with Luc Bossé and his talented roster of artists and writers (Zviane, Samuel Cantin, Michel Hellman, Alexandre-Fontaine Rousseau) and of Vincent Giard and Sébastien Trahan with their publishing imprint la mauvaise tête. To that list I could add publishers Front Froid, Lounak, and the revamped mécanique générale and artists Iris, Cab, Michel Falardeau, Christian Quesnel, Stanley Wany, Delaf & Dubuc, Julie Rocheleau, Jean-Sébastien Bérubé, Thierry Labrosse, and so many, many, more.... In a decade, the scene has literally exploded! As of 2017, the Quebec comics scene has had an amazing documentary TV show (BDQC), countless articles and reviews in newspapers, a show at the Montreal Museum of Fine Arts ("15 ans de la Pastèque"), a re-energized festival in Quebec City thanks to Thomas-Louis Côté and a new festival of Comics in Montreal (MCAF\FBDM). Now, it needs a few thick books that can survey the growth of the scene viewed from the many angles emphasizing our diversity: genre stories, literary and experimental art comics, a slew of Quebec artists working for European and American publishers to the thriving BD auteur scene.

Any short articles will always cut people out (and rightly frustrate some neglected artist's contribution) and we've seen that the current memory of the Internet/print journalists (because of time and money) rarely goes back in time to more than ten years. So Andy Brown was right, republishing the whole thing has value and I thank him for his foresight.

— Marc Tessier

POSTSCRIPT 2017:

Time shuffles along, and what began as bitter debate becomes fuzzy memories. All too often, heated arguments erupt without all parties possessing a full sense of the context. As one of the authors of "The replies" I've often felt that *something* was lost in the ensuing kerfuffle.

Many people have expressed quite strong opinions about the schism that supposedly divided the Montreal comics community as a result of the replies to the article. It has been said that, because we responded and criticized, we caused great harm to the community and its unity.

But a lot of those comments were made behind people's backs as hearsay, mere rumour. Not everyone has had in hand the issue of *The Comic Journal* where the main article appeared and even fewer had access to its two responses. The book-style *TCJ* was quite pricey, and not everyone can read English.

Furthermore, even if what we're discussing is the history of Quebec comics (with a local focus on Montreal), the greater context is American. It's the self-image that we were communicating to North America's most important journal of comics news and criticism. *The Comic Journal* is known for its lengthy, in-depth interviews with comics creators, its acerbic editorials and scathing reviews of the products of the comics industry.

In the late 90s (I'm going from memory here: it's quite a challenge to research material from a long-gone message board!), the *Journal* had shown interest in publishing coverage of the Montreal scene. On the TCJ message board, writer Milo George suggested that this was something worth covering, but that they had no idea on how to go about it. Bart Beaty, who'd been residing in Montreal for several years and covering European comics (likely purchased from our local book shop) for the *Journal*, had never parlayed his geographical advantage to focus on the local scene. A few Montrealers did convey (again, on the message board) to Milo George the names of journalists or reviewers who might be suitable. We felt that solid coverage from various perspectives over several articles could do a good job. Many styles tackled from many points of view over several articles. And it seemed important that the authors not be directly involved in the topic at hand, to avoid the conflict.

Eventually, we did learn that Marc Tessier was to write a report, and make it a personal one, basically a memoir.

Milo George commissioned the article from Marc but left his position of editor-in-chief before it saw print. Dick Deppey took his place in 2004, and when I inquired with him as to the possibility of "beefing up" the coverage to consist of more than a single article, in order to feature a variety of voices, he admitted to having no knowledge of what was in the pipeline at the time.

Even though I'm sure Marc worked hard to do a very good job, and he did, it remained a partial one and many actors barely recognized the scene they were part of. The scene as shown became a small coterie, a handful of artists like the Surrealists or the Fort Thunder group.

We gathered that the multiple articles that we had hoped to see would have to be written by ourselves and as responses to the article in the *Journal's* letters section, "Blood and Thunder." "We" being a group comprising Kurt Beaulieu, Richard Gagnon, Jane Tremblay, Jacques Boivin, Francis Hervieux and myself.

We opted to write an article focusing on what was missing from Marc's article and not to nitpick too much. Basically to cover what was left uncovered. And an important thing was to jointly sign the text in solidarity. I wrote a considerable part of the first draft of that one and a few of us polished it up and made revisions and additions.

In light of much back and forth and discussion, the group decided that a second text was needed to critique Marc's article and correct the factual errors it contained. We divided our efforts.

The second text was written in a way to ensure its being ideal fodder for "Blood and Thunder." It had always been a very opinionated and combative space and we took pains to make the piece an ideal fit, one that Gary Groth and Dick Deppey would deem worthy of publication in that forum. Otherwise, it would be a waste of everyone's time.

If there is one thing that I regret especially, it's that I would have hoped for a way to be critical without being needlessly hurtful. My initial choice was to only cover what was left unsaid in Marc's article and to avoid sounding bitter. But it was important as a group to jointly sign the letters, even if I could clearly feel that it might hurt Marc's feelings.

Basically, except for a lot of chattering, nothing much happened. There was no great, permanent split in the local "scene" and my opportunities and friendships did not suffer because of it. The scene continued to evolve along the natural course of things. The notion that a great big cobblestone had been callously tossed in the placid pond of our unified scene only makes sense if you believe that there actually was unity to begin with.

That being said, a lot of water flowed under the bridge and Marc and I have since then collaborated on a few projects, mainly around his *Trip* anthology. We've run into each other a few times at conventions and festivals and have enjoyed cordial conversations. I sincerely think that Marc is the bigger man, as he was first to cross the aisle and hold out his hand. If we must look at specific things, we'd probably still find ourselves disagreeing quite a bit, but he wisely chose to look beyond such trifles.

It takes plenty of class and maturity to do that.

— Éric Thériault

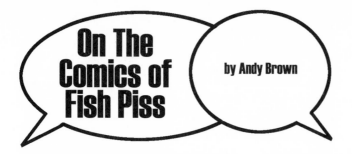

On The Comics of Fish Piss

by Andy Brown

A study of the comics in the pages of the seminal zine *Fish Piss* is an excellent primer on the unique field of bilingual comics in Montreal in the 1990s. Edited by Louis Rastelli *Fish Piss* ran from 1996 to 2006 for 11 issues (plus three limited bonus editions) and started as a mash up of the anglophone spoken word community and the comics community, both French and English. In fact, *Fish Piss* is a calling card to a time and place that has been called Canada's last authentic bohemia.[1] It also featured literary material, essays, non-fiction, biographies, radical politics and music, but the subject of this analysis is the significance the comics played in establishing a "contact zone" of cultural production.

Fish Piss arose from the DIY zine aesthetic of the 1980s and early 1990s as exemplified by such publications as *Factsheet Five* (1982-1998), *Punk Planet* (founded in 1994), or *Maximumrocknroll* (founded 1982). In fact, editor Rastelli cut his teeth on a Montreal music zine called *RearGarde*, then later worked as the editor of *Flaming Poutine*, which transformed into *Fish Piss*, an archa-

ic term for ink. Rastelli on the origin story: "I meant to keep it going but the old editor had collected money for ads for the issue that never came out and the advertisers wanted refunds. I decided to change the name for that reason. *Fish Piss* was one of the title ideas I had, after reading too much McLuhan. It is a metaphor on how consumers of media affect each other constantly without realizing it, much like fish may not notice that their own piss is in the water they swim around in. That the initials would remain FP clinched it."[2]

The publication went from a 24 page photocopied zine with "no advertising" to a 160 page magazine with silkscreened covers (by comic artists) and worldwide distribution through Tower Records. Rastelli describes the editorial mandate as "pluridisciplinary freeform loose-themed collective work." But, throughout its run, the space devoted to comics remained relatively consistent.

Fish Piss did not play by the traditional rules of publishing fields, as outlined in Thompson[3] and based on Bordieau's fields of cultural production. Thompson outlines four sources for capital available to a publisher: economic capital (access to funds), human capital (access to staff), intellectual capital (access to rights), and symbolic capital (the status or brand recognition of a publishing house).

Although *Fish Piss*, in its later issues would trade on its symbolic capital, it operated totally outside this paradigm. The idea of a publishing "industry" was totally anathema to its DIY values. In fact, it could be argued this DIY aesthetic forms its own publishing field. Valuing community engagement over distribution, valuing openness and diversity over sales figures. What is perhaps more useful is to examine the zine through the lens of a fifth type of capital, linguistic capital, which is an addition Lina Shoumarova makes in

Louis Rastelli in the Archive Montreal offices.

her thesis on linguistic properties of the book publishing field in Montreal.[4] Shoumarova posits that it is the uniqueness of Montreal itself, what she calls a "contact zone", that allows for the greatest opportunity for further discussion of the field.

Traditionally a linguistic publishing field would operate within a rubric of geographic limitation (books published in English would be sold in English speaking countries), the selling of foreign rights (translations), or through partnerships with foreign publishers. Again, *Fish Piss* operates outside this field. Unlike a magazine that translates its own text and formats them side by side on the page (such as *En Route*) *Fish Piss* is truly bilingual, its comics and essays, poems, and stories exist on the page without translation. It is assumed the (local) audience is as bilingual as the editor. This is the contact zone to which Shoumarova refers, the two solitudes meeting on the page, or at least an audience willing to embrace "linguistic otherness." For Shoumarova language shapes a cultural field, whether at a political, economic, or cultural level. Montreal is an "intellectual nodal point" and *Fish Piss* becomes an "inter-cultural dialogue" which "confers an identity," to its contributors, or to put it in Thompson's terms, over its 11 issue run *Fish Piss* achieves "symbolic value," which is the process of representing a scene.

Shoumarova interviews French and English publishers, and examines their contact points but on the anglophone side focusses on those of the new generation, "la relève." It would appear significant that of the three anglophone publishers she interviewed only one is still active, Conundrum Press, and that it has adjusted its mandate to publishing exclusively comics (including French comics in translation), and that many of these comic artists were first published (and discovered by Conundrum) in *Fish Piss*.

So what about the comics in *Fish Piss*? Why were they so significant in the shaping of the linguistic and cultural field of Montreal? The linguistic otherness of Montreal, and by extension *Fish Piss*, runs parallel to the "otherness" experienced by comics themselves within the cultural field. But we also need to consider the linguistic capital of comics within both the English and French cultural fields. For English readers, these comics would be vulgar, messy, or classified as "underground", and not accessible to mainstream com-

ics readers. *Bandes dessinée* are a highly respected art form in French, but these bd operate outside mainstream Quebec culture, but also and especially, outside the Paris hegemony of the French linguistic cultural field.

There is not a homogenous linguistic market in Montreal, and *Fish Piss* embraces this "heteronormative linguistic field." In fact, both the French and English comics published in *Fish Piss* share more artistic attributes than separate them, they are both outsiders on an underground spectrum. Rastelli explains: "I think the fact that both English and French underground / DIY / independent culture is way off on the margins of the mainstream of either language makes them bond and cross-pollinate more."

As exemplified by Rastelli's unique curatorial process it is the comic artists who are prioritized in *Fish Piss*, they are the ones getting paid: "The one constant through the run as far as selecting /commissioning was deciding on a cover artist and a centrefold and/or illustrations. The only people who got paid were the cover artist, centrefold artist, and usually one artist per issue providing some commissioned illustrations." The fact that it is the silkscreen covers and comics that give the publication its "otherness" (even within the DIY field) is validated. But who are these comic artists?[5]

The cover of the first issue is a psychedelic fish drawn by Billy Mavreas, perhaps the ultimate

FISH PISS

NO ADVERTISING! $1

crossover artist from the French / English cultures but also the comics / spoken word communities. "I did the cover for issue #1, it was a time when I was enthralled by that intersection between drawing and writing, so I drew a fish composed of small calligraphic symbols."[6] Mavreas's contributions to *Fish Piss* predate his attempts at actual comic stories, and are more like illustrated texts, such as "Waiting for the Ride", the centrefold in issue #3, "Hanging with Jesus", and "Tuesday at the Office". This is an artist working out his style in the consecutive pages of a zine. "I think it was the Quebecois comix zines in general that are responsible for pushing me into making comics as opposed to graphics or spot illustrations. *Fish Piss* was part of it, it gave me carte blanche which is always good for a young artist."[7]

Mavreas hits the nail on the head with his comments about artists having a forum to work out their style, which in turn influenced other artists to work out their styles, and a loop of creativity is formed: "After creating the identity and style of *Fish Piss* in its first issues," says Rastelli, "artists had an easier time coming up with material that fit the magazine and it made it much easier for me to select stuff. In this sense artists like Mavreas, Valium, Suicide, Bell influenced many younger artists by being part of the first issues which forged the style and identity."

Also in the first issue and the cover artist of the second is Rick Trembles. His autobiographical strips were done specifically for *Fish Piss*, and appeared throughout the entire run. Trembles produced a music zine called *Sugar Diet* which pre-dated *Fish Piss* and morphed into a forum for his other autobio comics. One of the characteristics of his work is its two-dimensional quality, resulting from simple lines with no crosshatching. The characters appear to be constructed of blocks of wood. This allows the writing to be highlighted and in fact words often consume the page, his alliterative dialogue filling speech bubbles which become the entire panel itself. But for the comics in *Fish Piss* he simplifies, strips to the iconic, and privileges the narrative voice. The strips themselves are about seemingly random childhood memories which take on great significance in their retelling. Trembles explains:

"I was roommates with Louis after a midnight move that resulted in my having to temporarily store most of my belongings in my parent's basement. After settling into Louis' I gradually started bringing all my childhood belongings back, bit by bit, which started triggering memories from my past. I was worried about them fading from memory, so I took the opportunity to document them before they could vanish. One of my last entries in this series questioned the nature of se-

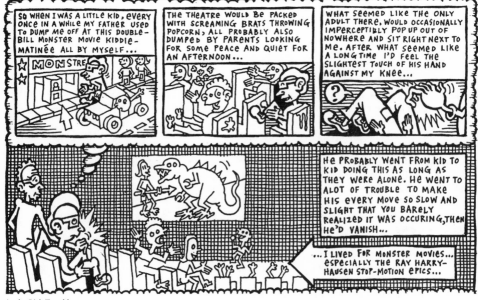

Art by Rick Trembles

lective memory, why certain inanities from one's past might resonate more than others, and why, no matter how hard you try, there's no guarantee you can deliberately instigate an event in your life in the present that will pass the test of time as worthy of recollecting years down the line."

Marc Bell was also known for autobiographical strips at the time, appearing in such publications as *Pervert*, *Mirror*, and later *Vice*. According to Rastelli: "*Guillotine* and *Pervert* had also just petered out. Looking at *Guillotine*, clearly the whole crew of contributors started cranking out the same sort of material for *Fish Piss*. When I say *FP* came out of a basic need to keep a publication going that people could submit to, it's the truth, someone else would have started up a similar thing if I hadn't." Issue #2 contains Bell's two pager about two incidents when he broke his glasses and walked around "in a fuzzy colourful fog for weeks." Like Trembles he "investigates the events," highlighting the important decisions that were made while in this state. His relationship fails and he "moves home" only to be beaten up and break his glasses again. Here Bell is delving into the traditional nerdy comic artist clichés, in opposition to the manly men, before his career took him away from the autobio and into the more abstract work of the art world. This is exemplified by his back cover for issue #4. Louis gives context: "I used to ask Marc Bell for autobiographical stuff all the time, he did a bunch of that, but then I think it pissed him off and he had his wild phase, these dense drawings with who knows what sort of thing going on." It would seem significant that the back cover of issue #4 was the last appearance of Marc Bell in the pages of *Fish Piss*.

However, the melding of the art world and autobio comics did continue in the pages of *Fish Piss* through the comics of Joe Hale. Louis describes his reactions to Hale's work: "His strips looked like some poor kid living in dysfunctional squalor scrawled them out but they were painstakingly perfected to look like that." These were later collected into a book edited and with an interview by Marc Bell.[8] Hale appears to be the most significant outlier of the artists published in *Fish Piss*, and he appeared in almost every issue. And whereas most of the cartoonists were happy to have a forum for their comics work, Hale came at the whole medium of comics almost as a performative artistic exercise. His real name is Joey Haley and he created the persona of Joe Hale to explore what

Art by Joe Hale

he saw as an exciting field of alternative comics, which was specific to Montreal. Disturbing in nature, these works often satirize the autobiographical position taken by many cartoonists of the day, including Bell. Hale's strip in issue #4, featuring a disembodied goose head in a hat, is eerily similar to Bell's Greedy Goose character. But there was more to it than that: these short stories transcend their small DIY format, reading like classic morality tales gone wrong.

When interviewed in *Love and Forgiveness* Hale reveals his intentions, like a curtain being pulled back on his artistic practice: "I wanted to satirize the autobiographical format, and present a character named Joe Hale who came from a world of unimaginable dysfunction. The formula for the humour in this collection is very dark. The reactions were extreme. For those who loved it, I felt concern for them. For those who hated it, they had my sympathy."

It is specifically Montreal where he·feels this comics experiment would thrive, possibly due to its value as a contact zone. "I was amazed at how organized the Montreal cartoonists were then. All the high-end stuff was francophone, in my opinion, and I wanted entry. And so, yes, I made Montreal an intentional destination for this pursuit."

Art by Mr. Graham Falk

Reading his one page comics at the time, in the pages of *Fish Piss*, one did feel a disturbed psychology at work. Comics like "Camp Cancer" or "I Get Wasted" were frank and brutal ("cause I got a pet monkey to beat up, a bag to shit in, and a floor to punch."). However, reading them today, with the knowledge they were satires, they make more sense, and become a type of gallows humour. But that does not diminish the powerful affect they had at the time, especially on the artists of Fort Thunder, who admit to being influenced by Hale.

The bizarre but hilarious Mr. Graham Falk provides one-page strips, which first appeared in issue #4 and continue in every issue after. His formula is to present a topic in a "how to" format, or like an advice columnist. "Suicide for Cowards," "Everyone Should be Healthy," "Correct Kissing," and "Show Your Pain" ("If you are being overworked then glue a globe of the world to the shoulders of your suit, this will arouse compassion in your co-workers.") are all hilarious in the gag cartoon tradition. Falk seems to

have disappeared from the alternative comics field, though a Google search implies he is now working in animation.

The cover of issue #3 is indicative of Howard Chackowicz's oeuvre. It features two children at a birthday party hitting a piñata, but instead of the piñata breaking open to reveal candy, it explodes in a bloody mess of red guts. The two-page silent strip "The Squirrel Lover" found in issue #2 has the opposite effect on the reader. An old man is broken hearted when the squirrels run away from him at the park. He then commissions a tailor to make him a suit out of bread. When he returns to the park and lies down, the squirrels surround him and literally eat his love as he cries tears of joy. These two works show the opposing sides of Chackowicz's art, the anguished and the poignant.

Also significant is the fact that "The Squirrel Lover" is silent or *sans parole*. The wordless strip straddles the linguistic field, opening interpretation to French, English, or anyone else. It is one of the methods to navigate the contact zone of Montreal, removing the language barriers altogether, and making the work totally accessible. The silent strip deals in the realm of a shared iconic language. Louis hints that this was an intentional choice for *Fish Piss*: "There were quite a few wordless strips in *Fish Piss* which readers did not count as anglo or franco." Many of the *Fish Piss* artists (including Trembles, Siris, and Suicide) contributed to the L'Association *Comix 2000* anthology which had a mandate to be silent. As Mavreas has said of the anthology: "the book is mute testimony to the potentiality of the medium."[9]

These silent strips were a bridge between linguistic zones and no one did it better than Eric Braün. Of German heritage but working in the

DERNIÈRE HEURE ©ERIC BRAÜN

COME ON PAT,
ONE MORE PAGE TO DO...

francophone milieu Braün contributed to every issue of *Fish Piss*. Braun produced one of the better comics anthologies of the 90s Montreal underground, *106U*, which featured covers made of metal or fake fur and highlighted Europeans next to the local artists. His *Fish Piss* contributions display a mastery of the iconic language of comics, often with a political message. The three panel gags are populated by characters who could have leapt right off the Monopoly board. As in the game itself these crooks and money barons deal with a world of simple symbols: a car, a house, a dollar sign, a hat.

Starting at issue #4 the francophone artists begin to dominate the covers (beautifully silkscreened) and more of the comics content. The cover of #4 is a street scene by Jean-Pierre Chausigaud who produced illustrations for many issues but no actual comics. Siris provided the front cover of #5 ("Future du Certain!") and Line Gamache[10] the back. The tagline for this issue is: "big variety true false mix o'... whatever." For the first time the francophone artists outnumber the anglos. Along with Brosseau and Siris are featured: Éric Thériault, Kurt Beaulieu, Eric Braün, Guim, Mr Swiz, Rose Beef, d. bilos, and Fidele (Genevieve) Castrée. Siris provides a silent three-page strip called "Traffic Calming" in which his chicken-headed avatar reacts to the urban chaos by smashing all the cars and bulldozing them away.

The cover of #6 is by Caro Caron, another francophone. More women cartoonists (almost all francophone) start contributing to *Fish Piss*, perhaps after seeing other women like Gamache represented in the earlier issues, essentially opening a safe space for their work.[11] The fact that Line Gamache edited an all-women anthology at the time called *Une Affaire Gigogne*, which featured many of the same contributors as *Fish Piss*, indicates an understanding of the traditional "boys club" aspect of the comics field and a willingness to try and rectify the situation. A teenage

Geneviève Castrée published some of her earliest work in the pages of *Fish Piss*.[12] Dominique Petrin (now exhibiting internationally) provided the back cover for #8. Hélène Brosseau appears on the back cover of #9, as well as contributing the logos for various interior columns.

Although never granted a cover or centrefold the comics of Richard Suicide can't help but shape the "style and identity" of *Fish Piss*. His heavy inking and claustraphobic panels perfectly encapsulate the urban anomie of his downtown neighbourhood in Montreal. His strip in #4, "Oeil de Veau le Cyclopique," is printed with an English translation beside it, the only time this happens in the entire run of the zine. Here Rastelli is testing out the contact zone, perhaps self-conscious that he is introducing anglophone readers to new francophone cartoonists, but ultimately decides not to continue the practice in future issues. Suicide's strips were later translated and collected into the Conundrum title *My Life as a Foot*.

The centrefold of issue #2 and the cover artist of # 6 is the legendary Henriette Valium. Within the context of the Montreal underground comics field Valium is considered the Pope, and his early contributions bring a real legitimacy to the zine. As Rastelli explains, "Valium is just a monument. Most of his contributions were exclusive pages from some of those oversized silkscreened "albums" he'd spend years and years on.[13] *FP* was also reasonably connected to the European zine and comics scene, and Valium was a rare bridge between them, he'd been published there a lot and brought some of that Le Dernier Cri industrial edge to *FP*." The dense, obsessive rendering of Valium's work helps *Fish Piss* attain another level of underground status, that of a bridge to the European comics field. It should be noted that Valium self-published his albums in both English and French, two different editions, embracing and helping to define the unique linguistic publishing field of Montreal. His latest over-sized album was

above: *Fish Piss* #4,
cover by Jean-Pierre Chausigaud

above right: *Fish Piss* Vol. 2, #1
cover by Henriette Valium

right: Art by Richard Suicide

published in English as a full colour hardcover by Conundrum Press. No French edition exists as of this writing. So it is the exposure in *Fish Piss* that allowed Valium to be embraced by anglophones and to bring his work to the North American book "industry" at large.

Which brings us back to the idea that *Fish Piss* acquired symbolic capital over its decade-long run, with Europeans, with anglophones, and with francophones.[14] This symbolic capital created a loop which caused more talented artists to submit. In this sense not only did Montreal shape *Fish Piss* but *Fish Piss* shaped Montreal (or the Plateau neighbourhood at least). But it also speaks to legacy building, the zine solidified a serious moment in 90s Montreal culture, what Trembles calls "a time-capsule of various artists' earlier work." The writers who cut their teeth in the zine have gone on to be embraced by the Can Lit canon. One example of many is that Heather O'Neill published her very first poems as a teenager in *Fish Piss*.

And it is the vision of Louis Rastelli that created this "big variety true false mix" that anyone interested in Canadian culture should now revisit. As Mavreas says, "I think *FP* is more important than we realize. Because Montreal doesn't mythologize itself in the same way as other Canadian cities do, we often lose count of the threads that helped shape not only the local scene but the national scene. I think Louis himself has not received the recognition for the work he continues to do[15] let alone all the work he has already done."

With his zine Rastelli provided a forum for a collection of comic artists and writers to explore, find their voice, and due to the fecundity of the contact zone that is Montreal, thrive. ●

ENDNOTES:

1. "Conundrum emerged from the closest Canada has come to a genuine creative underclass since the Bohemian Sixties scene in Toronto and Vancouver.": The Conundrum Curmudgeon by Hal Niedzviecki, Globe and Mail, Nov. 23, 2005… Or as Rastelli states: "Low rent, easy welfare, high unemployment, pre-Internet, four Universities parked around the mountain, there may have been a higher than average quantity of writers and artists and musicians than other places. I was one of the only people I knew working a day job at an office. But as per the 90s zinester cliché I got to use the office photocopiers and fax machines and mailroom."

2. All quotations are taken from emails with the author when compiling this essay in April 2017, unless otherwise indicated.

3. *Books in the Digital Age: The Transformation of Academic and Higher Education Publishing in Britain and the United States.* John B. Thompson, (John Wiley & Sons ,2013).

4. *Publishing in the Contact Zone: Linguistic properties of the book publishing field in Montreal,* Lina Shoumarova (Concordia University Master's thesis, 2007).

5. For the purposes of this essay I will only focus on comic artists who appeared regularly in *Fish Piss*, over more than one issue, and not one-offs.

6. Mavreas was doing the posters for the spoken word series YAWP. Conundrum Press noticed these psychedelic posters and published a collection of them called *Mutations* in 1997.

7. *The Overlords of Glee,* Mavreas's first book of experimental comics came out with Conundrum / Crunchy in 2001.

8. *Love and Forgiveness* by Joe Hale: edited, coloured and assembled by Marc Bell. (Swimmer's Group, 2014).

9. *Matrix* magazine #56, "Comix en ville" 2000.

10. Conundrum would go on to translate and publish two books by Gamache, *Hello, Me Pretty* and *Poof!*

11. It should be noted that women contributed their writing from the very first issue: Heather O'Neill, Golda Fried, Catherine Kidd.

12. *Susceptible* was published by Drawn & Quarterly in 2012.

13. *1000 Rectums* (1990), *Primitive Cretin!* (1996)

14. Also, due to the distribution deal with Tower Records, it had credibility within the music scene as well.

15. Rastelli continues to run Expozine, the Montreal Archive, and Distroboto.

MODERN TIMES

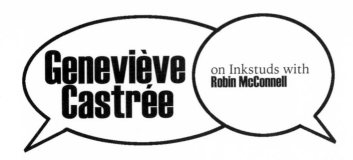

Geneviève Castrée

on Inkstuds with
Robin McConnell

Originally aired on CITR 101.9 FM in Vancouver, 2012.

Archived on www.inkstuds.org

My guest this week is Geneviève Castrée, her latest book is Susceptible *from Drawn & Quarterly. Her other work can be found in* Kramers Ergot, Drawn & Quarterly Showcase *and a bunch of early work including* Lait Frappé.

Robin McConnell: Thanks for joining me today, I very much appreciate it. It's interesting, you're not very far from Vancouver, but our paths have never crossed. You're in Anacortes, Washington.

Geneviève Castrée: Yeah. Anacortes, Washington, yes.

RM: I was looking at your blog, of your event, the Anacortes Unknown, and it seems kind of like an idyllic place to be.

GC: Yeah, it is. I mean, in the summertime Anacortes is very much a different place where a lot of people are like, "Oh man I want to go back there." But in the winter time it gets kind of bleak. It's sort of a retirement community, or I guess people call it a bedroom community too? It's the type of place where we don't have a college or anything to keep younger people interested in living here for expanded periods of time, and so there's not even really work for normal people, so it's very much retirees who are drawn to this place. Nowadays anyways, it didn't use to be that way.

RM: It seems like a mix between

retirees, and then young people who want to start a farm?

GC: Anacortes is strange. It's this weird place where you know the hip young people who want to grow their own vegetables. I fucking wish we had that here. We don't really. The farms are really north of here. It's unfortunate. I think it's just kind of too expensive around here. A beautiful place is always expensive but when there's no jobs, there's all these empty houses in Anacortes that have no renters, yet families that are homeless, and my friends had to move out of town because they couldn't get a job, and they couldn't afford a decent place to live here. It's a little bit sad.

RM: I read the comics I had of yours. When I read *Lait Frappé*, and then read all your work be-

Geneviève and husband Phil Elverum.
Photo courtesy Robin McConnell.

tween that and *Susceptible*, I kinda felt like those two really had a strong connection between them among all your work that I've read.

GC: That makes a lot of sense to me. That's cool that you got that.

RM: Is *Susceptible* a story you've been working through in your head for a long time, and trying to figure out how to tell it?

GC: I guess we can call it a story, but there's many ways to see it. It's my story, so it's just this thing, this weird soup that's been sloshing around inside of me for a very long time, trying to figure out a way out. It's this weird exorcism in a way. Had I done it ten or twelve years ago it probably would have been very very embarrassing, and ill prepared. But this time around, I think that maybe I have got enough of the skills necessary to turn it into a book that's passable, or acceptable for some people to read as a book. Around the time that I did *Lait Frappé* I would have wanted to make a story that was more like *Susceptible*, I just didn't have the perspective or the distance. So you know, I just made a book that just seemed to be about this girl, that wears striped sweaters all the time, and she's all messed up.

RM: Maybe give listeners a context of what *Susceptible* covers. It's about yourself, it's about part of your childhood....

GC: It's based on childhood memories from the age of about 2 to 18. And I just was trying to draw things that I saw with my own eyes. I mean there are a couple of exceptions in the book, things that I draw that I imagined, but otherwise it's very much as I saw it unfolding. Then I changed all the names, because that's always the danger with autobiographies. I always say this, but true 100% pure autobiography is impossible to achieve, and so I just felt out of fairness, I had to change the names, because they become characters no matter how hard I try.

RM: The names were really interesting. For the name of your mother, who was Amer, and then the stepfather, or the fellow, was Aman. I'm curious about those particular choices of names.

GC: In French those names, *amer* means bitter, and so I just had this female version of the adjective bitter for the mother character's name, and then the male version of the word bitter for the male step-dad character.

RM: I was also thinking about how Amer also sounds like "mere".

GC: I just wanted something that also sounded like it could be a person's name, because that's something that happens often, especially if you translate the book in another language, I mean I wrote the book in French initially, but then it got translated into English, and now its being translated in German. I wanted a word, it would seem plausible that it could be a person's name, in a strange other universe, you know? Especially now that people are naming their kids Apple and stuff.

RM: I was wondering about what language you originally wrote the story in, because the names work really nicely in that kind of pun-way. Like the father being "Tête d'Oeuf", so "Egg Head". It's interesting when you do translate work, what parts do you maintain in a certain language, and what parts don't you? And so for you it was mainly the names that you chose to keep.

GC: Yeah, I mean I feel very lucky that Drawn & Quarterly let me keep the names as is. I mean I think my English is pretty good? But I really wanted to have someone double check, especially with syntax and punctuation, because that's another struggle for me in English. So when they looked it over, that was one of the first reactions from one of the employees, "Well... these names are sort of unlikely," and also its very confusing, because there's not that much of a difference between the two names. But I'm glad that they let me go ahead with it. Because it would not have been as cool had I called them like, Bitter and Unhappy or something like that.

RM: Bitter-He, and Bitter-She...

GC: Yeah exactly! I wrote the book in French, and like, Quebec is not France, and it's not Belgium. English speaking Canadians know that Québec is this weird place. In the United States, not everybody knows that Quebec is this weird place but it's different. It's in North America, but it's not like an American State, and so I wanted to have like, in the French version of the book it was clear when you read it, there are nuances that a French person from France would read and be like, "Oh how colourful, this person is from Quebec." So I wanted to have something in the English version

"I feel like I am a trans-Canadian, because I moved out of Quebec when I was 17 and then I went and lived in British Columbia, and then, it never really occurred to me until I was 18, that I wasn't fully from Quebec."

of the book and the names and everything that would just be like, "Oh I am not reading this thing about a kid who grew up in Indiana, you know?" Like, it's a different place, and it was important to me to have that be obvious in the book.

RM: There was something on the back I was very curious about, it's called a trans-Canadian exploration. And I've never actually, being Mister Super Canadian, I've never heard that kind of term — trans-Canadian. I'm curious where that comes from.

GC: Oh yeah, that's funny actually because I didn't write that blurb on the back, that's the funny thing about those blurbs is they're in your handwriting but you're just transcribing something that the publisher wrote for you. And so, I wrote it down and I was like, "Oh... trans-Canadian. I mean that's cool." And then with Drawn & Quarterly we were discussing actually changing the text at the back of the book, and I was like, "I actually really like trans-Canadian." Because that's what I am. I feel like I am a trans-Canadian, because I moved out of Quebec when I was 17 and then I went and lived in British Columbia, and then, it never really occurred to me until I was 18, that I wasn't fully from Quebec. I was in Victoria, walking down the street, and there was this couple from Quebec talking to each other and I just went over to them, and we chatted, and then the guy in the couple looked at me and said, "So you're not really from Quebec are you?" And he was just like "Wow. Where's your dad from?" And that for the first time in my life, I realized that I am not 100% Quebecois. I am like half.

RM: That's where you're from, that's where you grew up, you spent the majority of your life there but because your father was not Quebecois at all, you have that weird distinction. It's odd to me, it's interesting.

GC: Oh it's super odd. I mean years ago I remember there was something in the *Globe and Mail*, one of those big Canadian newspapers, this lady, she's probably a big deal in Canada, I just don't remember her name, but she had written something about how in Quebec people still frequently use the expression "Pure Wool" (*pure laine*) to describe someone who's 100% of Quebec heritage, and how that wouldn't stick anywhere else in Canada. I feel like, listening to Canadian radio, they're constantly talking about how cosmopolitan, and what's the word that they always use? Just the Canadian diversity, like being Canadian is being from wherever, and just identifying as a Canadian. I'm into that, but in Quebec it's a little different; it's very important to be this person who can say, "My mom is from Quebec, my dad is from Quebec," whereas to me I grew up in Quebec, I was raised in Quebec, and I speak English with an accent, so I feel like I'm legitimately from that place.

RM: One of the things I was wondering about the book is, what do you use for the viewpoint as you're telling your story? Are you trying to tell it through the eyes of how old you would have been then? It doesn't seem necessarily as reflective as much as kind of experiential.

GC: Yeah, I mean I'm sort of re-experiencing... Putting myself back in the place, back in the time it happened. Like, "I'm walking into the kitchen and I see this person that I really love, she is doing drugs...." Everything is in the present tense. It was more about the experience rather than rehashing something. When you're a child there're these things that happen before your eyes that you don't necessarily comprehend fully until later on; you look back on these strange memories, no matter what these memories are. It could be like going to the amusement park with your friends, and then you saw something, and then you're not too sure, but when you're older you realize like, "Oh my god, that homeless person was shooting up!" You only really realize these things later on. I really like using the present tense.

As I get older, I meet other children who have a missing father who lives in British Columbia. It's like a mythical Kingdom where dads go to disappear.

from *Susceptible*. Image courtesy Drawn & Quarterly

RM: One of the things I remember, and I hope I'm not spoiling the book for some folks, but you'll make references like, "this is the last time..." but it wasn't. You feel this interesting finality, at different points that you're going through, like things just seem kind of stuck in a way? Not sure stuck is even the right word. It just feels like they're difficult points for you to get through in this book.

GC: Yeah, I mean they weren't the funnest things to talk about, that's for sure. But I also feel that finality is something that I've come to understand, and appreciate more now that I've finished the book. You know I finished this book, and then it came out like six months or so after I finished it, and then people talk to me about it. There's that thing where you've completed a work, and get to experience it through someone else's eyes, and get to understand all these things about this project you just worked on. Like there was all this stuff I wasn't aware of that I became aware of later on. So I guess finality wasn't something I was aware of when I was working on the book, but now I am because people talk about it.

RM: You've done a lot of really gorgeous colour work, and I'm really curious about the choice to do it in black and white.

GC: I was actually just talking about this with a friend of mine a few days ago; I love black and white so much, I mean I guess that it did occur to me that if I made my book in colour it would be more expensive? Also I'm kind of hard-ass on printing things on the continent as much as possible. I didn't want my book printed in Asia, and I think that's a big turn off for a lot of publishers. I mean I don't think that's in the author's hands, we should just be grateful that the person is publishing you in the first place, but I don't know, maybe it's my heritage or whatever but I'm just feeling very sensitive about how crazy the direction we're headed is; with factories burning down in Bangladesh so we can have fresh clothes. So anyways, I'm not saying that getting printed in Singapore is the equivalent of getting clothes made in Bangladesh, I mean I don't actually know what their working laws are like over there, but I just felt like it should be kept close to home. Talking to Drawn & Quarterly about publishing the book, it was like, maybe if we print in black and white we can do it in Canada. But generally, the reason is I love greys and blacks; really good blacks and using a lot of white, and all these different shades of grey. It speaks to me a lot because a lot of the comics I grew up with were in black and white. When I discovered underground comics in the 90s everything was in black and white. I just feel like the book, as an object, is becoming popular to the point where every asshole on the block has a book that's in colour, and sometimes it's the most magnificent object, where the artist is amazing, but once in awhile you look inside the packaging and you wonder, was this really worth $35? Is this work worth being printed in colour? Does that sound mean?

RM: I've had discussions about printing overseas with folks, because I myself have certain challenges with it, because I believe in a living wage model. Like folks being paid the proper amount to live off of. And the reason we're able to get cheap books in Asia is because they're not getting paid a lot. As consumers we make a choice of where we want to get our product. And I think if we make a choice, where you know the folks are being paid fairly, that's just as much a part of the process as any other component.

GC: You know it's funny to me because while you were saying that I couldn't help but want to make a joke about how much cartoonists make. I worked on this thing for two and a half years, and got paid $2000. I completely agree with you, and I also totally believe we just make the type of culture we believe in. I like making things on a smaller scale, because it's just easier to keep control of so that's another thing. To be published by somebody like Drawn & Quarterly is not Rupert Murdoch, but it's a bigger step, just the type of book tour I had working with them. They have a lot of people who know what they're doing, whereas with a smaller publisher you maybe have one person. They know what they're doing, and there's many more circulating, and there's more of a reason to justify a book getting published halfway across the world, but to me there's also the environmental perspective, it's a little intense to know that your book is going to travel all the way from China to here, and that even with the shipping, it's still cheaper than had you done it here in like Manitoba or something.

RM: It does seem then that local culture is important to you, like the music festival you do — the Anacortes Unknown, and then you're also on smaller record labels. Do you have something on K records?

GC: Yeah I do. I have a 7-inch, and then they

put out a book record of mine in 2007. Actually everyone should buy that if they like my work, because it's just sitting on shelves, but I need to plug it, because I don't think people know that it exists.

RM: What's it called?

GC: It's called "Tout seule dans la forêt en plein jour," but you can just call it "Tout seul" which means all alone. All the songs and the drawings are based on war, the idea of war, the different types of war. It came out in 2007, and it's a 60 page book, with an LP.

RM: I'm pretty sure Lucky's has one in Vancouver, for Vancouver folks listening.

GC: Yes, thank you.

RM: How long have you been doing the music festival?

GC: Well, the first time I came to visit Anacortes, I was playing at the second edition of a festival that was called "What the Heck." That year I wasn't involved, but the third year I was involved in organize it, and so the festival lasted a total of ten years, and then the Anacortes Unknown music series that happened last summer, and then I made one happen this spring, that I curated, and we're having another one this summer, in July. So yeah, for me already now it's ten years of my life. I never really think about it that much, and then the other day this artist that lives in Anacortes, I was reading her CD and she describes herself as a community organiser, and I realized, "Oh man... she has her shit together. I wish I was a community organizer." and then I realized, "Holy fuck! I am!" I never really thought of myself that way, so now I'm bringing it up because I kind of get tired of talking about my book.

RM: It seems that your music and your comics, is sort of a balance for you.

GC: Yes, definitely. They come from the same person. I get kind of weary, because people sometimes are like, "They compliment each other," and I'm like, "Yeah, they kind of do." I get weary maybe because I'm in my thirties now and I want people to take me seriously… or I'm having an existential crisis. Not to toot my own horn, but "I am a cartoonist, because I am published, and because I think that my stuff is alright," but then I also see myself as a musician. I don't like putting labels on myself, but I guess I just don't want people saying, "Oh! She's a singing cartoonist," or, "She's a cartoonist who plays music on the side," because I take my music pretty seriously. And if other people whose music isn't that great can consider themselves musicians then I'm allowed to get that little notch in my belt. I just talk about all the things I do at once.

RM: I got that idea from looking at your site, listening to your music, looking at your work. I don't really see you in one little section. And it's interesting, because it makes you a more full-bodied artist, there are different ways to express what you're doing, and sometimes cartooning is limiting.

GC: Here's the thing about comics versus music. I have a lot of music in my life again all of a sudden, and the thing is when I'm in a situation of panic, comics will always be what feels more natural for me to do. It might be sort of a rare thing, but I've known since a young age that it's what I wanted to do for a living. And a lot of people are fighting for comics to be recognized as a legitimate art form, and to me that's really funny, I'm just, "Whatever, just draw comics." I really like drawing, I really like doing this, and I don't feel like I have to prove to any fancy pants gallery people that it's a worthy activity, but in terms of music it helps a lot because it's very lonely to draw comics, especially if you do the type of drawings I do; they're very selfish. You zone out for so many hours just spending a lot more time than necessary on some pages. I appreciate music because it gives me an outlet and this opportunity to go out. I think of music as being so social, like people will meet the love of their life, or have one night stands going to music concerts, but

you're not going to have that reading comics at your house. [*Laughs.*] I mean there's weird social comics that are becoming popular, like you know it's exciting, it's really beautiful to look at, but I often feel like, when I see crazy insane, Le Dernier Cri style zines, I'm like, "Oh yeah, you could read those at your house, and still have time to go out and party." But if you're gonna read something like *Big Questions*, in order to sit down and read that brick, that's a lot of nights not going out with your friends.

RM: I almost feel like if you're reading a lot of Le Dernier Cri books, you've got to party pretty hard.

GC: Yes! In all honesty it's beautiful, it looks exciting, it looks awesome to make this stuff, but it doesn't speak that much to me. Everyone is like, "You got to go to the zine festival!" freaking out about it. I felt really embarrassed after it because I went, and maybe all the really cool stuff was sold out or something? Because by the time I finally made it there, I didn't really feel that inspired. I want to read a straight up novel with no pictures in it. That's the zone I'm in lately. I love books, and I love the fact that there's so much content in this really small thing; you hold so much in your hand, as opposed to these crazy books where it's like a splatter of this Iron Maiden Eddie looking guy, whose eyeballs are bouldering out, and it's in neon orange!

RM: I think I know what you're talking about.

GC: I feel like I'm saying really weird, negative things. [*Laughs.*] What's wrong with me?

RM: You're giving us Canadians a bad reputation, we're supposed to be the nicest people.

GC: Well I've been living in the United States for a while now, so maybe that's why.

RM: I'm curious about the time when you really started making comics, like *Lait Frappé*, because you mentioned being in Victoria. Was there a development period for you in terms of finding your voice in comics? Even though you wanted to do comics for a long time?

GC: Well *Lait Frappé* was my first book published by somebody else that wasn't me. And I was still young, a teenage cartoonist. Before that, I did some mini comics, you know I experimented. So I didn't put that in *Susceptible*, I didn't mention anything about when I started at 15, making zine-like anthologies, the type with all photocopied pages, and some ad for a tavern at the back of the zine. So I would do that with other people in the Montreal underground comic scene and I think that I did a lot of trial and error back then, some pretty embarrassing stuff. Like part of the underground comics is you don't really know how to draw women yet? I think that's a French thing. Even though I was a girl myself, I felt like when I would draw a sexy lady she would just look really stupid, and so I did a lot of these dumb, violent comics, with a lot of poop stories, and then sort of settled down, in this place of feeling fine with drawing stories that were a little more relatable or emotional. And so *Lait Frappé*, was my publisher Benoit in Montreal and my first work. He and I had talked about it. He had seen some of the other things I'd done that were a little bit smarter, and he was like, "Yeah, I'd love to do a book with you." So I came up with that story. But now I don't remember what your question was, sorry.

RM: That's okay. So Julie Doucet was a really big influence on you at one point, and she's someone who's work you're still very much into.

GC: Yes, for sure. It's funny because people mention her a lot when they talk about my work. When I was younger it would come up in ways that were much worse, whereas now it's fine. People say, "She was an influence," and I'm just like "Yeah, yeah." The first time I ever saw Julie Doucet's work was in a comic shop in Victoria, Legends Comics, you must know that store right?

RM: Gareth Gowden, I know.

GC: Yeah! He's such a nice guy, I haven't seen him or talked to him in a million years. But so yeah, he was there but there was also this other guy named Grant and he owned the store. I didn't know my dad, but then I turned 15 and went to visit him and we went into Legends — and I had never seen underground comics before

and I saw *Dirty Plotte*, and my dad said that if I drew comics, that's what I would draw. And so I looked at it, and was like "Holy shit!" because this was a comic done by a woman from Quebec, and I was just like, "Holy fucking shit. What is happening in the world." It blew my mind, because right away I knew she must be French. and Doucet sounds very much like a Quebec name. It was mind blowing because at the time Julie was having this double life. She was an artist from Quebec who was quite successful, but it was not a thing that was on the radar. It was a big influence, but also through that store I discovered Rene French, who was also a big influence, and Debbie Drechsler, I got some *Hate* comics, got into Chester Brown, *Ed the Happy Clown*, which was a huge mindfuck to me as a teenager. So yes, yes, Julie was an influence. What else do you want to know?

RM: One of the reasons I like to bring up Julie is because to me she's one of the most important Canadian Cartoonists. She's someone who's work I'm very fascinated with, like the work she's making now. And you did an art show recently, in Anacortes, where you had your work, Julie's work, and some other women. I'm wondering if you could tell me a little about that.

GC: I guess the most cartoony of all the work was mine, and then there was this other Canadian artist, who you should check out. Her name is Nadia Moss, and she is incredible. She does illustration work, and at this particular art show she had these paintings made out of dirt, like maybe she used stencils or something, and spray-on glue on her canvases? From far away it would just look like spray paint, but up close you would see dirt and twigs and stuff. Julie also had some collages, and I really love what she's been doing in the last few years because she's got this super legit ethic. Like you said she's one of the most important Canadian cartoonists in your opinion, and I think there's two things that we don't need to put in front of the word cartoonist when people talk about Julie. I really hate the fact that people say "woman" cartoonist, and in a way, saying "Canadian" cartoonist is the same thing, because as nice as it is to have some sense of geography, I just think she's one of the best cartoonists, I would say probably top three. So she's got this amazing thing where people will say, "Oh she was one of the very best at this." I mean as much as people are mourning not being able to read more comics by her, her art to me now is so fucking exciting.

RM: It's really amazing. Really neat use of... I don't even know how to describe it. It's like a collage, and it's a lot of commentary on gender identity... I just get very excited by her collage work, it's really interesting, and there's a lot of thought.

GC: Yeah! And it's also very often hilarious. She has a really good sense of humour. You know she had this thing where she made up some new country, and used some world atlases, and cut up all the pieces, and made a new map of the world with a new country that she invented, and

putting in these rivers, and these noodle shapes on top, and then silk-screening all of that. The silk-screening itself is very precise, and then she makes up a language, and then a dictionary, and then she writes a personal diary in that language. And so you have to have the dictionary to read her private, personal diary, and then you learn all these super private details about her. That in itself is super deep. Some real next level shit.

RM: If I remember correctly, the show was on space?

GC: The theme of the show you mean?

from *Susceptible*. Image courtesy Drawn & Quarterly

RM: Yeah...

GC: In Anacortes?

RM: Yeah...

GC: Here's the thing, I called the festival and the show ours, and the festival was sort of paying tribute to the exhibition because it was up for a month and a half, and it sounds so fancy saying it this way, but it's Anacortes, so like 100-120 people came to the actual festival, and then the gallery had more than that. But in terms of having an event in a town this size, it was very successful. But the show, I called it ours because you know I started working on the show in September. At the time there was all these moron republican dudes saying things about women's rights, all these ridiculous quotes. Anacortes is sort of split two ways. You have the aging hippies, and then on the other side you have the conspiracy theorists; people who are pretty right wing, the kind of people that will live in a compound or something. Pretty libertarian views, but not like in a Chester Brown way.

RM: We get them a lot on Vancouver Island, where my dad lives.

GC: Right, yeah, totally. I mean the weather, everything is very similar to Vancouver Island, and so at the time I just felt like having some sort of statement that was mildly political, and have something that said "ours". It's really inoffensive, but I really wanted to have just a little political flavour. I mean I invited all women artists, but I didn't make a big fuss of it; I didn't want people to be, "Oh it's an art show with all women." And so I encouraged everyone to give me stuff that they felt had some sort of political meaning. And most of us had some stuff that was very gentle, but still pretty badass.

RM: What did you have for your own work?

GC: I just had a couple of things... I honestly didn't have as much as I would have wanted to have in the show, because I was busy helping everybody else. I did the invitation cards, and it was a painting of this lady lifting a very heavy rock. The painting itself was based on, having read *Susceptible*, this photo I have of my mom as an 18 year old. She was part of this work program for teenagers, where you travel around Canada, and so she's wearing this checkered shirt and her hair is braided. It was based on this idea of my mom as a very strong 18 year old. To me that kind of comes full circle, because I don't always necessarily put her in the best light, but that was, to me, paying tribute to her in another way. And then I did this other big painting of a teenage-looking person, that's buried in snow in an above ground swimming pool. Do you guys have that? Is that a thing in the English speaking world? Do you know what I mean? They're these super shitty pools that people buy.

RM: Yeah, Yeah, they're round and...

GC: Yeah! And instead of being dug into the ground, they're above ground. So it makes this image that I'm using for a record that's coming out soon. I did the image for the art show, and I wasn't happy with it, so even now as we speak I'm redrawing it and I'm very happy with the new version.

RM: Do you have any tours coming up for your music? Any shows?

GC: I am going on tour, but it's not for me. I'm going on tour with some friends, playing bass in a different band. I'm leaving the day after tomorrow; we're going to Europe for a little over three weeks. I'm very stressed out about it. But I don't have any music tours for myself, it's really hard to choose, because I have to make a choice. I'm very excited for my next book, but I also have this music in me, which feels like all these zits I have to pop or something... This music I'm trying to get out of my system. I'm the type of person who works very slowly, but I have a lot of ideas. So I've got all these broken up ideas to catch up on. Just trying to keep it all together.

RM: Do you want to talk about your next work? Or is it all pretty nucleus as far as just starting out?

GC: It's not nucleus, it's just that I'm worried that the thing's not going to get made, and that I'll look ridiculous because I talked about it too much, and then I work so excruciatingly slow, and there's always a moment where everybody is expecting the thing, and it's not finished yet. I can say though that the book will probably be about the same length as *Susceptible*. My two next books will be just exploring this thing that I'm curious about. My dad, who is barely spoken about in *Susceptible* — I actually don't know what the state of his Pagan beliefs are at the moment — but when I did meet him again, he was like a sorcerer, just very into potions and spells and all kinds of witchcraft related things. I used to roll my eyes at him as a teenager, because I'm not a very spiritual person, but there's this really intense attraction now. On tour, I've been going to all these shops where they sell crystal balls and stuff, and I'm talking to all these people, and I always feel like such a fraud because I go in there and I'm so scared that they can tell that a part of me is like, "This is bullshit." But there's another part of me that's very curious about it. So these are the things I want to explore before my next book.

RM: Nothing wrong with being a little curious.

GC: Yeah, Victoria is actually the witch capital of Canada, and I didn't even know that when I lived there.

RM: That and Nanaimo.

GC: Nanaimo? Really?

RM: There's a big Satanist festival there or something.

GC: I mean I'm not drawn to a Satan collective. I'm not spiritual, and I feel like in order to believe in Satan you have to believe in the Bible. I think that to believe in upside down crosses, you have to believe in the power of right side up crosses. They just look too much the same. Not into that.

RM: I feel like we're at the end of our time here, and I wanted to thank you for taking the time to talk to me today. Thanks so much for chatting with me.

GC: Thanks so much for having me. I hope nobody steals my ideas. ●

Postscript 2017:

In the lead up to doing this interview, Geneviève and I exchanged a number of emails, discussing our common friends and community with vigorous sassing in my general direction for taking so long to interview her. We were hoping to meet in person, since she lived just two hours away, and suggested a number of things to do and see in the weird town of Anacortes. She really loved the oddity to be found there, connecting it to Twin Peaks. In an email she describes some of her locals: "Many amazing characters in town. May-Louise, the 'lady with the hats'. The lawyer who looks exactly like Leland Palmer. And this man who designs the full-size wooden cut outs of historical Anacortes figures. After a crazy car accident in his early twenties he became quadriplegic and opted to ride around in a strange vehicle rather than use a wheelchair. His name is Bill Mitchell. He is pretty wild. I told him I draw comics once and he got so excited, went on and on and on about R. Crumb like he was this unattainable life-force few humans had ever seen in person. To him cartoonists are not only celebrities, but celebrities from forty years ago that you'd have to travel back in time to meet."

Understanding Anacortes helps you understand Geneviève and how a West Coast Quebecois transplant was able to flourish creatively. I really enjoyed talking to her about her life and experiences. After the interview we continued to correspond. However, within the next year she was diagnosed with inoperable pancreatic cancer. She passed away in July of 2013, leaving behind her husband and young daughter. — Robin ●

189

Michel Rabagliati

Interview by
Conan Tobias

The following pre-interview was conducted by email as background for a profile of Michel Rabagliati that ran in Quill & Quire in May, 2016. It appears here in its raw form.

Translation by
Michelle Winters

Conan Tobias: Your childhood and your parents seem to have been big influences on your work. What did your mother and father do for a living, and what were they like? Tell me a bit about the neighbourhood you grew up in.

Michel Rabagliati: I was born in New Rosemont, in Montreal, a fairly new neighbourhood, where a lot of young families came to live in the 50s and 60s. My parents liked that it was a middle-class area with a lot of services and parks and playgrounds for kids. Right next to us was one of the first shopping malls in the province, which opened in 1953 — the Boulevard Shopping Centre. There was also a Steinberg's supermarket, which had a service station attached to it. My mother, who loved anything modern, adored that "newfangled" place.

My parents both grew up middle class. My mother worked for a long time in manufacturing, on production lines, for Avon, and also selling women's shoes. My father was a typesetter. He had the opportunity to learn his trade as an appren-

tice in his early twenties, and went on to become a "journeyman." That kind of teaching, right on the shop floor, provided by mentors or masters, doesn't exist anymore. My father loved his job, and told me a lot about it at home. He was a jovial, funny, and very affectionate man.

CT: I understand there were a lot of comics in the house when you grew up. What was it about these comics that appealed to you?

MR: I was very much drawn to comics as a kid. In Quebec in the 60s and 70s, kids weren't reading about American superheroes. French and Belgian comic distributors were all powerful in Quebec, and magazines for kids, like *Spirou*, *Tintin*, *Pilote*, and *Pif*, were cheap and easy to find. My parents got me subscriptions to those magazines, because they didn't know what else to get me. That's all that interested me. I also think they were happy that I was reading and using my brain. When I was around 10 or 11, I started copying comic characters out of those magazines to practice drawing. I also tried to make a few

from *Paul Joins the Scouts*

strips myself. But I found it difficult and labour intensive. I have to say that what I appreciated most growing up was the freedom I had: the freedom to dream, to play, or just to do nothing. I feel very lucky to have been able to do what I wanted with my time, and I'm grateful to my parents for that.

CT: Can you tell me a bit about your life as a graphic designer? How did you start out, what were your goals, what type of work were you doing?

MR: Graduating from graphic design school in 1980, I started working freelance right away. I haven't worked in an office or an agency in my life, except for a few months. I really admired Paul Rand, Saul Bass, Push Pin Studios, and, a little later, the world of Neville Brody. My dream was to do poster art for big cultural events, but I didn't actually get much opportunity, and did whatever fell in my lap just to survive: logos, printing, annual reports. I really enjoyed my job as a graphic designer, but with the advent of computers, around 1986, I found that things were getting a little too complicated and that the tasks of the graphic designer were getting heavier and heavier. So I veered off toward magazine illustration. Creating unique illustrations was a lot less complicated than worrying about printing problems, colour separation, and all that. So I worked in illustration until around 2004, and ended up abandoning my final clients to devote myself to comics.

CT: Before going into graphic design you originally considered becoming a cartoonist. What prevented you?

MR: It's true, that was what I wanted to do as a kid. My father dissuaded me and directed me toward typography, figuring I'd have an easier time making a living in that career. Fortunately, I could sense the wind changing and that typography as a career was going to disappear very soon, so I refocused my attention on graphic design and, later on, on illustration. I don't regret it. I really enjoyed those jobs, even if I was dreaming about comics.

CT: How did you end up working with La Pastèque?

MR: It all started with Pastèque in 1998, when, by chance, I was walking past a bookstore on St. Denis in Montreal. Two young booksellers, Mar-

tin Brault and Frédéric Gauthier, were launching a new comic magazine, *Spoutnik*. I proposed a comic to them that I'd been working on at the office to kill time, between illustration orders. It was *Paul in the Country*. They were very interested in publishing it, so I asked for some more time to add another story, "Paul: Apprentice Typographer." That's how it all started, in October, 1999. La Pastèque was my first publisher and I was their first writer!

CT: How did you end up working with Drawn & Quarterly originally? How did that result in them publishing the first Paul story?

MR: I worked on a logo for D&Q in 1990. They used it for about two or three years. But it was in 2000 that Chris Oliveros showed interest in translating my first book, *Paul in the Country*.

CT: Why did you end up leaving D&Q and moving to Conundrum?

MR: It was D&Q who dropped me when *Paul à Québec* came out in 2009. They opted out because they felt that anglophones would have trouble grasping the Quebec spirit, the humour and everything. I've always found that a strange and mysterious decision because, in fact, that book was my greatest success: 50,000 copies sold, a feature film, and unparalleled critical success in Quebec. It even won the Angoulême International Comics Festival's audience choice award the same year. So when I felt I wasn't getting any more support from D&Q, I went to Andy Brown at Conundrum Press.

from *The Song of Roland*

THE FIRST NIGHT, THERE WAS MAYHEM IN THE BUNKHOUSE. EVERYBODY WAS OVEREXCITED.

from *Paul Joins the Scouts*

CT: Paul is often referred to as the Tintin of Quebec. How do you feel about that, and why do you think people say it? Is it just the album format, because the stories couldn't be less alike. Paul has much more "Canadian" adventures, in that, compared to Tintin, his life is very ordinary. He's probably never going to go to the moon.

MR: I think they're referring mostly to the popularity of the character. It's true that Paul has become a sort of Quebec comic icon. For the moment, he's the best-known "local" comic strip character. His face is also very simple, like Tintin: round head, two black dots for eyes, simple nose, line for a smile. Hergé's simplicity. But for me, that's as far as the similarities go. Tintin's universe is entirely fictional, while mine is more auto-fiction.

CT: Many of the Paul stories end with a very emotional event: the doll at the end of *Paul Has a Summer Job*, the crash at the end of *Paul Joins the Scouts*. How many, if any, of those events are pulled from your life.

MR: Most of the events are 85% true. I add a little fiction to make things more interesting, but only a little. The part I fictionalize, or lie about, the most is in the chronology of events. I reprogram the sequence of my real events to amplify the dramatic effect. I change the order of facts to give them greater impact for the reader. I'm always thinking about the reader's pleasure. It's important for me that the reader is having a good time reading my stories. So you have to work as a director. Straight ahead autobiography doesn't especially interest me.

CT: What was it like making the movie of *Paul à Québec*?

MR: I was involved in the production of *Paul à Québec* on a number of levels. I was the one who initiated the project at the beginning, in 2010. I contacted a filmmaker I really like, François Bouvier, and just asked him if he'd be interested in making a film based on one of my comics. He accepted, and we started work on *Paul has a Summer Job*. Then we changed focus to work on *The Song of Roland* [the English title of *Paul à Québec*]. So I co-wrote the script with the director. Also, at one point in the movie, Paul, played by François Létourneau, is drawing onscreen. It's actually me — my hand — drawing in those scenes. While we were filming, it was funny, because when they needed me they'd yell, "The hand!" I'm also shown singing in a choir, because I'm a choir singer in real life, and that's my actual choir performing in the movie. I also worked on the opening and closing credits, which are cartoons. Those cartoons are the work of Luc Chamberland, who directed an excellent documentary about Seth [*Seth's Dominion*] at the National Film Board. The film was critically and commercially successful. A lot of people said that we stayed very true to the spirit of the comic.

CT: Do you have a rough idea of what stories you'll tell of Paul in the future, or do you decide book by book?

MR: It depends on a number of things: on the story I feel like telling, on what I feel like drawing, and how I feel in my personal life. I know

that my next few books will be fairly different, because I've finished with the character's stories of childhood and adolescence. I'd like to write a story where Paul is 55 years old. That's where I am right now in life. It might not be very funny, but that's what I think I feel like doing. I'd also like to one day write stories that other people tell me. I'm not that eager to keep talking about myself for the rest of my days. ●

from Paul Up North

Originally published in:

Trip #8, 2014

Translation by
Aleshia Jensen

Interview by
Jean-Michel Berthiaume

In March 2014, we had the privilege of meeting with artist and cartoonist Zviane to talk about her work, her influences, and her never-ending quest for renewed creativity.

TRIP: Writing a book like *Le Bestiaire des Fruits* isn't something you start on a whim. It's not as simple as heading to the fruit aisle and trying everything you find.

Zviane: When I started trying different kinds of fruit, I actually wasn't planning on making a comic. I didn't even have a blog. I just like trying new things; and actually, if you look at my books, I often end up changing mediums. For a long time I used Rapidographs, like in *L'ostie d'chat*; they're architect pens that give you a consistent line thickness, always the same width. I finished everything off with a solid orange fill on the computer. The blog sketches I did at first were done with Microns or Staedtlers — cheap pens everyone uses because they're not that expensive but that actually don't last very long, so they cost more in the end — and grey markers. I used Rapidographs for *Going Under*, too, but with grey and black fills, no shading; it was a different graphic style. I used pencil in *For as Long as It Rains*, and something I'd never used before: a kind of giant mechanical pencil with a huge lead — like, 1.4 millimetres, a mechanical pencil I brought back from Angoulême and thought was cool because it was yellow. [*Laughs.*] The giant lead is good because it gradually becomes bevelled so you can get both a broad and fine stroke. It was a kind of square feel, with somewhat rough angles; it was a different feel drawing with it, so I wanted to try using it. But it was a crappy idea… [*Laughs.*] for a lot of reasons.

TRIP: Do you feel the pen you use affects your work?

Zviane: Yes, for sure. And it's also that you're changing the environment, because you're changing the feel in your hand, your way of thinking. When I "ink" in pencil, I'm a lot more careful about the order I draw things in so I don't brush my hand against the graphite, which means I don't draw things in the same order. And that's another problem I have: I'm left-handed. When I ink, I often go from right to left so that I don't smudge the ink or graphite. The thing is, I often start inking at the right-hand panel, then I go backwards, which means I don't really reread as I ink because I'm doing it out of order. Sometimes I wait until the panel's dry and go from left to right because it always turns out better when I go in reading order… except then I risk smearing the page with my hand.

TRIP: Let's talk a bit about your influences. You seem to draw on ideas from so many different places that they're hard to pinpoint. Has manga had a strong influence? And animation?

Zviane: Yes, for sure animation! That's what I wanted to do, but it's so time consuming. I took a year of animation at Cégep du Vieux Montréal. I still do a bit — I make animated gifs. I discovered manga a lot later, and I regret not having read it before. I watched Japanese anime, and at some point, I discovered these amazing manga series and thought, "How come I've never read these?!" For instance, I read *Dragon Ball* last year and was like, "OH MY GOD, it's SO good!" I read it and really regretted not having discovered it before, but I don't know if I would really have appreciated it if I had. While I was reading *Dragon Ball*, I was doing a comic for *Papier* (a comics magazine published by Delcourt), and I did a Dragon ball-style kick panel.

TRIP: Is that how your influences generally come into play?

195

Zviane: Always. I'm pretty much a sponge. I don't really have an original style. I'm pretty much cribbing ideas left and right. I imagine most people are kind of the same, but the thing is, I don't feel at all bad about copying other people. If people complain, I don't care; it just has to work. I read something somewhere that reassured me and I totally agreed with what the person said (because, when you steal things left and right, you end up asking yourself about your drawing style, about what exactly it is: "Is there a real me?" and that kind of thing). It was, I think, a Flemish guy who was presenting at Angoulême, who said, "In the end, you can copy style, but you can never really copy content." The things that can be plagiarized are things like graphics, ways to tell a story, but not the story itself. The story, it's so much a product of my own experience; I can't steal what someone else feels. That's why I'm never afraid people are going to copy me, because if someone is going to copy stuff, it's going to be a drawing or an idea or a layout, but they're never going to be able to copy anything in terms of story. All that to say, I copy a lot.

TRIP: So you're inspired by the world and what you read?

Zviane: One of my favourite things is just observing people. Even when I'm travelling, I like wandering the streets and people watching. I find going to museums almost boring. Maybe I'm just not there yet; I'm still a bit sleepy-eyed. [*Laughs.*] I'd rather watch people.

OK, I'm not a visual person; I'm really a musician. I realized this recently. There's something truly weird happening at the moment: I'm doing comics and it's starting to become my career, but I should really be in music. Because I have a really good ear and a crappy eye. I know I have a crappy eye; I don't recognize faces, because, five seconds ago, I couldn't have told you the colour of your shirt or your eyes! I don't retain that type of thing. And I talk to plenty of cartoonists and they notice everything. Iris said to me one time, "You're, like, blind!" because I don't even notice the colour of people's skin. At some point I realized that I'm barely able to draw without a reference, that I can't draw from memory. That's one of the reasons why I draw so rarely, because it requires so much effort.

However, with music, I have an excellent memory for pitches and rhythm. I don't have perfect pitch, but I do have relative pitch — relatively good [*Laughs.*] Good enough to get an exemption from my solfège classes in university. I could really develop my ear and do mixes, or whatever; I have the physical ability. More than for comics, but making comics is free, and you can work alone. I would have liked to work in animation but you can't work alone in animation — it's just not possible. That's what I like about comics: you can make a book by yourself. Which is not necessarily the case for many other art forms.

At the same time, I say that, but someone lent me a decent sound card and I'm trying to build a kind of mini studio at home, with a sound bank and my piano hooked up to my laptop, to get back into playing music. But in the same way I do comics. I was so used to the university contemporary music scene, where you have no choice

from *For As Long as It Rains*

> **"I should really be in music. Because I have a really good ear and a crappy eye. I know I have a crappy eye; I don't recognize faces, because, five seconds ago, I couldn't have told you the colour of your shirt or your eyes! I don't retain that type of thing. And I talk to plenty of cartoonists and they notice everything."**

but to depend on others, but, if you make electroacoustic music on your computer, you don't need performers, and you don't need to organize concerts, you make music like you make comics! That's what I'd like to do eventually: start a music blog.

TRIP: You said you want to make music the way you make comics. But do you make comics the way you make music? I'm curious to know how your music background has affected your creative process.

Zviane: I'm making a book about that right now [*Laughs*.], a zine. I made some blog sketches on the subject at one point. It's going to be called *Ping-Pong*. It's about the fact that there's a sort of ping-pong between the arts. Like things I sometimes do in music become similar to what I do when I draw. When I encounter problems, sometimes the solution is elsewhere: it'll be another field that helps me out. Like story-writing solutions. I realized at one point that it would be a good idea to do the composition exactly the same way I do animation: I do my key poses first and then my in-betweens. I do a rough sketch then add the details after. It's similar to what I do when I write music. I never go in a linear way; there are structures I'm a bit more comfortable with and that's pretty much what I'm trying to do in terms of writing the story: I do my key poses and my in-betweens. The same way I write music, the same way I write a story, the same way I animate.

TRIP: Coming back to your creative projects: do you work from home?

Zviane: At the start I worked from home, then in 2009, I went with the whole gang to 5555. There were ten of us: Sébastien Trahan, Michel Hellman, Catherine Genest, Vincent Giard, Julie Delporte, David Turgeon, Luc Bossé, me, my brother, and his girlfriend. It lasted almost a year. Then they moved to 7070, to the Maison de la BD. I was at that studio too. I went back to working from home for almost a year, a complete hermit. After that, in late 2011, I spent three months at 7070; it was fun — really fun! There were a ton of authors and we had dinner parties together. We worked on our comics (I was working on *L'ostie d'chat* a lot at that time) and someone would say, "Hey! We're making dinner. Who's in?" And we would all go grocery shopping and cook a big meal. It was super fun.

TRIP: There were a lot of people during that time, and we can see the work that came out of that period.

Zviane: That group is pretty much all people from Jimmy Beaulieu's *Vestibulles* workshop — it's kind of the common thread. In 2009, almost everyone knew each other through that workshop. Jimmy, the great uniter! [*Laughs*.] In late 2012, I moved into an apartment with Luc Bossé. We turned the biggest room in the apartment into an office for the two of us, and it was really fun working there. Recently I thought to myself, "Hey, it would be fun to go back to working in a studio." It's fun to having a workspace outside of your home. It helps create a boundary with work. But, whatever, at the same time, I keep working when I get home anyways. [*Laughs*.] I also find that when I'm around other people who are working, I can work for longer stretches, and I work more efficiently.

TRIP: And just like the pen you use and such, working in a studio must have an influence on your work.

Zviane: Right now, I'm just working on the script. I'm placing my Lego blocks. My approach is to kind of change styles, and that's something that's carried over from the very first comic I did. I see comics as being very similar to plays, which I think is evident in my work. I read once in an article that my comics have a lot in common with cartoons, and I pretty much agree with that. However, I took theatre all through high school, and comics are a bit like theatre. So, when I come up with my scenes, I often write dialogue with scene directions. Panel where she lowers her head, then looks to the right... It's written out — my first draft is written out, not drawn. Often, like for *L'ostie d'chat*, I had enough information with my written dialogue that I didn't have to draw up the layout. There weren't a lot of backgrounds, so I didn't need to do that much research. I had a good handle on my characters, so I went straight to pencilling; they were tiny pages, little pencil drawings. In *For as Long as It Rains*, I mostly blocked

it out as I went (I decided on the layout at the same time as I wrote the dialogue). When there was a lot of dialogue, I wrote it down on a separate page, but when there weren't many words, I drew the layout right away. But I'm a bit less comfortable with that method; I prefer writing rather than drawing; it was more to try it out, because I like trying things. But the thing that can be a trap with writing it out is that I often find myself narrating the same way, and certain scenes sometimes need to be narrated differently. With that method — writing things and laying out panels — it's hard not to default to a three-panel layout. For example, you'll rarely see a giant square panel with three little panels, and four little panels beside it, or a page with four-panel strips; those are things that my system doesn't allow me to do. In *For as Long as It Rains*, the storyboard was done on cardstock pages that were cut all crooked. The drawings were super messy too, roughly sketched stick figures. But I worked on loose pages. I used spiral notebooks before, but changed, because I wanted to be able to move pages around and add more — something I couldn't do with a spiral notebook. It let me skip pages, change the order, add pages, and there are also a lot of pages I cut out or just removed altogether. I redrew the sex scene three times. It wasn't working because there was no progression. At some point, I realized it was just people having sex. I was too preoccupied by "how I should do this." It's already a huge challenge to write choreography, and the sex scene also had to recap the book's entire story.

TRIP: The musical score, the buildup...

Zviane: You can't think it all up at once, the sex scene with the musical score; the first thing I thought was, "I want to have a sex scene with a score." I started by writing the scene, then dealt with the score after. I checked out some porn, took notes, because at some point, you question how you're going to do it; touching the face and things like that are nice in theory, but what do people actually do? I didn't want anything too weird, either. It had to be pretty banal. I wanted there to be something happening too, a sort of buildup to a disagreement. I thought, "What do I want, first of all, in terms of time." I figured, in terms of pages, that two pages at the start would be reader-friendly, and then something happens, and then, back to reader-friendly for another two-three pages, then, whoops, it would be cool if there was a spread with the score (something I do all the time in my books!), but that you feel like the score is the same thing as the comic. It would just be graphic symbols that tell you what's going on. And it would serve as an ellipsis, otherwise the scene would have been too long. I wrote up the scene and then I thought, "OK, let's invent a notation system." It didn't take long, because I knew exactly what I wanted. I wrote the score, I showed it to a few people who said, "Hey, it would be cool if the key was in the inside cover flap." To invent the notation, I thought, "What are the parameters?" The parameters for intensity, contact, positions, and speed. At first, I wanted to make sure the musical staff represented parts of the body. The upper lines would be the upper body: the first line would be the head and the second, the shoulders, etc. but that system was too imprecise! When you see a score, the lines

or spaces represent pitches; that's not how a sex score should work. In fact, what it should be, is the height on the staff should correspond to the degree of intensity. If you just graze with your hand, or if you punch, down low is more delicate, and up high, more intense. I used the height on the staff to show intensity, rather than write f (for *forte*), p (for *piano*), or write in crescendos. I represented the parts of the body with a schematic, a pictogram that looks like a body part, for example, a semblance of a hand. Each pictogram has a little black square that's a bit like the round part of a note, the part which indicates its position on the staff. Two pictograms side-by-side are two parts of the body that touch (touching themselves or their partner). Like for musical scores, above, there are tempo indications; I left those in Italian. I also put the sexual positions above the staff, to indicate the environment, and how the two characters were positioned. Also, the movements (the movements — that's one thing that could use some reworking): there was the solid line (stay there) and the dotted line (a movement from here to there). Once I'd written the scene and had the notation system, all I had to do was transcribe it. The spread where we only see the score without the drawing was the toughest part to figure out, because I wanted it to be precise, to have a progression — it's far from being just whatever! And if someone looks at the spread in detail and decodes everything correctly, which no one is going to do, they'll realize that the guy, he slaps the girl.

TRIP: No?!

Zviane: Yes! And it's completely clear that he's slapping her. This is why the girl gets really angry, and when you turn the page, the couple is fighting. It was important for me that, even if no one reads it, that it works. The score is there, part of the comic too. Musical scores are practically comic art anyways, they're pictograms — graphemes, if you like — that indicate movement, that have a certain meaning: it's a language. Musical scores and comics aren't that far from each other. 🌑

L'ostie d'chat

Shared Spaces: The Making of a Collaborative Comic
by Eric Bouchard

Originally published in:

Trip # 7, 2012

Translation by Helge Dascher

L'ostie d'chat [*The Fucking Cat*] is above all about two characters: Jasmin Bourvil and Jean-Sébastien Manelli, twenty-somethings whose friendship goes back to the start of high school, with all the usual highs and lows, especially once women come into picture. There's also Legolas, a ridiculous, mangy cat whose care they share as they sort through life's many other frustrations. A pathetic excuse of an animal, it's the legacy of a time when they lived with a couple of roommates, including Steve, the cat's former owner, who went on to commit suicide. Also populating their world are girlfriends, ex-girlfriends, Jasmin's musician friends, Jean-Sébastien's programmer pals, the regulars at the bar, girls with borderline personality disorders, and difficult family members. It all goes down in the ambience of the crooked-floored apartments around Montreal's St-Denis and Mont-Royal streets, complete with near-empty refrigerators, six-packs of beer, overflowing trash bins, unwashed dishes, and blocked toilets.

But the world of L'ostie d'chat steers clear of pathos. Balancing out the drama is a joyous succession of doomed plans, Jasmin's awkward blunders, and Jean-Sébastien's jubilant ego trips, as well as sexual escapades as complicated as they are uninhibited. It's a chronicle of the life and tribulations of young adults on the cusp of settling down, although it sometimes seems like they'll never get that far.

While the arc of the story is straightforward, what makes it so engrossing are the incidents and interactions among the characters. But L'ostie d'chat also presents a number of innovations that deserve attention, especially around the dynamics that result from its alternating authorship.

Going digital

There is no real term in French to describe the product of Iris's and Zviane's unusual collaboration. Webcomics — digital comics posted in regular instalments on the Web — are well-established in the English-speaking world, but francophone cartoonists are still hesitant in this area, so much so that the French language has no equivalent word for the medium. While an entire cohort of francophone cartoonists keep comic blogs in which they bare their souls on a daily basis, very few use the method to create long stories in a serial format (a notable exception is Thomas Cadène, creator of *Les autres gens*).[1] This is especially true in Quebec, where L'ostie d'chat stands out as a pioneer.

Of course, the paper version of L'ostie d'chat gives it a whole new lease on life. This phoenix-like revival was launched the same week as the appearance of the digital version's epilogue, which ended an adventure that lasted two and a half years and some 500 pages, and enjoyed a following well beyond Quebec's borders. With 800 to 1,000 visitors per instalment, an online Korean translation,[2] and publication under Lewis Trondheim's acclaimed "Shampooing" imprint, L'ostie d'chat, a joint creation by Iris and Zviane, is the first real success story of Quebec's comics blogosphere.

This is not the first time that the two cartoonists have seen their online work end up in bookstores. Published in 2006, Iris Boudreau-Jeanneau's *Dans mes rellignes* presents a collection of daily pages she posted on *Monsieur le blog* the previous summer. And compilations of the strips posted by Sylvie-Anne Ménard, aka Zviane, on the blog she has kept since 2006, were published in two large volumes entitled *La plus jolie fin du*

201

"Webcomics – digital comics posted in regular instalments on the Web – are well-established in the English-speaking world, but francophone cartoonists are still hesitant in this area, so much so that the French language has no equivalent word for the medium."

monde (2007) and *Le quart de millimètre* (2009).[3] But how did the two cartoonists come to create a collaborative project? They obviously share a kinship in terms of age, style, and approaches to distribution, but what role did geography play? To what extent was neighbourhood, which is a theme in the story, also a factor in its creation?

A digression on neighbourhood

There was a time when what could be described as a school of Quebec comics, or at least a movement — the Montreal comix scene around Henriette Valium — practically had a physical address. It should be said that the tormented life of the streets was one of the subjects it explored with special verve, with many of its cartoonists sharing a predilection for describing a motley, decadent, cursed bunch of urban dwellers caught up in various dependencies. The language was inflected by *joual* (Montreal's spoken French) and brazen misspellings, and the style was emphatically inventive and imbued with often obscene humour.

Most of these artists haunted Montreal's Centre-Sud: they lived in the neighbourhood and also found in it the ideal theatre for their artistic concerns. Zooming in, one would have seen that one of its epicenters was the stretch of Cartier Street between Sherbrooke, Ontario, and Lalonde – an interzonal space between the gentrified Plateau-Mont-Royal and the imagined wildness of Centre-Sud. In the late 1980s, a number of the movement's most representative artists, including Siris, Richard Suicide, and Caro Caron, lived in the area, some even as roommates.[4] They paid a kind of homage to it in comics such as *Le zoo de la rue Cartier*[5] and *Chroniques de la rue Cartier*. In a short biography that appeared on the website of the event Nuit blanche sur table noir, Suicide made a point of specifying that the "centre of the world" was located at the corner of Cartier and Ontario. It's worth noting that Julie Doucet lived right there, on Ontario between Papineau and Cartier, from 1987 to 1993, a time when she was working on her zine *Dirty Plotte* and publishing

English-language work in *Weirdo*, a magazine edited by Robert Crumb.

The neighbourhood, a hotbed of creation in which a community of comic book artists lived their real and imaginary lives, may have had the highest-ever density of comic book artists per square kilometre in Quebec.[6] This proximity and creative intimacy fostered a certain cohesiveness in one hub of the Montreal comix scene. But did it also lead to the emergence of joint projects, other than collectives? Unfortunately, with the exception of a few collaborations in magazines and zines of the day, little remains of the work that generated the most interest at the time.[7]

Getting back to our subject, it seems that a new mini-epicenter has recently emerged just one street east of Cartier, on Dorion Street. Iris, who has always admired and felt an affinity for the creative world of Centre-Sud, was the first to move there. A year later and a few houses down the street, she was joined by her friend and fellow-cartoonist Zviane, who had previously lived far off-centre in the city's Villeray neighbourhood. That's all it took for talk about collaboration to come up between the new neighbours (or pseudo-housemates). As such, could it be that this idea of neighbourhood was the basis of their joint project?

A stylistic autopsy

Shared spaces: shared pages? Some people claim that the two cartoonists have similar styles; and yet even a cursory reading of their respective pages in the edifice they have constructed together reveals the opposite. In fact, stylistic consistency would have been surprising. In several works of tenant-themed fiction, even authors working on their own switch voices as they move from one apartment to the next. In *La Vie mode d'emploi*, Georges Perec passes through every unit of an apartment block at 11 Rue Simon-Crubellier, shifting literary styles as he goes. In *Cages*, Dave McKean takes us into the apartments of the tenants of Meru House, adopting a different visual style for each.[8] In the case of Iris and Zviane, what stands out at first glance is the very different way they each approach the tabular space of the page.

Zviane and the Italian operetta

It's no secret that Zviane has an all-consuming passion for classical music, as well as for musical notation, a system used not only to indicate pitch but also to manage time — a formal concern that has inevitably worked its way into the composition of her comics. She also has a strong interest in Japanese comics, with their kinetic energy and tendency to feature micro-sequences, silences, and moments that linger like suspended musical notes. One could say that Zviane favours *meaningful* layouts; in fact, even her regular layouts seem intended to convey a specific dynamic.

Thierry Groensteen, who reorganized Benoît Peeters' typology of layouts (he considered Peeters' parameters – conventional, decorative, rhetorical, and productive[9] – too restrictive), would classify Zviane's tabular composition as *ostentatious*.[10] This is because in Zviane's work, as mentioned above, even a *regular* layout[11] is not necessarily discreet; its regularity becomes a deliberately visible device in a compositional approach aimed at pacing the story.

Zviane

The fact that a character of Italian origin is paired with Zviane gives her further opportunity to indulge her musical inclinations. While Jean-Sébastien Manolli comes across as *forte*, his family registers as *fortissimo*: its members include an uncompromising and authoritarian father, a fawning but intrusive mother (she wields an iron fist in a velvet glove), an extroverted brother, and a powder keg of a sister, prone to bouts of madness. Their family environment is rarely calm, and the home is all the more theatrical when the verbal fireworks break out in Italian, the language of passion. Unsurprisingly, it's all reflected in Jean-Sébastien's impulsive and self-centered personality. And stylistically, the various elements combine to give Zviane's narrative space

in *L'ostie d'chat* the feeling of an Italian operetta.

This combination of theatre and classical music, with its blend of comedy, song, and dance, is especially apt to describe Zviane's extravagant, modulated, and capacious "phrasing." Though the word "dance" may seem surprising here, it captures her interest, not only in aspects of time, but also in the drawn representation of movement. Another influence in this regard was a university course in animation, which led to various experiments that Zviane posted on her blog, as well as one of the most delightful sequences in *L'ostie d'chat*, which unfortunately could not be reproduced in the paper version. But the kinetic impulse inherited from animation still comes across throughout, giving expressive life to both the expansive and the restrained movements of her characters' bodies in space.

"Iris and Zviane's pages can be understood as two avatars of the abstract universe that is L'ostie d'chat, like two tips of a giant iceberg poking out of the water."

Iris and cartoony comix

Enter Iris Boudreau, whose influences are rooted in comix culture. Her pages mark a change of register: their sensitive and elastic drawing and discreet layouts reveal a more intimate approach to comics.

Boudreau is known for her involvement in the world of zines, where self-publication isn't synonymous with exclusion, but a value in itself. Often photocopied and stapled by the authors, zines lay claim to a status that is inaccessible to industrially published books: while printers and distribution channels can become intermediaries or filters that make a book "anonymous," zines, with their small runs, retain an element of soul. Every copy has its own individuality and its own flaws, and the work produced is somewhere between a book, a work of art, and a happening.

Despite having put out noted professionally-produced comics (*Dans mes rellignes*, *Justine*), Boudreau has self-published since the start of her career, and she shows no sign of letting up.[12] As crystallized in vivid and political terms by Alex Baladi in *Encore un effort*,[13] the world of zines is often — and unfortunately — considered to be the minor leagues, like a preliminary circuit prior to professional publication from which artists need to free themselves, when in fact it can (and should) also be seen as a creative laboratory. It is a fertile space precisely because it is free and personal. For Iris, the DIY zine, or *carnet*, remains the medium of choice for creating comics. First, the *carnet* (a French word derived from the Latin *quaternum*, meaning folded in four) offers a workspace whose size is equivalent to that of the printed page, unlike the oversize drawing page

that is the standard in conventional comic book production. In the case of zines, the printed (or digital) result provides a more honest reproduction, avoiding the effects of reduction, which alter the original drawing. In addition, the format introduces a certain spontaneity to the page and the drawing. Often, the tedious work of penciling is bypassed; the style is economical; the functional layout gets straight to the point. Since Iris is interested above all in storytelling, the distinctive space represented by the *carnet* takes on what may be its original function: that of a small portable medium intended for note-taking, or, given the spontaneity it demands, for a certain *automatic* way of writing.

In Iris' work, spare and functional does not mean inexpressive. This is where her connection to comix culture becomes evident. Her synthesized system of representation allows distensions and deformations to insinuate themselves, underpinned by a situational sense of humour rooted in Anglo-Saxon culture. In emotional situations, limbs twist or soften, and faces go from discreetly rounded and semi-realistic to compressed, passionate, and geometric — an approach that calls to mind the styles of contemporaries like Peter Bagge and Matt Groening.

Comics in close quarters

L'ostie d'chat is a shared space in more than one way: it is a common living and meeting space for two artists who are also neighbours; a narrative space leased and occupied by two cartoonists; a tabular surface that moves back and forth between two distinct graphic styles; and a story inhabited by the personalities of two characters.

There are other examples of well-known cartoonists who work in tandem, including Philippe Dupuy and Charles Berbérian, Eric Warnauts and Guy Raives, and, more recently, the couple known by the joint pen name Kerascoët, all of whom work in silent alchemy, with both contributing to the same drawings and building every image together. By contrast, the "fusion" of Iris and Zviane occurs at the level of the storyline, a space in which the extravagant personalities of these two young artists are offered fertile ground to develop the adventures of their many characters; it does not, however, extend to the drawing. The two cartoonists take turns producing short chapters of the same story, which follows its path independently of their distinct graphic styles. Of course, the chapters they create are coloured by their respective styles and approaches to composition. But while each of the main characters has a designated creator, the arrangement is not absolute, and as characters pass from one pencil to the other, their "skin" changes a little, too. For instance, Zviane gives Jasmin a more Latin touch, and Iris has Jean-Sébastien looking more cartoonish.

Iris

Because of this, it can seem in *L'ostie d'chat* as though the characters were swapping out their creators, and not the reverse. Given that Jasmin, Jean-Sébastien and the rest are all equally capable of switching between the looks given to them by Iris or Zviane, and of evolving in both a Boudrellian and Menardian space-time without significant distortion to their nature, readers come to see the characters as claiming their own existence, independent not only of the cartoonists' graphic styles, but also of their imaginations. The characters seem to evolve in an abstract space, unknown to their creators, that allows them to adopt multiple poetic and aesthetic identities, and to exist in parallel worlds that are often tangential, since points of contact can happen at any moment. To use an analogy from television, it's as if two TV stations were tasked to produce the

same soap opera, and the viewer, with no remote control in hand, were exposed to abrupt but regular channel changes without losing the narrative thread, as though the story had a "will" of its own.

In *Le cadavre et le sofa*, Tony Sandoval uses a narrative process that suggests a similar analogy. Readers witness the evolution – albeit somewhat static, and for good reason – of Polo and Sophie, two bored teens who spend a summer in the country (a well-used theme if there ever was one, thanks to the introspection it allows). With no other distractions available, they spend their days sitting either on a couch in the middle of a field, next to the corpse of a young man, or on another couch that belongs to Sophie, who has a television with 180 channels. Or is it a television that has turned 180 degrees to look in on itself? As Boris Vian put it in a song: "I turned it around... / The other side was captivating..."

Sandoval's chameleon-like virtuosity is on display in the comic: the graphic treatment shifts according to mood, leaving readers with a sense of constant stylistic zapping. As Polo confides, he wants nothing less than to watch every channel, but he becomes so obsessed with Sophie's beauty and nonchalance that he quickly sees "the 180 channels [move] into the background." Into the background or onto the same plane as the story itself? A strange metonymy presents itself, in which the medium seems to have internalized the media element at the heart of its story.

But despite the cartoonist's stunning virtuosity, the characters in *Le cadavre et le sofa* remain tethered to their creator; Jasmin and Jean-Sébastien, by contrast, seem to belong only to themselves, with no other anchor.

While Sandoval switches between styles, Daniel Goossens' early work offers examples of *narrative* zapping. On a single page, and sometimes within a single strip, unexpected breaks disrupt the narrative continuum, while other scenes (often interrupted) are suddenly sutured. The coherence of these disparate collections finds its legitimacy, not in the logic of the narrative sequence, but in the *thematic* thread of the subject at hand. It is as though Goossens were playing a single-handed round of exquisite corpse (a Surrealist method for collaborative image-making), with each new scene governed by the concealment of the last.

Although zapping exists in *L'ostie d'chat*, it operates only at a stylistic level; the narrative thread remains essentially intact. Still, a dimension of the exquisite corpse method is discernible in the work, to the extent that a "pass it forward" logic governs its production and publication.

Manifest traces

The above reflections all lead us to the ellipsis, the central narrative device of comics. Whether it's a question of changing channels, places, styles, or panels, a comic takes form as the set of all manifest traces of a void, that is, of an absent, potential, immaterial world. As such, Iris and Zviane's pages can be understood as two avatars of the abstract universe that is *L'ostie d'chat*, like two tips of a giant iceberg poking out of the water.

A whole online community will be mourning the end of the regular and entertaining instalments of the collaboratively created story. No doubt somewhere in the cartoonists' minds, other avatars of Jasmin, Jean-Sébastien, and the rest still subsist, not entirely Zviane-esque and not entirely Iris-esque either, but evolving on their own, independent of their creators. ●

ENDNOTES:

1. http://www.lesautresgens.com; paper edition published by Dupuis.

2. South Korea is key international market for online comics. The Seoul International Cartoon and Animation Festival (http://www.sicaf.org), which grants awards for best international productions, in 2010 received some 3000 submission from 32 countries.

3. *Dans mes rellignes* (Mécanique générale, 2006), 104 pp; *La plus jolie fin du monde* (Mécanique générale, 2007), 304 pp; *Le quart de millimètre*, (Grafigne éditions, 2009), 337 pp.

4. Friends and occasional collaborators were also neighbourhood regulars.

5. Siris, *Baloney*, t. 2: *Le zoo de la rue Cartier* (Zone convective, 1997), 32 pp.

6. Excluding, of course, the co-operatively run studios. Of these, the most significant today is probably the studio at 7070 St-Hubert (http://atelier.aencre.org).

7. Among titles still available today are the short stories with a Centre-Sud feeling by Caro Caron and Richard Suicide, published in the first two issues of *Cyclope* (Zone convective, 2000 and 2003); Suicide's stories in *My Life as a Foot* (Conundrum Press, 2007); and, of course, compilations from Julie Doucet's *Dirty Plotte* period, such as *My Most Secret Desire* (Drawn & Quarterly, 1995) and *Ciboire de criss!* (L'Association, 1996).

8. Georges Perec, *La Vie mode d'emploi* (Paris: Hachette, 1978), 641 pp; Dave McKean, *Cages* (Northhampton, Mass.: Kitchen Sink Press, 1998), 500 pp.

9. Benoît Peeters, *Case, planche, récit: Lire la band dessinée* (Paris: Casterman, 1998), 41 ff.

10. Thierry Groensteen, "Chapitre 1.11 – De la mise en page," *Système de la bande dessinée* (Paris: PUF, coll. "Formes sémiotiques," 1999), 107-119.

11. Groensteen prefers the word "regular" to Peeters' "conventional;" both refer to what can simply be termed a "grid."

12. Examples include *Comment j'ai raté ma peine d'amour* and *Tear in my beer* (2008); *Occupez-vous des chats, j'pars* and, with Zviane, *Stie qu'on est ben* (2009); and *Petites histoires – Numéro un* (2011).

13. Alex Baladi, *Encore un effort* (Paris: L'Association, coll. Éprouvette, 2009), 80 pp.

The Sacred and the Profane:

Obom on Making Comics in Montreal
Interview by Helge Dascher

Never before published

Translation by Helge Dascher

A wondrous, wistful world takes shape in Diane Obomsawin's comics and animations. I've translated a few of them, always awed by their combination of simplicity, humour, and resonant depth. Often their protagonists suffer harm through no fault of their own. A transformative imagination helps some endure, like the foundling in the graphic novel *Kaspar* (which Diane also made into an animation) and the child in the autobiographical short film *Here and There*. Hurt flows into hope in the stories of first love and coming out in *On Loving Women* (adapted into the animated short *I Like Girls*). A combination of tenderness and vaudeville panache runs through everything: a flying carpet crosses the sky with verve, Jaws' toothy mouth opens into an abyss of woeful sorrow, roses bloom with éclat.

Diane was born in Montreal and raised mostly in France, attending a succession of schools in the transatlantic back-and-forth between her divorced parents. In her early twenties, she returned to Montreal for good. With roots in graphic design and editorial illustration, she came into her own as an animator and cartoonist in her thirties. Out of a meandering stream of activity have come acclaimed animations and graphic novels, as well as illustrations, installations, sculptures, gifs, and other creations, all marked by her gentle humour and masterful sense of storytelling.

When I first met Diane, aka Obom, she lived in a nineteenth-century greystone building in Old Montreal that was inhabited by an assortment of artists and shady characters. Nothing was up to code. The apartment was strangely angular, but its high ceilings gave it a feeling of generous spaciousness. A bird feeder hung in front of its large windows, and when these were open, birds flew in and out, familiar and unconcerned. With its low rent, the apartment was one of a series of charmed spaces that have given her the freedom to develop as an artist.

We got together for the following interview in the apartment that is her home and studio today. It is in the Plateau neighbourhood, in a vine-covered building surrounded by greenery that conveys a similar sense of connection between the worlds inside and out. I came wondering about the influences that helped shape her unique voice and how life in Montreal has played into it all.

Getting started

Helge Dascher: Let's start at the beginning. Have you always drawn?

Diane Obomsawin: Yes, always. I drew the way all kids do. It goes back so far I don't remember when I started. But the thing is, at some point I decided not to stop. I had an older step-brother who had gone to the École des Beaux-Arts in Paris, so I knew that you could study art and eventually do something with it. And I told myself: okay, that's what I'll do. I'll keep drawing and at some point I'll just slide into art. It was like not growing up, but without being self-destructive, because I knew there was a future in it.

HD: You moved around a lot when you were young. Was being good at art part of your identity as a kid?

DO: Not at all. I was 17 or 18 before anyone considered me good at art. When I was little, it was more like, "What a vivid imagination!" It wasn't: "Oh, this is so beautiful!"

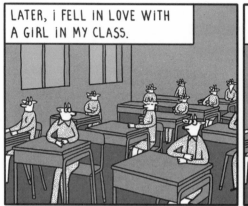

from *On Loving Women*. Image courtesy Drawn & Quarterly

Actually, recently — yesterday, in fact — I discovered that I still don't know how to draw. I came across an article where a bookseller recommends *Kaspar* and *I Like Girls*. She says: "Don't let the primitive style put you off." That was still fresh in my mind this morning, and I thought, "I really wish I knew how to draw." I have a good graphic sense so I can get by, but knowing how to draw is a whole other story. I was playing Pictionary one day and nobody could guess what I was drawing. [*Laughs.*] I can't draw – it's a fact.

HD: So how would you describe your graphic style?

DO: It's very naïve, very simple, very primary. I've been thinking a lot about it lately. I'd like to deconstruct my drawings completely: no mouth, no details, just silhouettes. A bit like Keith Haring. Or just squares and geometric forms. I did a comic a while back using nothing but circles. The panels were so small that I couldn't draw tall characters, so I drew them as balls. It was fun to do, and their roundness gives them a nice graphic quality. I'm looking closely at things right now and thinking about what direction I could go in.

from *Cyclops*

HD: Where did your interest in comics come from?

DO: It started thanks to my step-brother in France. He was into *Spirou*, so he asked my step-father for an allowance. And when he got an allowance, my brother and I got one too, and every Saturday, we'd do a comics run to the little corner store. I'd buy a *Pif* and a few Carambar candies.

So I read *Pif* and later *Pilote*, but I also made comics. They had a kind of double purpose. On the one hand I wanted to make my mother laugh. I'd draw stories about everyday life and take her side in things. But there was a flip side as well. I used comics as an outlet, because our family got on my nerves.

HD: Did you show her your comics?

DO: Yes. She didn't like the ones about the annoying family at all. But the ones that showed her in a good light made her laugh. When my mother laughs, she laughs until she cries – it's very encouraging. I still love showing her my work because her response is so great.

HD: How old were you when you were drawing those?

DO: About 11. After that, I left France to live with my father in Montreal. It was difficult because I didn't see him a lot — he worked at night and I was at school all day. He enrolled me in an English-language "New Canadians" class. I was young, I got my period for the first time, I couldn't speak to my father about how I was feeling. I was lost, really lost, in every way, and I used comics to express how lost I was.

HD: Did you draw comics with friends?

DO: No, not at all. It was a very solitary activity. I didn't show them to anybody, either. So that was a tough time, and I eventually went back to France. My mother was angry because I'd gone to live with my father, plus I'd basically missed a year because of the New Canadians class and she didn't know what to do with me. My old school finally agreed to take me back, and I ended up with an incredible teacher. She changed my life. She had us write poems in class. The first one I handed in was very short, and she wrote an entire novel on the back in red ink, with recommendations about books to read — the Surrealists, Raymond Queneau, and so on. She basically opened the door to who I still am today. I started drawing comics again and I'd send them to her.

HD: In those comics, were words as important as the drawings?

DO: Yes, always. And they still are for me. I'd even say that writing comes first. When I worked

"On the one hand I wanted to make my mother laugh. I'd draw stories about everyday life and take her side in things. But there was a flip side as well. I used comics as an outlet, because our family got on my nerves."

on *Kaspar*, I was worried that I might be short on time. I told myself: I'll write, I'll place the text in the panels to work out the rhythm, and if I run out of time, I'll draw stick figures. I was willing to do that. So writing comes first, and I deal with the drawing after.

HD: How did you first come into contact with underground comics?

DO: Through my mother. She went on a trip to the US, and she brought back a book of American underground comics for me. That's how I discovered Robert Crumb. I don't remember the others, but Crumb really stuck with me. I was into dark humour, and my mother gave me books from the French underground, too.

HD: Did they interest you right away? Did they influence you?

DO: Absolutely. And it was the spirit of the times, as well. There was *L'Écho des savanes*, with Gotlib, which shattered all kinds of taboos. It was such a rich moment. Julie Doucet has said that it was thanks to *Charlie Hebdo* that she gave herself the permission to do what she was doing. She told herself: if they can go there, I can go anywhere, I can say whatever I want. So it was a magnificent time — a time of real expressive freedom.

Growing as an artist

HD: How old were you when you came to live in Montreal?

DO: I was about 23 when I came back for good. I lived in an apartment that cost $45 a month. It was in a small wood house with a wood stove. And I found a small studio. It had a front door I loved, all covered in posters. When I met the artists there, we really hit it off.

HD: Was their work commercial or underground?

DO: They were totally underground. Before I joined the studio, there was a speakeasy in the basement, just to give you an idea of the atmosphere... and one of them, Benoît Fauteux, had built a cabin with a wood stove on the roof. So there was the speakeasy in the basement, the cabin on the roof, and this totally unconventional studio. There was a lot of sharing of ideas, a lot of alcohol (which backfired on me), and a lot of doing nothing much at all, just playing cards.... It wasn't great for making money, but it was a brilliant place to grow as an artist. Especially in the beginning.

HD: That was in the 1980s. Did you know Julie Doucet at the time?

DO: Yes. She was working at a photocopy shop, Copia, on Rue Ontario. I traded with her: I gave her a drawing, and she gave me all her *Dirty Plottes*. I still have them. I even have the envelope I got them in.

HD: Did you know Sylvie Rancourt's work back then?

DO: I did, actually. I found out about her through a friend. That was back when she was drawing the books herself. They were absolutely fascinating.

HD: Were you making comics too?

DO: No, I wasn't making comics at all. I was doing editorial illustration, which was the freest thing I could find at the time. When I arrived in Montreal, I went to see a few advertising agencies, because I'd worked in advertising in France. One guy did me a real favour. He said: "I like your work, but it's too distinctive. Keep doing what you're doing. Follow your own path. Your creative universe is already too precise. It's not adaptable." That was a real gift in a way. After that, I decided I'd try animation. I knew nothing about it, but I got a job and figured I'd do basic stuff, learn, and eventually make a film. Except I wasn't very fast at drawing acetates. And the same thing happened. They said: "Don't waste your time with us. Do your own thing, make your own films. We'd rather help you with your projects than see you waste your time with us – and have you wasting ours."

Julie was self-publishing back then. She had a PO Box in which she'd get all these letters. I thought to myself: if I had a PO Box, I'd get letters from around the world too. But of course she did more than rent a box. She was doing a good job distributing her fanzines, she travelled a lot, and she had a style that was so provocative. It was really influential. The freedom she got through *Charlie Hebdo*, she passed on to others.

The PO Box really impressed me, but I didn't go that route. In my case, it took a publisher for me to start making books, and the publisher was Benoît Chaput. I had made comics to illustrate three placemats for the snack bar La Paryse. Benoît saw them there and he liked them a lot. I had made them very freely, and he thought there was something poetic about them.

HD: What was the first book you published with him?

DO: The only thing I could publish with him were my dreams. I had all kinds of ideas for comics, but he was interested in the dreams. It was only after Benoît gave me the green light for the dream book that I started making comics more seriously. And I really adored the process, the perseverance and diligence of making a drawing every day, and having the drawings add up to a book. After the dreams, it was *Kaspar*.

HD: So all that happened quite far along in your life…

DO: It did. Comics came quite late.

HD: And what about animation?

DO: Animation appeared more or less at the same time. A friend convinced me to go to Concordia University. I'd already made one short animation, *Le microbe abominable*, for my first grant application to the Canada Council. So I had that to apply to Concordia with. During the application interview, a prof asked me why I wanted to do animation. I didn't know what to tell him. And so we watched my film, and when it was done, he said: "Forget the question. You're com-

ing with us. We're going to have fun." So comics and animation came one after the other, and my life opened up from there.

Wendy Tilby, who received a Palme d'Or for *When the Day Breaks*, was one of my professors there. Working with her was lucky for me. I had already done a lot of illustration, and I was always making things. So I came to Concordia with a certain background. I had a naïve way of animating, and she wanted me to learn, but she didn't want me to become "deformed" — she didn't want to inhibit my inventiveness. She was a good match for me. And it was thanks to her that I ended up at the NFB [National Film Board].

HD: You did three or four contracts for the NFB, and those opened the door for you doing a project of your own. And along the way, your style got a lot more minimal.

DO: Yes. At a certain point in the underground, I was getting scared of myself. I was stuck in a kind of — not irony — but darkness. One time, I took a *Life* magazine and stuck little drawn heads on every person. I made thousands of drawings using group photos from *Life* magazine — groups of miners, swimmers, dancers — and I'd put heads on all of them. And suddenly I was afraid that when I'd die, I'd have to face all those heads, those horrible heads with their missing teeth. So I threw my *Life* magazines in the garbage and told myself: no more heads. The fact of putting those heads on people — scratching them out, in a way — suddenly seemed disrespectful. That was when I was in my thirties. I moved from that black humour to a kind of tenderness. In a way, it was like going from the profane to the sacred.

Dealing with subjects like love, gentleness, or kindness can be a challenge, though. When you talk about something that's joyful, it doesn't seem to hold up the same way as something that's dark. It's as though something that's dark is truer. I'm like Tintin's dog, Snowy. I've got my little devil saying: "Art has to be provocative." And then the good Snowy says: "No, keep doing what you're doing. The art you make is more about consolation than provocation."

HD: *On Loving Women* is about lesbian first love and girls discovering their sexuality. But you de-dramatize and de-stigmatize it. You make it accessible. And last week, the animated version, *I Like Girls*, won the children's choice award at the FIFEM children's film festival.

DO: Yes! I get goose bumps thinking about it. It was great. And actually, that's exactly the word the kids used. Two of them said that the film de-dramatizes the subject. And they said it was good to see characters who take responsibility for themselves. I was really touched by it.

HD: Right now, you're working on a 14-pager for a magazine in Vienna, and you're giving yourself the space there to deconstruct things.

Julie Doucet, Genviève Castrée, and Diane Obomsawin at Drawn & Quarterly bookstore for the launch of *On Loving Women*, February 2013.
Photo courtesy Drawn & Quarterly.

DO: Yes, absolutely. I think that's the thing: I need to have more than one playing field. I need a place where I can take it all apart, but I also want to keep making things that have a kind of tenderness.

Stories and structures

HD: You often work with existing narratives, like a story by Ovid, your friends' memories, or your dreams. In all those cases, the narrative is pre-established. It's as though the thing that interests you is the idea of stories themselves and the structure of stories.

DO: Yes! I'm doing a comic right now that's based on an existing story. It's for the 375th anniversary of Montreal, and it's about Saint Philomena and a Montreal church dedicated to her. A vial of her blood was discovered in her tomb. It was the term "vial of blood" that got me interested… I like that the story starts in Rome in the 1st century AD and ends in Quebec in the 1960s — it's funny that it can travel through time and space like that.

HD: How do you go about articulating and condensing a story like that? Do you do it in your head? Do you break it down on paper?

DO: I think a lot about the story first. And then I sit down in my black armchair. It's not really a work chair – it's more for relaxing. And that's where I do my research. I read as much as possible about the subject – for instance: Saint Philomena, the church, the neighbourhood. I take notes in a little notebook. I write and write. Anything goes. And then I let it all rest.

After, I trim it down and I decide how I'll start. Then everything goes very fast. I write quickly, I draw quickly, I try to see how many panels I'll use. That's where the fun starts for me. When I did the research about Saint Philomena, I read that her remains were in a glass coffin, which made me think of Snow White. The glass coffin, the vial of blood: those kinds of images are starters for me. So just for a laugh, I added the seven dwarves. Saint Philomena says, "Sometimes people mistake me for someone else," and you see the seven dwarves file in. I came across incredible *ex votos* to Saint Philomena. One person thanked her for helping them win their battle against drugs, sex and poker. That's so full of colour — I couldn't have invented it. I need to start with a lot of information that's anchored in reality. I can't invent everything — I'm not made that way.

Making comics in Montreal

HD: If you had to describe what's specific about the Montreal comics scene, what would you say?

DO: That there's a new generation of young artists coming up like mushrooms…. We're going through a real boom.

HD: And why's that?

DO: I'm not sure. For a long time, people here had a complex that the only things that mattered were happening in Europe. But that's changed completely. Not just in Montreal — right across Canada, with artists like Michael Deforge and Marc Bell.

And Montreal has all these French-language publishers: La Pastèque, 400 coups, Pow Pow, La mauvaise tête. There's the magazine *Planches*. And there's Vincent Giard, who's a really enterprising young guy. It just takes one or two…. Chris Oliveros was so important that way, too. Vincent Giard and Julie Delporte were behind the "48 heures de la bande dessinée," Montreal's 48-hour comic project. There's a theme, everybody works together, and when the 48 hours are up, an album that gets printed during the night, like a newspaper. It's distributed at Expozine, a comics event that brings together the whole underground francophone and anglophone comics scene. The 48-hours experience got artists together and talking, and they went on to rent a studio space together. Jimmy Beaulieu, Zviane, Catherine Lamontagne, Iris, Vincent Giard, and Paul Turgeon are all there. It's a huge loft with many small offices, a big kitchen, and a good atmosphere. Pow Pow's Luc Bossé is great too. He'll get everybody to rent a van and go to the festivals together.

I wouldn't join a studio anymore — I need my little space. But once in a while I enjoy events that bring people together like that.

HD: A lot of young women are making comics in Montreal today. I'm assuming you and Julie opened the way for them?

DO: Julie especially. I feel a bit outside the comics scene. Maybe because I want it that way. I make comics, but they're published by a poetry press. I'm an animator, but that's not all I do. I'm in more than one group, and I need it to be that way. It's not a conscious decision, but it suits me.

HD: Your English-language publisher is D&Q. Anything to say about that?

DO: When D&Q recently asked me to make a comic, they gave me complete freedom from start to finish. I really appreciate that trust.

HD: Chris and D&Q have always had huge respect for an artist's work.

DO: It's great. Benoît Chaput at L'Oie de Cravan is the same. Working with the two of them is a perfect arrangement for me. L'Oie de Cravan is a small press, so there's a slowness, you can take your time. It's about poetry, not about making a consumer product. And then there's D&Q, which has the same respect for the work, but also great distribution, so the books get out there and reach more people.

HD: Okay, so when you think of translation, what is the thing that matters most to you?

DO: I don't want to control the process. I'd rather go on trust. It's better that way. I don't want to compare versions and make changes. I have a sense of humour that hangs on a very thin thread — I don't even understand it myself. So I just hope the sensibility comes through — that the person who translates it gets me. ●

214

from *Mile End* by Michel Hellman

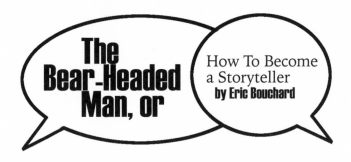

The Bear-Headed Man, or

How To Become a Storyteller
by Eric Bouchard

Originally published in:

TRIP #8, 2014

Translation by Helge Dascher

In 2010, Michel Hellman made an impressive debut in the world of Quebec comics with *Iceberg*.[1] Minimal and evocative — the images are made of torn and cut pieces of loose-leaf on a black background — it depicts a nuclear disaster in the far north that was long kept secret. Hellman comes to comics from art history, and his book reflected an open take on the form, whereby comics don't have to be drawn, but can be made of any sequentially organized images, including photographs of people (as in *fumetti*), as well as photographic or digital representations of other art forms (such as the layered-paper images used in *Iceberg*).[2] It also showed his ability to engage readers through bold pairings.

This approach returns in *Mile End*, Hellman's most acclaimed release to date, but with a focus on content, not form.[3] As such, the drawing style is simple, although its loose and busy feel is far from bland (the work of Jean-Marc Reiser comes to mind). Hellman — a Quebecer born to an American father and a French mother — applies his unique storytelling talent to the narrative itself, with a hybridizing aesthetic that plays out at many levels, whether the subject is the neighbourhood where the action takes place, the apartment in which the first-person narrator rents a room, a unique bestiary of hybrid creatures, or the narrator's own metamorphosis.

From setting to spectacle

A case in point is the introductory scene, in which Hellman adopts a technique used by Robert Crumb in his famous wordless strip *A Short History of America*.[4] Crumb's twelve horizontal, static-shot panels record the transformation over time of a patch of land, its trees progressively cut down to make way for a city and all the excesses of the "progress" it brings. In Hellman's version,

we see the Mile End area's evolution through the ages, from colonization and deforestation (lumberjacks and log drivers at work) to industrialization (factories and telephone poles), urbanization (multiple-story buildings and the arrival of cars), immigration (Jewish, Greek, Portuguese, and hippie), gentrification (condos, yoga, and fair trade coffee), and finally apartment sharing. Cycling through his future adoptive neighbourhood, the narrator-protagonist, a bear-headed man, catches sight of a room-for-rent ad — one of the natural parasites of the neighbourhood's dominant wood species, the telephone pole.

Once he moves in, he finds his attention drawn to the local characters, a constant and entertaining source of distraction for this student who initially wanted a quiet place to write his master's thesis.[5] The colourful, storied neighbourhood has an irresistible presence: every event is imbued with a unique charm, and soon the charm itself starts to work on the narrator. As the narrative it inspires veers off on fantastical tangents, the procrastinating student becomes an enthusiastic storyteller.

As such, the vignettes often begin with the act of writing itself, articulated around the figure of the blank page in one of its two contrary forms. There is the (inner) one on which nothing happens: the computer screen, page, or book that stares blankly back at the thesis-writing student, and from which he is easily lured. And there are those that seem to offer endless potential as narrative frameworks: local storefronts (the narrator sometimes sits in front of an antique dealer's shop or Wilensky's diner[6] with a roommate, waiting for something to happen); the narrator's sleep, from which he is often abruptly woken; and even his apartment itself, which always seems ready to boil over with unexpected events. Whether the narrator is struggling with

"In fall, a formation of umbrellas takes flight for warmer climes. In spring, as the sap starts to run, telephone poles wake up and march down the street."

from *Mile End*

"On the dedication page, addressed to the cartoonist's young son, a newborn is carried in a black-and-red-checkered scarf by a moose-stork. With origins that go back to both Hans Christian Andersen and Quebec folklore, the flying moose heralds a storytelling world that is itself hybrid."

"Hellman — a Quebecer born to an American father and a French mother — applies his unique storytelling talent to the narrative itself, with a hybridizing aesthetic that plays out at many levels, whether the subject is the neighbourhood where the action takes place, the apartment in which the first-person narrator rents a room, a unique bestiary of hybrid creatures, or the narrator's own metamorphosis."

writer's block or simply daydreaming, the Mile End "muse" is never far away.

The evocative power of place

Street sounds help summon a fantastical world. They announce the arrival of its "actors:" the rumbling of a garbage truck is a call to watch the performance of the hip-hop-dancing garbage collector; a ringing bell accompanies the approach of the knife sharpening truck and brings on a pang of nostalgia. Little by little, the various sounds spur the narrator's imagination: a fire truck siren inspires the creation of a new word, "pyropire," and in one of the book's most memorable sequences, the wail of a tow truck in a snowstorm triggers a wildly inventive vision of the impending snow removal operation (pp. 73 to 79).

Quebec's seasons, a natural cycle of metamorphoses, not only lend the book's sections their distinct qualities, but also offer fertile ground for this inclination to transform and exaggerate. The transmutations they bring include the usual seasonal ones (the day after the snow removal operation, "the big piles of snow have been replaced by puddles of slush"), as well as imagined phenomena (a glimpse of the effects of climate change, p. 94) and those that come with the changing seasons (in the area framed by Parc, St-Laurent, Van Horne, and Laurier streets, the arrival of summer coincides with a literal infestation of the neighbourhood by its local characters; the narrator draws up a list of them, and ultimately adds himself, pp. 113-115).

The narrator's apartment is a constant site of spectacle as well. Though decrepit (with leaky ceilings, peeling plaster, and questionable wiring), chaotic, and overstuffed, it has "a certain bohemian charm." The roommates all lead irregular lives:

one, a party-loving musician, comes and goes at the most inopportune times; the other, who shows up unannounced one day and never leaves, works from home revising porn movie subtitles, "never showers, and pees on the toilet seat." Ironically, these agents of distraction keep prodding the narrator to get back to work on his thesis.

With one thing leading to another, the apartment undergoes various transformations as well. An old captain's wheel turns the balcony into the prow of a ship, and the apartment changes from cocoon, to cave, to palisaded lookout, complete with a campfire. In its final incarnation, it morphs into the boat-shaped wicker basket of a hot air balloon, whose fabric is a patchwork of city festival banners — an extended metaphor for the author's buoyant imagination, which finds itself carried away one last time.

Bestiary:
from folklore to Star Wars

The spirit of metamorphosis also operates at the level of a bestiary of hybrid creatures that includes the bear-headed narrator. On the dedication page, addressed to the cartoonist's young son, a newborn is carried in a black-and-red-checkered scarf by a moose-stork. With origins that go back to both Hans Christian Andersen and Quebec folklore, the flying moose heralds a storytelling world that is itself hybrid. The next moose to appear has no body, and its trophy-head is attached instead to the roof of a car. Animals, objects, and machines mix and merge, giving shape to the *Mile End* bestiary.

The creatures that live in the narrator's apartment are all denatured as well. Among the animals are a turd-factory of a domestic rabbit that chews on power cords, a rat that lives under a stove burner, a neutered cat, and a foe-tus-like polymer dinosaur that expands in water. There are hybrid machines, too, including a mesmerizing and cynically engineered pig-shaped alarm clock that doubles as an automatic bacon cooker. A poignantly outdated and underperforming anthropomorphic laptop is unplugged by its user and stashed away in a closet, where its keys have become "cold as ice." Forgetting its strength, the senile computer accidentally crushes the mouse it is playing with: "I… I like petting soft things," it says, quoting Lenny from *Of Mice and Men*.

It's no different in the neighbourhood. In fall, a formation of umbrellas takes flight for warmer climes. In spring, as the sap starts to run, telephone poles wake up and march down the street. But the most spectacular mutations occur in winter. There's the skeleton of a vertebrate snowmobile… and, during a night-time snow removal operation, the loud equipment outside turns out to be a four-legged, snow-removing AT-AT, followed by a fleet of NASCAR-style, tracked sidewalk plows engaged in a terrifying race.

Hybrids of all kinds abound. Just as the neighbourhood stirs the protagonist-narrator's imagination, the creation of *Mile End* brought out a surreal streak in its author, inciting him to turn the elements of his day-to-day life into the surprising creatures that populate his urban legends.

From thesis-writer to bear-man

But the ultimate metamorphosis is that of the protagonist-narrator. Having moved to Mile End to write his thesis, he is soon distracted by the local goings-on. Though a researcher and historian, he rarely refers to his academic interests (exceptions include a digression about checkered lumberjack shirts, and a self-portrait as a cultivated, fez-wearing pipe smoker). Instead, he begins to chronicle his neighbourhood, whose contagious vitality soon turns him into a storyteller. Tips on how to dress for the cold, for instance, quickly veer into the absurd: initially mundane and methodical (wool scarf, fur hat), they become increasingly bizarre (newspaper is used for extra insulation), and everything ends in hyperbole: "In extreme cold, leather boots harden and explode." (p. 63); "At these temperatures, tears will solidify on contact with the skin, causing our eyes to weld and stay shut until spring." (p. 64)

In the course of his transformation, the narrator also blends into the neighbourhood. As noted above, he comes to think of himself as one of the locals. He learns to adapt: he limits his diet to minted potatoes to save money, finds a way to stock up on beer without going outside in winter, and calmly ushers a date out the door after battling a rat in his kitchen. When he finally finds a girlfriend, adaptation gives way to something more primal. We see him ensconced in his cave-apartment, wrapped in blankets and napping by the radiator. Toward the end of his girlfriend's pregnancy, he adopts the role of male protector. Here, the narrator and his visual and totemic representation finally become one: a bear-headed man, he is a creator with his feet on the ground, inspired by day-to-day life, but with an imagination animated and animalized by an untamed, wild, and fantastical universe.

The shifts all seem to follow a pendulum-like movement: the protagonist-narrator's environment inspires a fantastical world, which he then projects back onto the environment, before succumbing to it and finally making it his own. On the last page, this autofictional cycle comes full circle: personified by his own creation, the bear-headed man can finally escape the pages of his book. ●

ENDNOTES:

1. Initially self-published in a limited print run, the book was reissued three times. At the 2011 Shuster Awards, it was nominated for a Gene Day Award for Self-Publishing.

2. Though abandoning the comic book format, Hellman used a similar technique in *Le petit guide du Plan Nord* (L'oie de Cravan, 2013), with images made of cut garbage bags. In the context of picture books, the approach is not unconventional; drawing is not the default medium in the field, and media are naturally varied. Classic examples include Leo Lionni's *Little Blue and Little Yellow* (1959) and Christian Voltz's photos of assembled objects (1990s onward).

3. Luc Bossé, editor of Pow Pow Press, told us in February 2014 that *Mile End* was his best-selling comic at the time, with 2500 copies sold.

4. Initially published in the magazine *Co-Evolution Quarterly* in 1979. The version published in the Snoid Comics collection (Kitchen Sink, 1980) included an additional three-panel epilogue.

5. The terms "masters" and "thesis" recur throughout the book.

6. Historic local diner immortalized by Mordecai Richler in *The Apprenticeship of Duddy Kravitz* (1959).

Art by Michel Hellman